Contemporary History in Context Series

General Editor: **Peter Catterall**, Lecturer, Department of History, Queen Mary and Westfield College, University of London

What do they know of the contemporary, who only the contemporary know? How, without some historical context, can you tell whether what you are observing is genuinely novel, and how can you understand how it has developed? It was, not least, to guard against the unconscious and ahistorical Whiggery of much contemporary comment that this series was conceived. The series takes important events or historical debates from the post-war years and, by bringing new archival evidence and historical insights to bear, seeks to re-examine and reinterpret these matters. Most of the books will have a significant international dimension, dealing with diplomatic, economic or cultural relations across borders. in the process the object will be to challenge orthodoxies and to cast new light upon major aspects of post-war history.

Titles include:

Wolfram Kaiser
USING EUROPE, ABUSING THE EUROPEANS
Britain and European Integration, 1945–63

Keith Kyle
THE POLITICS OF THE INDEPENDENCE OF KENYA

Adam Lent
BRITISH SOCIAL MOVEMENTS SINCE 1945
Sex, Colour, Peace and Power

Spencer Mawby
CONTAINING GERMANY
Britain and the Arming of the Federal Republic

Jeffrey Pickering
BRITAIN'S WITHDRAWAL FROM EAST OF SUEZ
The Politics of Retrenchment

Peter Rose
HOW THE TROUBLES CAME TO NORTHERN IRELAND

L. V. Scott
MACMILLAN, KENNEDY AND THE CUBAN MISSILE CRISIS
Political, Military and Intelligence Aspects

Paul Sharp
THATCHER'S DIPLOMACY
The Revival of British Foreign Policy

Andrew J. Whitfield
HONG KONG, EMPIRE AND THE ANGLO-AMERICAN ALLIANCE AT WAR,
1941–45

Contemporary History in Context
Series Standing Order ISBN 0–333–71470–9
(*outside North America only*)

You can receive future titles in this series as they are published by placing a standing order.
Please contact your bookseller or, in case of difficulty, write to us at the address below with
your name and address, the title of the series and the ISBN quoted above.

Customer Services Department, Macmillan Distribution Ltd, Houndmills, Basingstoke,
Hampshire RG21 6XS, England

Hong Kong, Empire and the Anglo-American Alliance at War, 1941–45

Andrew J. Whitfield

palgrave

First published 2001 by
PALGRAVE
Houndmills, Basingstoke, Hampshire RG21 6XS and
175 Fifth Avenue, New York, N. Y. 10010
Companies and representatives throughout the world

PALGRAVE is the new global academic imprint of
St. Martin's Press LLC Scholarly and Reference Division and
Palgrave Publishers Ltd (formerly Macmillan Press Ltd).

ISBN 0–333–79333–1

This book is printed on paper suitable for recycling and
made from fully managed and sustained forest sources.

A catalogue record for this book is available
from the British Library.

Library of Congress Cataloging-in-Publication Data
Whitfield, Andrew J., 1973–
    Hong Kong, Empire and the Anglo-American alliance at war,
    1941–1945 / by Andrew J. Whitfield.
        p. cm. — (Contemporary history in context series)
    Includes bibliographical references and index.
    ISBN 0–333–79333–1
    1. World War, 1939–1945—China—Hong Kong. 2. Hong Kong
    (China)—History—20th century. 3. United States—Military
    relations—Great Britain. 4. Great Britain—Military relations–
    –United States. I. Title. II. Contemporary history in context series
    (Palgrave (Firm))
    D767 .W45 2001
    940.53'5'5125—dc21
                                                       2001021750

10   9   8   7   6   5   4   3   2   1
10 09 08 07 06 05 04 03 02 01

Printed in Great Britain by Antony Rowe Ltd, Chippenham, Wiltshire

Contents

General Editor's Preface

In a lecture in May 1943 Britain's Deputy Prime Minister, Clement Attlee, reflected that the US should learn to appreciate that states which ape their constitution are not necessarily democracies: 'A study of the history of Central and South America should help this process.' He went on to observe that while US Secretary of State Cordell Hull seemed blithely to assume that all colonies were anxiously awaiting their version of 1776 and self-determination, many were small and, certainly at the time, were seen by the British as unlikely to prove viable on their own.

One such small colony which, in the way it became something of a political football, well illustrates these differing attitudes towards Empire, and also China, of the British and Americans during the Second World War was Hong Kong. Under Japanese occupation from Christmas 1941, the issue of the future of the colony was, as Andrew Whitfield shows, a running sore in Anglo-American relations in the Far East theatre. It even became a matter of debate in the corridors of Whitehall. Despite the disparity in power between the two Allies, however, it was the British who won out.

Roosevelt may have favoured the return of the colony to China on grounds of visceral anti-imperialism, a fairly crude Wilsonian view of the world that assumed long before Francis Fukuyama came along that American-style liberal democracy and self-determination was the end to which all peoples were tending, and the expectation that this would materially benefit US trade by turning Hong Kong into a free port. He could, however, be challenged on all of these counts. Attlee was not the only British minister to hint that a glance at American history would suggest that the Americans were pots calling the kettle from whence they sprang black. And as Whitfield demonstrates, American attempts to portray Chiang Kai-shek as a democrat were at best wishful thinking, while on the last point they were mistaken, as Hong Kong was already a free port. That the British thought Roosevelt was wrong did not, however, mean that they were going to win the argument.

In explaining how and why they did so Andrew Whitfield provides a detailed, entertaining and persuasive account of a relatively neglected aspect of the Second World War. Analyses of the wartime alliance tend to focus on the European theatre. China has usually been portrayed as an essentially American show. To a considerable extent it was. However, as this book points out, the Americans did not get things all their own way. This had significant long-term consequences. Had Hong Kong been incorporated into Chiang's China it would have gone with the rest of the mainland in 1949. This would have deprived the West of a window on China, deprived Hong Kong itself of its post-war prosperity and helped to ensure that China was more isolated than was in any event the case. These realisations were to dawn upon American policymakers themselves come the 1950s. By then, however, they were already having to come to terms with the consequences of the failure of their wartime strategy in China. Truman may have been the first President to suffer the effects of the 'Who lost China?' syndrome that was subsequently to haunt Washington and play a major role in shaping the mentalities of the cold war. As Whitfield eloquently shows, the seeds of this failure had, however, already been sown by his predecessor.

PETER CATTERALL
London

Acknowledgements

Many people have helped in the writing of this book. In particular, Trish & Gess, Richard Robinson, Alex Marshall, Adam Dunning, my colleagues (you know who you are) and my family, especially, Susanna. Research was conducted with financial assistance provided by the Humanities Research Board of the British Academy and the University of Birmingham. Special thanks to the Public Records Office, Kew, and the Roosevelt Library, Hyde Park. The final credit is to Scott Lucas, without which none of this would have been possible.

List of Abbreviations

BAAG	British Army Aid Group
BOT	Board of Trade
CA	China Association
CO	Colonial Office
COS	Chiefs of Staff
FO	Foreign Office
HK	Hong Kong
HKPU	Hong Kong Planning Unit
KMT	Kuomintang, Chinese Nationalist Party
OSS	Office of Strategic Services
OWI	Office of War Information
PM	Prime Minister
SD	State Department
SOE	Special Operations Executive

Chronology

1842	Treaty of Nanking: cession of Hong Kong island
1860	Convention of Peking: cession of Kowloon
1899	Lease of New Territories for 99 years
1940 July	Evacuation of women and children from Hong Kong
1941 August	Atlantic Charter signed
1941 7 December	Japanese attack Hong Kong
1941 25 December	British surrender Hong Kong
1942 February	British surrender Singapore
1942 September	Lord Cranborne agrees to negotiation of Hong Kong
1942 September	Extraterritoriality negotiations resume
1942 October	Churchill's Mansion House speech
1942 November	Chinese ask for negotiation of Hong Kong
1942 November	Oliver Stanley appointed Colonial Secretary
1943 August	Hong Kong Planning Unit formed
1943 November	Cairo conference
1943 November	Generals' coup attempt against Chiang Kai-shek
1944 April	Japanese launch Operation Ichigo in China
1944 November	Dismissal of General Stilwell
1945 February	Yalta conference
1945 12 April	Death of President Roosevelt
1945 April–June	San Francisco conference
1945 July	Potsdam conference
1945 July	Clement Attlee becomes Prime Minister
1945 14 August	Japanese surrender
1945 30 August	British re-enter Hong Kong
1997 1 July	Britain returns Hong Kong to Chinese rule

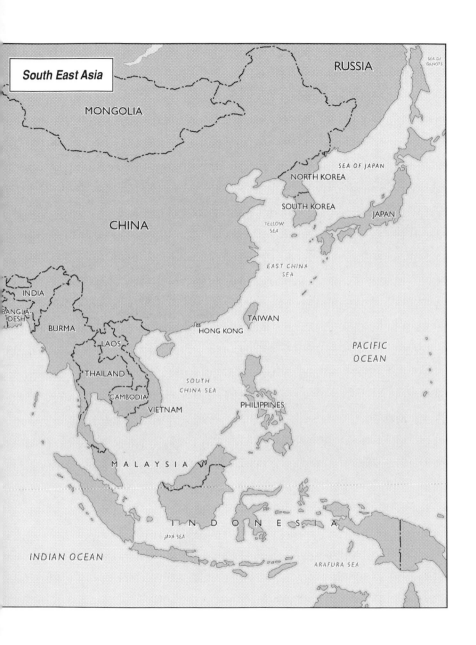

South East Asia

RUSSIA

MONGOLIA

SEA OF OKHOTS

NORTH KOREA

SEA OF JAPAN

SOUTH KOREA

JAPAN

CHINA

YELLOW
SEA

EAST CHINA
SEA

INDIA

BANGLA
DESH

BURMA

TAIWAN

HONG KONG

PACIFIC
OCEAN

LAOS

THAILAND

SOUTH
CHINA SEA

CAMBODIA

VIETNAM

PHILIPPINES

MALAYSIA

INDONESIA

JAVA SEA

INDIAN OCEAN

ARAFURA SEA

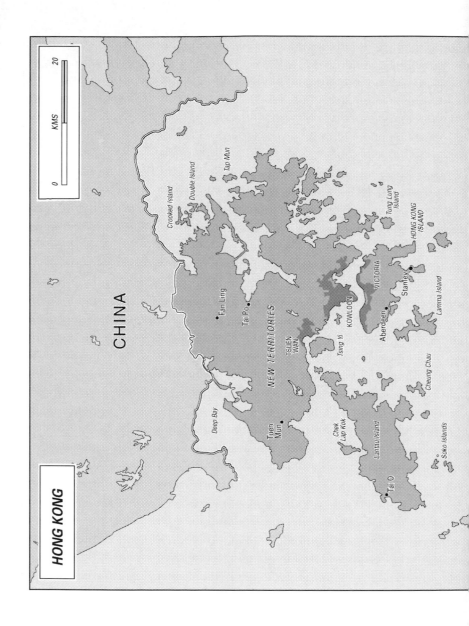

Introduction

I would love to be around in 1997 to see with my own eyes
Hong Kong's return to China.[1]

Deng Xiaoping, 1984

The empires of the future are the empires of the mind.[2]

Winston Churchill, 1943

At the end of the twentieth century Hong Kong held an emotive place
in the British conscience. As Britain's last significant colony it represented a reassuringly modern and sophisticated China for Western
visitors; the China that could have evolved had communist rule not
intervened. But lost in the enormity of the Second World War is a
hidden history every bit as dramatic as the growth of Hong Kong into
its modern, urban self. The story has been understandably overlooked
since 1945 as politicians came and went and the world had new, more
pressing complications to catch its attention. These remain, however,
interpretations. Only one thing is for certain; Hong Kong's place now
rests in Chinese history.

The fall of Singapore in February 1942 marked the nadir of the British
Empire during World War II. It was the surrender of Hong Kong to
the Japanese in December 1941, however, which started the rot. Dis-
proportionate to its small size, the colony became critical in Britain's
battle to retain her Far Eastern empire. Ironically, though, the threat to
British sovereignty came not from Japan but from her own allies, China
and particularly, America. Under the leadership of Generalissimo
Chiang Kai-shek, the Chinese attempted to reclaim the colony with the
active support of Washington. At times emotions would run so high
that it was almost like a replay of the American War of Independence

1

with the colonists arranged against the colonialists. Ultimately, of course, Chinese exertions came to nothing, but not before the triangle of British, Chinese and American relationships had all been dragged through the mire.

Britain may have been down but she was not yet out. The Chinese were unfortunate to find that the Hong Kong issue could not be viewed in isolation by the British authorities. Whatever indifference the British had viewed the colony with previously, it became increasingly inseparable from the destiny of Britain's wider Empire. As the balance of power shifted inexorably against Britain during the war, she clung ever more tightly to the idea that her power was intrinsically tied to the survival of the British Empire and her colonies. In many respects, Britain's real war was not with her declared enemies but with her main ally, America, who held it in her power to deny Britain her Empire.

If Britain's over-arching war aim was not readily apparent this was understandable. Raymond Seitz, American Ambassador to London half a century later, noted that the British appeared to have a deep attachment to understatement and obfuscation:

> I remember my first encounter with British understatement shortly after I came to live [in London] in the 1970s. There was a rowdy demonstration at Stirling University when Prince Charles visited there one autumn day, and several people were hurt in the ruckus. On the television news that evening, the screen showed a picture of two plain-clothes cops kicking a long-haired student who had fallen to the ground. The news reader, using his most serious good-citizen voice, said, 'A man is helping police with their enquiries.'[3]

Whatever the problems of deciphering British intentions, conscious or unconscious, her inability to find tangible meaning in Empire is more interesting. British political leaders implicitly accepted that this uncoordinated and motley collection of lands and islands fitted together into some mysterious whole, providing the source of British strength. Deeper analysis of Empire was rarely encouraged, and no one wondered whether it was a military or economic liability; it was always an assumed asset. During the Second World War few British leaders deviated from this point of view. Winston Churchill's vociferous and eloquent defence of the Empire was shared throughout the British establishment, with disagreement usually stemming from his method, not his message.

The British chose to defend and rehabilitate their Empire during the war by using any means at their disposal. Beggars could not be choosers and, reluctantly, Britain was drawn towards the need for some sort of alliance with America. No longer materially strong enough to project the power which they once did, the British hoped that American industrial might could be forged in common cause with British imperial aims. The war had ripped through any pretence that Britain could sustain the enormous responsibilities of her Empire alone. And yet British leaders still pretended that the Empire could be put back together without a price to be paid. Of course, this was wishful thinking: the Americans were traditionally arch anti-imperialists, never missing an opportunity to recall their war of independence a century and a half earlier. A common language misled many British politicians into thinking that Britain and America could share common foreign policy goals. Oliver Harvey, Anthony Eden's private secretary, wrote in his diary that:

> The US Government is becoming very baffling to us, more and more secretive. They invited Madame Chiang Kai-shek [China's First Lady] to visit Washington and smuggled her by air through India, including a night on route without letting either us or India know anything about it all! These are not the manners of a Great Power . . . Why? Don't the Americans trust us? Are they afraid of our disapproval? . . . Do they think they can run the war without us?[4]

Instead, America was pursuing her own informal hegemonic agenda with the term 'democracy' substituted for 'empire'.

The Anglo-American relationship was a different creature according to its regional context. On the western front, for the most part, it worked relatively well for the simple reason that Britain had traditionally remained detached from European issues; there were few British interests in dispute. The Far Eastern war was a different matter. Here the real clash of empires was played out. America had long coveted a special role in Asia, illustrated by its strong missionary presence in China. With her predominant military strength America attempted to displace the old imperial influence, and replace it with her own. Unfortunately, however, both Britain and America had grown accustomed to having things their own way and compromise did not sit comfortably in their psychologies. The Americans were naive to expect that they could uproot a century's imperial legacy in one fell swoop or that they could win the war alone, not to mention whether or not the natives would welcome them. Many of these accusations could also be levelled at the British. The scene was set for a turbulent alliance.

Hong Kong was key to British efforts to resurrect her Empire in the Far East, and in a wider context, sustain British imperial ambition worldwide. The colony, which barely covered 300 square miles, had little in its favour save for a deep water port and proximity to China. Yet size was not everything. It became a diplomatic test case because of the political claims which converged on it: the Chinese Nationalists claimed the British colony as an integral part of China, and in this they were supported by the Americans. The British, on the other hand, had ignominiously lost the colony to the Japanese in December 1941 and now attached their imperial pride to regaining Hong Kong. Malaya, Singapore and Burma did not have these claims. The British Prime Minister and his Foreign Secretary quickly realised that if Britain was forced to relinquish Hong Kong, it would set a precedent for her other colonies. For the British the objective was to marry their imperial ambition with an Anglo-American alliance. It is not, therefore, an exaggeration to maintain that British foreign policy in the Far East was frequently seen through the prism of Hong Kong.

Note on historiography

There are already several books on the Anglo-American relationship during the war in the Far East, but none that specifically deals with the question of Hong Kong from the British perspective.[5] Although the Anglo-American relationship is an important component of British policy, the book is not from its inception a narrow study along those lines, but seeks instead to integrate wider economic, social, cultural and political strands. While Chinese sources remain scarce due to political sensitivity, copious British and American documentation provides (to a certain extent) an understanding of Chinese policy. Detailed use has been made of the private and political papers of senior British policy-makers, including Anthony Eden and Winston Churchill. The relevant Cabinet papers have also been consulted with emphasis on frequently overlooked departments such as the Colonial Office, Special Operations Executive (SOE) and Board of Trade. American material has been extracted from the Roosevelt papers and the National Archives, including State Department, Office of Strategic Services and Joint Chiefs of Staff files.

Chinese transliterations have used the Wades-Giles system, common to the period.

1
Return and Departure: the Fall and Recapture of Hong Kong, 1941 and 1945

Although no eyewitness accounts exist, disappointment must have been etched across Admiral Cecil Harcourt's face as he entered Hong Kong harbour on 30 August 1945. Arriving as the commander of a British naval task force it was evident that Britain's colony had been devastated by three and a half years of war; first by the Japanese attackers, then the Chinese looters and finally the American bombers. This was not the glittering prize of concrete and steel which the British would return to Chinese rule. Little did they know it, but fifty-two years of uninterrupted British rule was about to begin.

Greeting the British fleet with the first peacetime edition of the *South China Morning Post* was Franklin Gimson. He had endured four years of privation in the prisoner of war camp perched on the opposite side of Hong Kong island. As Colonial Secretary, the second most senior post in the British colonial administration, Gimson had given much of his adult life to administering the Empire. He also possessed the most unfortunate timing, arriving in Hong Kong the day before the Japanese invaded. What he and many other British and Commonwealth subjects were doing on this inhospitable rocky island, several thousand miles from home, was a question which has rarely been posed.

Hong Kong history

Hong Kong's place in official British history books began in 1842. It was in this year that Hong Kong was ceded from the Chinese Manchu dynasty, marking the beginning of Western encroachment on the Orient. The conflict that precipitated British rule over this barren island off the south China coast was perhaps an inevitable clash of power, trade and cultural differences as British merchants sought to exact trade privileges in the Far East. As anyone familiar with the origins of the British Empire will know, there was nothing strange about this; the informal British trading empire often moved onto a more official footing as conflicts arose.

Although the Treaty of Nanking, which legitimised the 1842 agreement, was not wholly exploitative of Chinese weakness it laid the foundations, symbolically at least, for a century of extraterritorial rights or 'unequal treaties' for China. From 1842 onwards China was effectively carved up between the Western Powers, remaining in existence, perhaps, only because it provided a useful administrative mechanism through which to facilitate foreign rule. China had to concede spheres of influence and special diplomatic immunities for foreign traders, epitomised by the International Settlement in Shanghai which allowed for a whole area of the city to be exempt from Chinese law and to have its own foreign council and police. The treaty system that developed from Britain's seizure of Hong Kong later became a valuable propaganda tool in Chinese domestic politics, symbolising national humiliation. Nonetheless, as John King Fairbank points out,[1] the expansion of foreign rule, or to give it its technical term, extraterritoriality, was no worse than the restrictions that the Chinese had imposed on foreigners before 1842: Western industrial development and military might had simply reversed their relative positions.

Prior to 1842 foreign visitors had to present themselves to the Chinese court to pay 'tribute', which was an elaborate admission of the superiority of Chinese culture and civilisation. Western diplomats had to prostrate themselves before the Chinese Emperor, performing three kneelings and nine prostrations. This is where the term 'kowtow' originates. According to Fairbank, 'The formalities of tribute relations were developed into a mechanism by which barbarous regions outside the empire might be given their place in the all-embracing Sinocentric cosmos.'[2] The tribute system stood at the heart of China's complex foreign trade relations, reinforcing the Emperor's ultimate power whilst maintaining China's superior position in the face of 'barbarians' from the West and elsewhere. The Treaty of Nanking in 1842, however, marked the beginning of China's transition from tribute to treaty relations, often to China's detriment and the erosion of her sovereignty. This development, moreover, was not smooth and involved further conflicts with the West in 1858 and 1860.

The existence of Hong Kong, therefore, became a potent symbol for Chinese politicians of the 'unequal treaties' imposed by imperialistic foreign powers. It frequently served as an excuse for Chinese failures and disappointments. Chiang Kai-shek, the Nationalist Chinese leader during the Second World War, wrote in his book *China's Destiny* (published in China in 1943 and in translation in the West in 1947) that foreign incursions into the Orient were the root of all China's modern ills: moral, economic, psychological and philosophical. The collapse of the old imperial powers in the Far East after the Japanese onslaught of December 1941, however, opened a new chapter of Western relations with China. Although contemplated before the eruption of the Sino-Japanese war in 1937, the abolition of extraterritoriality in China needed the impetus of the Pacific war, and was agreed in January 1943. Hong Kong, however, was not included in this joint Sino-Anglo-American treaty.

After an uncertain start as a British colony in the 1840s when the London authorities questioned the utility of a barren island with few natural resources, the colony began an intrepid expansion which transformed it into a modern commercial centre. Hong Kong's deep water harbour facilitated its development into a focus of British trade in China, offering proximity to Canton and shelter from unpredictable Chinese jurisdiction. In 1860 the peninsula opposite Hong Kong island was obtained through the Treaty of Peking, and later, a much larger area called the New Territories was leased for ninety-nine years from 1898. By the turn of the century Hong Kong had become what Norman Miners has described as 'one of the ten first-class colonies in the Empire': it was a fully integrated component of the sprawling British Empire.[3] Even so, London's interest in the intricacies of colonial rule was sporadic, and the colony was usually left to its own devices. A Labour Party official characterised this rule from a distance as one of letting 'sleeping dogs lie'; avoiding the scrutiny of 'deep-seated troubles' and only taking action 'when a riot or the like compels attention to its deeper causes'.[4] Japan's occupation of Hong Kong in December 1941 provided such a shock: it shattered Britain's imperial complacency and rekindled the question marks over British sovereignty. With the benefit of hindsight, it also marked the beginning of Britain's struggle to redefine the meaning of Empire in the cold war era.

The defence of British Hong Kong 1939–41

With the outbreak of war in Europe, the Far East became precisely that: far removed from the British mind. Logistically stretched on the Western front, British politicians hoped a Japanese attack on British possessions in the Far East would never happen. The imperial defenders in the colonies were, perhaps, even more culpable; they assumed the Japanese were incapable of such an action. It was unsurprising, therefore, to find British defences in poor shape. The gradual deterioration of the situation over the preceding years appeared, however, to alleviate the need for urgent action. The Japanese had, after all, been involved in four years of indecisive fighting in China and had tied down two million of their own troops without seizing control of the whole of China. Nevertheless, with the landing of Japanese forces at Bias Bay, thirty-five miles north-east of Hong Kong in October 1939 the colony had effectively become a hostage to fortune, completely surrounded by hostile forces.[5] The closest the British defenders of Hong Kong came to the realities of the situation were in the crowded cinemas of Kowloon where they witnessed Japanese atrocities perpetrated on the Chinese mainland. And yet within two years the British had lost the colony to a numerically inferior enemy, with ample forewarning.

The question of defending Hong Kong was not a new dilemma and had been broached in the less troubled times of 1937 and 1938. This planning was conducted on the basis that there would never be a Japanese invasion of Hong Kong or the Far East, and if there was, Hong Kong would not be militarily significant. The Chiefs of Staff attempted to explain to Winston Churchill, as the fighting raged in Hong Kong in December 1941, the choices they had faced: 'At that time it was confidently expected that soon after the outbreak of war with Japan it would be possible to dispatch a powerful fleet to the Far East, which in certain circumstances might effect the relief of Hong Kong.' The Chiefs listed three available options: (1) demilitarise Hong Kong, although this was 'inadvisable at the time'; (2) pour such resources into Hong Kong as to make it a self-sufficient fortress, although this was deemed too expensive in men and *matériel*; and (3), the chosen option, retain a sufficient garrison in the colony to hold out until relief could be brought.[6] It all came down to keeping up appearances.

Defending Hong Kong with a large and well-equipped armed force was a daunting task at the best of times. One look at a map should have highlighted the defensive problems facing the colony quickly and pointedly. The nature of the terrain and the miles of coastline and border meant defensive forces would find it hard to 'funnel' attackers into a favourable scenario. The obvious advantages and options available to an attacker meant that to cover all contingencies the British would have required overwhelming troop numbers in their favour, elaborate minefield and wire entanglements, and strong air cover, all of which they lacked. To think that the island of Hong Kong could have held out for two weeks, never mind the 90 or 130 days envisaged, was ludicrous. Once the Japanese had succeeded in conquering Hong Kong's hinterland, the tiny island of Hong Kong with its narrow harbour presented little obstacle to the attackers while confining the defenders so they could be strafed and shelled more easily.[7] Quite what it was assumed the Royal Navy relief force would find on its arrival in the harbour, had all their ships not been sunk or torpedoed, was uncertain.

Logistically the navy had no means to rescue the defenders; no battlegroup was going to be sacrificed on what would have been a suicide mission or be in a position to take offensive action that far east after only four months of a two-front war. Therefore, the role of the garrison was in essence one of prestige only. They would have to fight for the prestige of the Empire, and considering the likelihood of relief, for their lives. The third, military, option chosen by the Chiefs of Staff was therefore misleading; there could be no holding out for the time envisaged, and certainly there was little chance of being rescued. The defenders could not even console themselves with the belief that militarily the battle would have great consequence, albeit for themselves. The Chiefs of Staff, to be fair, were in an unenviable position, having too many commitments and not enough troops. The Empire was not in the habit of scuttling and running, and sacrifices had to be made. But there was little excuse for actively encouraging a greater loss of life, which is what occurred.

As the Battle of Britain reached its climax in August 1940, London's military planners had one last pang of conscience. The deteriorating situation gave the Chiefs of Staff cause for a radical reappraisal of their Hong Kong strategy. The Chiefs painted the position of the colony in surprisingly honest terms for the first time, advising that:

> Hong Kong is not a vital interest and the garrison could not long withstand Japanese attack. Even if we had a strong fleet in the Far East, it is doubtful whether Hong Kong could be held now that the Japanese are firmly established in the mainland of China; and it could not be used as an advanced naval base.
>
> In the event of war, Hong Kong must be regarded as an outpost and held as long as possible. We should resist the inevitably strong pressure to reinforce Hong Kong and we should certainly be unable to relieve it. Militarily our position in the Far East would be stronger without this unsatisfactory commitment.[8]

The Far Eastern situation was now bleak. Indo-China had fallen to the Japanese, preventing the Royal Navy operating safely that far north, as was painfully demonstrated when Japanese torpedo-bombers based there sank HMS *Prince of Wales* and HMS *Repulse* on 10 December. Even had a British task force performed an epic journey to relieve Hong Kong it would have found that there was not a dock capable of accommodating a capital ship.[9] Furthermore, Singapore was the main priority for British Far Eastern strategy and what few modern aeroplanes there were, were filtered into Malaya to provide defence in depth. The earlier strategists had also ignored the importance of air support in defence, as they had in the Mediterranean, and of course there were no airfields on Hong Kong island itself. The exposed position of the mainland RAF aerodrome at Kai Tak would soon become apparent. The only glimmer on this dark horizon came from a conversation which the British Foreign Secretary, Anthony Eden, had had with Harry Hopkins, President Roosevelt's special envoy. There, the implicit promise of American support for the defence of Hong Kong was insinuated, although it is hard to see what material difference this could have made to the final equation as the Americans were as unprepared for a Far Eastern war as the British.[10]

The resolution of the Chiefs that the colony was a hopeless cause, though, did not last long. The culprit, if there can be one, may be Major General Grasett. He was Commodore in Chief of Hong Kong from November 1938 until 19 July 1941. On his return to Britain he decided that, after all this time, the level of troops and anti-aircraft guns were inadequate even for a holding operation.[11] In Air Chief Marshall Brooke-Popham, the new Commander in Chief Far East from October 1940, he found an important ally.[12] Visiting the colony to inspect the defences personally, Brooke-Popham failed to appreciate the nature of its strategic position and with the encouragement of Grasett requested two more battalions. Winston Churchill, now Prime Minister, was one of the few who, despite his workload, correctly read the situation. Churchill, who had perhaps consulted a map, failed to be impressed by a call for more troops:

> This is all wrong. If Japan goes to war with us there is not the slightest chance of holding Hong Kong or relieving it. It is most unwise to increase the loss we shall suffer there. Instead of increasing the garrison it ought to be reduced to a symbolic scale. Any trouble arising there must be dealt with at the peace conference after the war. We must avoid frittering away our resources on untenable positions.[13]

The Chiefs reciprocated Churchill's common sense, informing Brooke-Popham that Hong Kong was indeed 'an undesirable military commitment'. But since they had missed the opportunity to evacuate in less troubled times, it would have to be held for as long as possible in order to bolster Chinese morale. Even increasing the garrison from 'four to six regular battalions would be unlikely to influence such a decision by the Japanese and could not affect the ultimate result'.[14] Major Grasett, however, would not accept this and set about swaying dissident opinion.

On his return to London, Grasett was instrumental in securing the dispatch of two Canadian brigades to the colony by using his personal contacts. Stopping in Ottawa en route to London, he met his friend, the Canadian Chief of the General Staff.[15] Scheming and pragmatism converged as the Canadian government was keen to aid the British war effort. The result was an offer of Canadian troops for the defence of Hong Kong. With the Chiefs of Staff support the Canadian offer was passed on to the weary Churchill who annotated, 'I approve – unless the F[oreign]S[ecretary] demurs.' Anthony Eden, in fact, 'warmly welcomed' this dispatch of reinforcements, oblivious to the likelihood of its one-way nature.[16] Conspicuously, any reference to 'prolonged resistance' and 'relief' were now absent from memoranda.

Although Churchill would later lament this decision in his *History of the Second World War*, the looming debacle was far from the Hong Kong Governor's mind. Buoyed by the prospective reinforcements from Canada, Sir Mark Young exuded imperial confidence, diminishing the precariousness of his own position. His letter to Sir Cosmo Parkinson of the Colonial Office, close to the time of the Japanese attack, exemplified the complacency so prevalent amongst the British establishment:[17]

> You mention the possibility of Hong Kong being well to the fore in the South if war with Japan. [sic] They are pretty well conscious of it here, in fact in some cases the consciousness is getting stale; but I am satisfied that really first class work has been done on the defences: the new General – nearly as new as I am – inspires the utmost confidence; and the latest news, still very secret, about reinforcements has made an immense difference . . . to [our] prospects, which as you know, has not up to now been very comfortable or conducive to the maintenance of prestige.

His correspondent, Parkinson, replying on 2 December, joked prophetically that 'if war breaks out with Japan it will be on a Sunday, or perhaps

Christmas Day will be a nice inconvenient time for it to happen! These things generally start at some unseemly time.'[18] Such a 'hope for the best, and it won't happen' attitude stifled any energetic attempt to prepare the defences of the colony. Just as Neville Chamberlain believed he could appeal to Hitler's better nature, so too, did the British assume that the Japanese would not inconvenience them by going to war in the Far East. For the British to seriously consider such a scenario meant contemplating the imperial over-stretch and strategic self-deceptions on which British policy was built.

As tensions mounted in the Far East, and as America imposed economic sanctions on Japan, Hong Kong was bursting at the seams with refugees fleeing the mayhem on the mainland. But besides this, an air of surreal normality permeated the colony. Although a reluctant Foreign Office had agreed to the evacuation of European and Indian women and children in July 1940, there were few other acts of preparedness.[19] Unpopular decisions, such as enlistment, were avoided in the belief that war would not come to Asia, even though there were numerous Japanese infringements into British Hong Kong territory during the period 1938–41, which could have acted as a forewarning.[20] Inaction was justified for fear of provoking the Japanese. Fifth columnists and Japanese spies roamed relatively freely around the colony, so that when the invasion came the attackers had remarkably detailed maps. The Japanese would know the British order of battle and defensive plans before their attack even commenced. The chopping and changing of key personnel did not much help either, be it Grasett's return to London, or Sir Mark Young's appointment as Governor on 10 September 1941. When the axe did fall with the attack on Pearl Harbour, however, the blame cannot be laid on a single individual; it was the culmination of a general complacency amongst the British 'Hong Kongers'. The pain and suffering following defeat would, though, raise the first real questions as to what was and would be the future relationship between the colony and Britain.

The Japanese attack: December 1941

On Saturday 7 December the colony was lost in its usual heady pursuits. The Happy Valley racecourse was filled to capacity, with the Royal Scots providing a musical interlude. Down the road the Middlesex Regiment were playing rugby, the game followed by a party at the Hong Kong Hotel. When the Japanese began their first air raid on Kai Tak airport at 8 a.m. the following day, there were already a few sore heads.[21] Even in the reality of war many of the British were unable to believe what was happening. The persistence of racial stereotypes, reciprocated by the Japanese,[22] added to a litany of miscalculation regarding their enemy. Some thought that the Germans were attacking because they assumed that the Japanese were unable to fly and dive-bomb accurately! Others dismissed the idea that the Japanese would be able to mount amphibious landings because the Japanese had no sense of balance and were susceptible to seasickness.[23]

The Japanese attack was swift and well executed. The main defensive position on the hinterland, called Gin Drinker's line, was quickly breached. The 2000 newly-arrived Canadian reinforcements, the Royal Rifles of Canada and Winnipeg Grenadiers, found themselves in the heart of this fight. Homesick and malaria stricken, they were hardly what the Chiefs had in mind when they allocated reinforcements. Indeed, the Canadian government had classified the two brigades as 'unfit for combat', fulfilling a political expediency rather than any practical use.[24] Accordingly, the battle-hardened Japanese quickly gained the upper hand. Within days the Japanese controlled everything bar Hong Kong island itself. As night drew in, the Allied defenders on the island listened in dread as the Japanese set about brutalising the local populace.

During the short siege which ensued, the island was shelled continuously by the Japanese. Even now, however, an air of unreality prevailed among many of the defenders. When David MacDougall, an Australian, parked his car amid heavy gunfire in downtown Hong Kong, a passer-by insisted on discussing the merits of parking his car elsewhere! 'The scene was too familiar to form a convincing background for deeds of violence. Even when it reached the stage of stepping over dead bodies on the street, the dream like atmosphere remained unchanged.'[25] As if the Japanese were not causing enough trouble, the defenders also had to buy off the Triads who were threatening to kill all the Europeans in a 'Celebration' on the 13 December. After frantic discussions and a considerable amount of money changing hands, the Triads agreed to call off their threatened massacre.[26]

The anticipated invasion arrived shortly when the Japanese launched a night-time amphibious assault on the island. Once ashore, the Japanese ran amok, butchering civilians and soldiers alike. With the defensive position crumbling, Sir Mark Young asked for surrender terms on 21 December, sensing the futility of further resistance. Winston Churchill, however, requested a greater sacrifice. He sent a personal telegram to Young which simply stated: 'The eyes of the world are upon you. We expect you to resist to the end.'[27] The surrender was nonetheless signed on Christmas Day 1941, 18 days after the first shot had been fired. Some British commanders were staggered by Sir Mark Young's offer to surrender. Brigadier Wallis, stubbornly resisting the Japanese at Stanley on the southern tip of Hong Kong island, refused to believe the news as it was 'unwarranted by the local situation', eventually surrendering on the 26th.[28]

The fall of Hong Kong was eclipsed in the British public consciousness by the wider deteriorating situation in the Far East which would culminate in the fall of Singapore. Britain's Commonwealth allies, though, took note. As those Canadian and British troops who had been lucky enough not to have been bayoneted were marched away into Japanese captivity, the Canadian parliament asked what this sacrifice had been for: few people could answer. Unwittingly, the Japanese had bequeathed the British a diplomatic time bomb as policymakers began the struggle to reassert their rule over this pocket-sized colony.

In defeat

Defeat was characterised by blame and dissent. Commonwealth nationals had particularly sharp knives. Lieutenant Colonel Ride, commanding officer of the colony's Field Ambulance Unit, believed that the British in Hong Kong had been 'psychologically defeated' well before the colony had actually fallen. Like a rusty hinge waiting to collapse, he described the colony's government as a hotbed of 'apathy, inertia and self-complacency . . . rotten to the core, its people [having] no confidence whatsoever in their leaders'.[29]

Undoubtedly, though there were pockets of gallantry where the Japanese met stiff resistance, on the whole the defence of Hong Kong was a black episode in British military history. The former press secretary to the British ambassador in China, James Bertram, captured in the fighting, had his own answers to the colony's fall. 'Nobody really cared enough about Hong Kong to rally to its defence that last reserve of human spirit that has, at certain moments in history, enabled men to hold out against impossible odds . . . And the one main group that might have defended Hong Kong with real passion, the Chinese, was never called upon.'[30]

General Maltby, the commanding officer of Hong Kong and the man who had inspired 'the utmost confidence' in the Governor, was unwilling to shoulder much of the blame. On the operation as a whole he felt that, 'strategically we gambled and lost, but it was worth the gamble'.

The Canadian Grenadiers, however, were 'the worse for the drink' at the Republic Bay hotel while the Royal Rifles of Canada were defeatist and almost refused to fight; views which would do little for inter-Allied harmony. To this he added unfavourable comments concerning Chinese enlisted drivers and the (unrealistic) promise of a Chinese counter-offensive to be launched in January 1942.[31]

The official British military historian wrote that:

> In the event of war with Japan the isolated outpost of Hong Kong was always doomed to fall. It could have been demilitarised in the early 1930s without loss of face, but such a course was not thought to be politically advisable. The colony had no strategic importance, and the few extra days of resistance which were gained by the presence of the two reinforcing battalions sent at the eleventh hour could not, and did not, have any effect on the course of events. The despatch of these reinforcements proved to be a lamentable waste of valuable manpower.[32]

The Commander in Chief of India was in no doubt as to the cause of Britain's failure in the Far East; it was the 'continued frittering away of our assets in small pockets' such as Hong Kong and Singapore.[33] Whatever the merits of such arguments, Hong Kong was now a Japanese possession.

2
The Meaning of Empire: Imperial Consensus, Whitehall and Hong Kong

To say that our Empire is 'bone of our bone, flesh of our flesh', is not to express an opinion but to assert a fact. So long as Englishmen retain at once their migratory instinct, their passion for independence, and their impatience of foreign rule, they are bound by a manifest destiny to found empires abroad, or, in other words, to make themselves the dominant race in the foreign countries to which they wander.[1]

Edward Dicey, 1877

I have never thought myself that the Empire needed tying together with bits of string. I agree . . . that natural development, natural forces, mysterious natural forces, will carry everything before them, especially when those forces are fanned forwards, as they will be, by the wings of victory in a righteous cause.[2]

Winston Churchill, 21 April 1944

Empire defined Britain and yet there was no agreed definition of what it actually meant. Sometimes it was a financial imperative, on other occasions it could be a strategic position. It could be personal attachment, it could be emotional. The multitude of colonies which constituted the British Empire meant that it could never be a homogeneous entity.[3] Nevertheless, in the British consciousness Empire became Britain's strength and purpose in the world. Rational assessment did not always support this sentiment but, as is so often the case, beliefs became self-fulfilling.

The basis of British strength lay in the forging of this imperial consensus which underpinned Britain's governmental bureaucracy. It was a consensus because so many British policymakers and military commanders shared a common set of beliefs and backgrounds, holding that the survival of the British Empire was pre-eminent. Regardless of political persuasion, there was a united ambition to return British rule to Hong Kong. The consensus was rarely founded on financial, geographical or strategic factors except when they appeared to substantiate the argument for the retention of the Empire by her Allies or among British personnel themselves. Without an explanation and analysis of this consensus, a deeper understanding of British motives and policies is impossible, and such an analysis lies at the core of this book. Of comparable importance is an understanding of the bureaucratic dynamics that controlled the British government system, known as Whitehall: the successful (and unsuccessful) interchange of information and ideas between these government offices determined London's planning to return to Hong Kong. Furthermore, behind the facade of bureaucratic anonymity stood individuals who frequently affected the course of Britain's Hong Kong policy in their own right: statesmen like Winston Churchill and Anthony Eden, alongside lesser known figures such as Sir Maurice Peterson and Franklin Gimson. The influence of these people needs to be clearly drawn out in the narrative as a balance to the 'inevitability' of bureaucratic momentum. Britain's successful reoccupation of Hong Kong was by no means assured; in fact, in 1942 it appeared highly unlikely. That Britain achieved her aims, for better or worse, rested ultimately in the hands of these individuals.

Hong Kong through imperial eyes

On the basis of financial and strategic measurements, Hong Kong was unimportant. From Britain's point of view, the colony was neither hugely profitable nor highly defensible; instead like the rest of the Empire, it just happened to be 'there'.

The British Government, however, needed no deep philosophical reasoning to justify its sovereignty over the colonies. Ever since Lord Aberdeen, as British Foreign Secretary, had decided to retain the island of Hong Kong in January 1843 the *causus belli* for Britain being there had ceased to be an issue. Aberdeen informed his plenipotentiary Sir Henry Pottinger in Hong Kong that 'as soon after the exchange of the Ratifications [of the Treaty of Nanking] as may be convenient, you will assume the Government of the island of Hong Kong, then [it will] become a Possession of the British Crown'. Indeed, the only debate within the British government over the future of Hong Kong had occurred in 1842. When Pottinger, at Nanking, had demanded that the Chinese cede Hong Kong to the British he was directly contradicting Aberdeen's orders. Hong Kong, in fact, was not the obvious first choice for a British settlement near China: it was barren, sparsely populated and malaria ridden. In short, there were plenty more desirous spots available. It was not without reason that when the Chinese negotiated the Treaty of Nanking, and accepted the loss of Hong Kong, they merely remarked, 'Is that all?' Aberdeen's decision in January 1843, therefore, settled the matter. Hong Kong would, from that day forth, be part of the British Empire and its position within it was no longer questioned.[4]

Forging the consensus

When the British Pacific Fleet re-entered Hong Kong harbour on 29 August 1945 they carried with them, in spirit at least, the vast majority of the British people, politicians and civil servants. The reassertion of British sovereignty over Hong Kong raised little controversy and much praise in the London press, being symptomatic of a strong belief in Empire which permeated public life. Few people would have been brave enough to argue that Britain's heterogeneous assortment of colonies were as much a liability as an asset to Britain's world ranking as a Great Power.

The forging of this sentiment was a complex process. Interestingly, Britain's defence of her sovereign rights was not fundamentally driven by any perception of tangible British economic or strategic interests. Instead, this implicit imperial consensus was frequently motivated by such abstract terms as 'honour', 'respect' and 'pride'. Representative of this resolve was Sir Maurice Peterson of the Foreign Office, who stated in 1942 that: 'In view of the ignominious circumstances in which we have been bundled out of Hong Kong, we owe it to ourselves to return there and I personally do not believe that we will ever regain that respect in the East unless we do.'[5]

Sometimes financial considerations were presented to support Britain's position in Hong Kong but we shall see that they had more to do with wishful thinking than hard-headed economics. Strategic arguments in favour of the colony likewise usually proved fallacious upon closer inspection. As is often the case when people hold deepseated beliefs, they usually find the answers they are expecting; the same was true of British civil servants attempting to justify the existence of the Empire. The consensus itself had been chiselled into the British psyche through decades of shared cultural and educational experiences which were not easily overturned by military or financial arguments. Perhaps we should not expect self-awareness or analysis from these people; it is only in retrospect that we can decipher the existence and basis of this conformism. For most British people at the time, the equation of Empire with power was an unconscious tenet of life which appeared a successful formula.

A strategic liability

Hong Kong's isolation from other British colonies, and its proximity to the country which laid the foremost claim to the territory, did not promise the most secure strategic base in the British Empire. History would prove this thesis correct. One thousand, four hundred and forty nautical miles from the nearest imperial naval base of Singapore, the colony's security rested chiefly upon its own resources, which geography did little to assist. The coastlines in the colony appeared infinite, the land mass favoured the attacker, while Hong Kong island's strategic position was nullified in the twentieth century by its lack of an aerodrome. The swiftness of Japan's victory over the British and imperial defenders in December 1941 provided a clear example of Hong Kong's vulnerability.

The Governor of Hong Kong in 1922, Sir Reginald Stubbs, foresaw that the eclipse of British naval power in the Pacific would imperil the colony's security. At the conclusion of the Washington Naval Conference in the same year which set limits on American, British and Japanese naval construction, Stubbs argued: 'This is the beginning of the end. I told you the other day that I believe we should hold Hong Kong for another fifty years. I put it now at twenty at the most.'[6] Not only had Britain willingly forsaken her naval dominance and become reliant on American cooperation in the Pacific, but she had also agreed to the prohibition of Hong Kong's naval defences. The failure to renew the 1902 Anglo-Japanese alliance arguably left the colony isolated and exposed to any future Japanese aggression, but now it would also be defenceless. Hong Kong's viability was, as one British newspaper correspondent maintained twenty years later, dependent upon the acquiescence of an impotent mainland power. He argued that: 'If the mainland power is weak or friendly, all is well in Hong Kong. But if the mainland power is strong and hostile, it is untenable.'[7] This strategic assessment, was in fact generally accepted in London even before the war. The Foreign Office saw little of strategic importance in Hong Kong and did not consider it a 'vital interest', while the Chiefs of Staff remained realistic about its defensibility. Still there was never any serious consideration of a British withdrawal from Hong Kong. There were even pockets of dissenters who held the colony was a defensible outpost with the Admiralty prepared to argue that Hong Kong was a linchpin in its pre-war naval strategy.

As a strategic base for naval offensives against Japan, Hong Kong played a central role in the British Admiralty's planning during the 1920s and 1930s.[8] Christopher Bell maintains that until the advent of Japanese airpower and the seizure of surrounding Chinese territory in 1938, the colony was intrinsic to British strategic plans in the Far East against Japan. In the Admiralty's 1931 war memorandum, it was stated that the 'loss of Hong Kong will force us to undertake its recapture before any effective further operations can be undertaken against Japan'.[9] However, with the growing realisation in London that war with Japan was conceivable at some point, Winston Churchill and the Chiefs of Staff never deviated from a pessimistic assessment of Hong Kong's chances in war or its value to British strategy. In spite of this, when the opportunity to evacuate the colony was presented to politicians in London, they were unable to withdraw from this imperial outpost. A mentality had been created amongst British politicians that ranked British 'prestige' and 'honour' before sensible strategies. Not even the Japanese capture of the colony after only 18 days could strip Hong Kong of the term 'strategic asset'. To believe it would do so is to underestimate the resilience of this imperial mentality: it did not ultimately matter whether the defence of Hong Kong was sound because the sentiment behind it – the attempt to safeguard British property – was the backbone of British policy. When the British talked in terms of the colony and strategy they were merely attempting to find a use for Hong Kong, and belatedly justify its existence. The fact that the justification was a bad one, was neither here nor there to the British!

Economics and Hong Kong

The association of Hong Kong with finance is not a particularly modern phenomenon. British merchants such as the Jardines and Mathesons were strong advocates of Hong Kong's seizure in the mid-nineteenth century as a base for their China trade. When Canton was open to Western traders in the summer, the British merchants would locate outside the Chinese city in the 'godowns', or warehouses. It was in winter, when Canton was closed to the foreign traders, that Hong Kong proved its real worth. No longer did the British merchants have to while away the winter in Macau and accept the humiliation of Portuguese rule. Instead, thanks to Sir Henry Pottinger's truculence they now had their own colonial trading base.[10] Yet, despite the influence of trade in Britain's occupation of Hong Kong, before 1941 the colony never became more than one of many imperial trading posts dotted around the globe. Its real economic importance came only after the Second World War. Prior to the outbreak of war, British investments in the colony were relatively small, while China trade was unimportant in comparison to other British trading patterns worldwide. In short, it was more of a financial liability than an asset, similar to other British colonies. This, however, did not matter to London: once the colony was established, trade, like strategy, became a subsidiary motive for retaining Hong Kong.

'A barren rock that will never make a mart...'

On the surface Hong Kong gave every sign of being a bustling, commercial asset. Since Britain wrested Hong Kong island from the Manchu Dynasty in 1842, the colony had grown to represent the industriousness of the Empire. From 'a barren rock that will never make a mart' (according to Lord Palmerston) to the main transhipment port with the Chinese mainland in Southern China, Hong Kong was living proof that Britain's mission was trade and not enslavement. Frank Welsh's *A History of Hong Kong* paints a picture of a Chinese colony, run by the British and drawing strength from the dynamism of mercantile trade and the stability of imperial rule.[11] Primarily, Hong Kong was built for Britain's China trade but it was not the only location for interaction with the Orient; Tientsin and Shanghai in the north of China, both flaunting their extraterritoriality, were equally attractive. Nonetheless, firms such as Jardine Matheson and Swire & Son came to value Hong Kong as a place subject to British law in which to conduct business. Logistically, moreover, the colony was well positioned; it was much closer to home than the north Chinese ports, and nearer to the opium cultivation areas in India.[12] At the outbreak of the Pacific war, these investments were still in place although the ongoing war in China had drastically curtailed the commercial lifeblood of the colony. A look around Hong Kong, though, would have shown the permanence of British rule: the Governor's mansion, the wharves and 'godowns', the Happy Valley racecourse, the golf course, the large buildings of the Hong Kong and Shanghai Bank.

During the war these investments would be referred to by many civil servants and business organisations, notably the China Trade Association, the Board of Trade and the Colonial Office. There was much speculation about the future trade prospects of the 'enormous' China market, and about Hong Kong's role in exploiting such a market. In a 1945 paper on commercial policy in China, the Board of Trade stated without blinking:

> British trade with China has been of substantial importance to this country in the past, although small in relation to the size and population of China. It is obvious that a very slight per capita increase in the productivity and purchasing power of China's vast population could mean a very large increase in her imports . . . It would almost certainly be a mistake to wash our hands of the China market.[13]

Scrutiny of trade and investment figures, however, showed that a lot of the wartime discussions were exaggerated or based on pure delusion. Indeed, utilising the Colonial Office's own financial figures for Hong Kong, printed in their annual 'Blue Book' for the period 1937–40, it is clear that British Empire exports into Hong Kong never rose above 17 per cent of Hong Kong's total imports. The vast majority of imports (34–38 per cent) still came from war-torn China despite the Japanese trade embargo.[14] On the scale of European or American markets, the China market was insignificant; its lowly per capita income putting consumer goods beyond the means of most of its huge populace. Even as a potential market the prospects were not exactly rosy as China struggled to rebuild itself after 15 years of continual war. This is not with the benefit of hindsight either. Reliable trade figures were openly available at the time and they allowed a different interpretation to that made by the Board of Trade. In fact, the Treasury refused post-war credits to China for the very reason that the China market was unimportant.

The illusion of China trade

Occasionally Foreign Office personnel such as the assistant under-secretary, Victor Cavendish-Bentinck, could be as forthright as the Treasury in denying the importance of the China market. In March 1945, Cavendish-Bentinck stated that 'China is not vital to the maintenance of our Empire and we can do without our China trade. So long as we maintain control of the seaways, a direct threat from the direction of China is not serious.'[15] Ernest Bevin's Far Eastern review in December 1945 corroborated this view, believing that 'trade with China was never large' and the China market 'seems still to be far off'.[16] The reason that the Foreign Office felt comfortable disparaging China trade was because Britain's continued presence in Hong Kong did not rest upon commerce. In fact, Whitehall bureaucrats frequently held an anti-business bias, believing that it was beneath their more cherished pursuits of uplifting native peoples and enforcing British sovereignty. Widespread ignorance of economic factors remained prevalent even at high levels within the British Government. Anthony Eden, for example, did not even realise in 1945 that the colony's attraction for international trade had previously rested on its free port (no duties) status. Among the comments of his civil servants he minuted, 'I had not known that Hong Kong was a free port.'[17]

The assumption that Hong Kong was a major economic asset must therefore be treated with a great deal of scepticism. The colony only needed to be assumed a financial asset in Whitehall, and not proven to be so. Financial facts were peripheral to the overall discussion on colonies in general, with Hong Kong being no exception to that rule.

Occasionally junior personnel within the Foreign Office would try to move policy formulation onto a more rational basis, asking for an assessment of the colony's economic and strategic worth (since they felt unable to offer one themselves). In January 1943 Sir John Brenan of the China department suggested 'that the various departments might be invited to consider seriously what importance they attach to the indefinite retention of the colony from (a) a military and (b) a commercial point of view.' His head of department, Ashley Clarke, agreed, believing that:

> without such an investigation it is impossible to form a sound judgement as to whether Hong Kong under British sovereignty will be an asset or a liability, and without knowing that we cannot be sure what policy will best serve British interests. It would seem to be for the Colonial Office to take up this suggestion with the Chiefs of Staff and Board of Trade.[18]

This enquiring attitude remained distinctly a minority point of view because it fundamentally misunderstood the wider basis of British imperial policy. It should have been little surprise that the China department's suggestion was quietly laid to rest. The fact that a strategic assessment of Hong Kong had to be suggested at all illustrated the British authorities' nonchalant attitude to the financial and military costs of the colony. Earlier English 'free-traders' in the late nineteenth century had advocated similar 'rational' ideas to those of Ashley Clarke and Brenan, but for the Empire as a whole. Richard Cobden had argued that little or no economic advantage accrued to Britain from the establishment of a formal Empire, while there was an increased likelihood of becoming involved in expansionist wars of dubious justification. These so-called 'free-traders' held that political control of foreign lands with all the associated defence and administrative expenditures was unjustifiable. Paradoxically, however, none of these people seriously contemplated the dismemberment of the existing Empire: they too subscribed to the belief that Empire and Britain were irrevocably intertwined![19] Times had not changed much.

Colonies were not measured principally in pounds and pence or in commercial utility. Instead, the basis of Britain's claim to Hong Kong was almost spiritual, and could be found in the hearts and minds of the British people. Colonies were perceived as an inheritance to treasure and nurture; they were a source of pride and strength, and not the millstones which Rudyard Kipling alluded to in *White Man's Burden*. Oliver Stanley, Colonial Secretary from 1942, like many other British ministers believed that economics were not of supreme importance in colonial debates. Arguing against the notoriously penny-pinching Treasury for increases to the Colonial Development and Welfare Act, he made 'no pretence . . . that this is going to be a profitable transaction on a purely financial calculation. The overriding reason why I feel that these proposals are essential is the necessity to justify our position as a Colonial power.'[20]

An imperial mentality: the cornerstone of British consensus

A consensus of any sort does not develop overnight, and the same was true of Britain's imperial consensus. It was the product of decades of shared educational and cultural experiences which originated in early Georgian Britain. Between the period 1750 and 1918 an empire was constructed that was so immense that it covered one-fifth of the land mass of the globe and incorporated 410 million people. It was the biggest empire the world had ever known.[21] At school, children learnt the names and locations of the multitude of heterogeneous Dominions, Crown colonies, and dependencies that constructed the empire. The term 'empire' was itself appropriated by the British to become 'Empire', a shorthand for the British Empire. Whatever the various motivations behind these annexations, British society was profoundly affected by the all-pervasive Empire. In its construction the British people found a deeply-rooted pride and fulfilment that manifested itself in an imperial mentality. William Gladstone went as far as stating in 1879 that: 'The sentiment of Empire may be called innate in every Briton.'[22] With the passing of time the British Empire had ceased to be the burning issue in the public consciousness it once was and had become an accepted feature of British life. By the eve of World War Two the conscious conviction of the superiority of British civilisation had increasingly mellowed to become an implicit belief in Empire. Nevertheless, the potency of this understanding was not diminished and underpinned British Hong Kong policy during the war. Through a set of shared beliefs and backgrounds a broad church of colonial agreement, incorporating voices as disparate as those of the socialist leader, Clement Attlee, and the arch-imperialist Winston Churchill, governed the acceptable limits of Hong Kong policy across the British 'Establishment'. For all the personal and political differences within the British Government, the indispensability of the Empire was settled; Britain would reconquer her lost Far Eastern colonies.

Education: 'A veritable rock of salvation in a drifting world . . .'

The seeds of imperial thinking were instilled early on in life. When a child started school, history and geography played a central role in the school curriculum. This was a generation used to viewing a globe of the world painted pink, and knowing that Britain stood at the zenith of her power. The education process of the governing classes was even more strongly biased to inculcate the moral and philosophical aspects of imperial thinking. This fact was exceptionally important because Whitehall, the London government system, drew its applicants from an extremely narrow class that invariably had a public school and Oxbridge education.

Most upper-middle class and upper-class parents sent their children, as they themselves had been sent, to public school. The public school curriculum was skewed towards the liberal arts, and discouraged practical and financial skills. Interestingly, the Empire was not presented in economic or strategic terms but from a moral point of view. If not quite as 'trusts from God', the colonies were at least perceived on a ethical basis; it was commonly held that Britain had a duty to civilise the world. The term 'mother country' itself implied the filial relationship of the colonies to Britain. Colonies would be ruled in trust for their 'backwards' inhabitants until they had sufficiently matured to take care of their own destinies.

From the public schools, the children of the elite passed to a complacent Oxbridge where, according to Correlli Barnett, 'amid the silent eloquence of grey Gothic walls and green sward, the sons of engineers, merchants and manufacturers were emasculated into gentlemen'. Oxbridge continued the liberal arts bias, placing great emphasis on academic and moral skills rather than practical knowledge. This was the finishing school for a governing class who would see 'the British Empire

. . . less as a repository of resources to be exploited than as a great instrument of civilisation and enlightenment, the successor to Greece and Rome; their own role as being that of super-prefects, administering the Empire justly in the interests of the governed.' [23] These were not people who enjoyed the cut and thrust of the commercial world, or the intricacies of a balance sheet. Instead, they preferred philosophical detachment and academic argument in a life of civil service. The application of this analysis to the Foreign Office, for example, helps explain why financial arguments imposed themselves so rarely upon discussions of Hong Kong's future. A senior member of the Hong Kong Government interned by the Japanese wrote cuttingly of his anti-business feelings. He recorded in his secret diary:

> I had a long talk with Sloss on the outlook of the Hong Kong mercantile community towards post-war reconstruction. They cannot appear to consider any other world than the one in which they can make money and retire. How they can imagine the youth of England sacrificing themselves just to permit the Hong Kong merchants again to recuperate themselves by ill-gotten dividends I cannot conceive. It appears to me a total misapprehension of the origins of the war if the pride of the youth of Britain is to be sacrificed for the securing of ill-gotten dividends. This statement is in my opinion no exaggeration and merely typical of the egotistic materialism of Hong Kong.[24]

The homogeneity of background did not just apply to members of the civil service within Whitehall; parliament was also dominated by public school and Oxbridge educated males. The use of political loyalties to differentiate MPs in isolation from other factors disguised the widespread agreement on the fundamentals of British foreign and colonial policy. Although Winston Churchill led an ostensibly coalition government during the war, senior Labour and Conservative members shared similar educational backgrounds. Some even knew their opposite counterpart from school or university. Clement Attlee, for all his socialist posturing, was a middle-class product of the old liberal public schools and Oxford,[25] as were Anthony Eden, Winston Churchill, Alexander Cadogan and Sir Stafford Cripps; the list was endless. A non-Oxbridge education was very much the exception in any Whitehall or government position.[26] A member of the Foreign Office observed this phenomenon (of which he was himself a part):

> The entire Government machine on the foreign side, outside No. 10, was at the beginning of the war dominated by old Etonians . . . Eden, Halifax, Cadogan, Vansittart, Neville Henderson (regrettably) . . . Macmillan . . . even the two Ministers successively responsible for SOE, Dalton and Selborne.

But he insisted that this was not necessarily a bad thing, in fact he argued that it probably 'did do something to facilitate relationships and thus promote efficiency'![27] The view that this conformity was a benefit and not a hindrance to the Empire could also be found within the Colonial Office. As late as the 1920s, for example, the officer in charge of recruitment to the Colonial Service regarded the public school 'as the spiritual child of chivalry', producing exactly the kind of person he wanted for 'a really crusading service'.[28]

Once the products of the public schools and Oxbridge had ascended to government service, the influence of their narrow backgrounds inevitably began to exert itself. Social improvements were often sponsored in the colonies as a means of bringing civilisation to 'backwards areas', even though it was of no immediate economic benefit to Britain herself. The sanitary improvements in Hong Kong and the control of prostitution and *mui-tsai* (child slavery) were small examples of such social conscience. It was, perhaps, sweetly ironic that the Chinese, who elaborately maintained that they had already attained the pinnacle of civilisation, found themselves on the receiving end of the West's 'barbarian' social improvements.

The burdens (and the financial and military costs) of Empire were readily accepted by the British Establishment because they had been conditioned to accept them. More than this, the costs were inescapable because the Empire *was* British power. Oliver Stanley, as Colonial Secretary, made this point repeatedly. He told the Cabinet in late 1944 that money for colonial development was essential:

> I am not pretending that the assistance to the colonies which I propose will not impose some burden upon this country. I do,

however, feel that the Colonial Empire means so much to us that we should be prepared to assume burdens for its future . . . If these sums are widely spent . . . there will in the long run accrue considerable benefits to us . . . But I am not basing my argument on material gains for ourselves, important as these may be. My feeling is that in the years to come, without the Commonwealth and the Empire, this country will play a small role in world affairs.[29]

The homogenous backgrounds of British policymakers with their antipathy for business should, therefore, make it unsurprising that these people put the stability of the British Empire before all else. Faced with an increasingly desperate need to defend Hong Kong in 1940, the Deputy Chief of the Naval Staff appealed to imperial glory rather than strategic necessity. He reasoned that the Chiefs of Staff's sensible relegation of the colony to a mere outpost 'was fundamentally wrong and not in accordance with our position as a great maritime power . . . Hong Kong is our most exposed outpost and we should do all we can to defend it without too many arguments; if it comes to war we should man the defences and fight as our forefathers did in many similar positions.'[30]

While the reality of British power may have waned, the mindset within Whitehall was still firmly rooted in the nineteenth century.

Individuals and Whitehall: reinforcing the consensus

An imperial consensus without a mechanism for self-enforcement would have only a theoretical existence. As it was, however, the London government bureaucracy in Whitehall provided a mechanism to translate British imperial sentiment into action. Through its system of government offices a rigid and hierarchical structure was established to coordinate British foreign and colonial policies, including Hong Kong's. Individuals, moreover, could not be ignored. Whitehall was not an empty bureaucratic edifice staffed by faceless civil servants. Senior civil servants, in particular, had as much, if not more, influence at certain times than the elected politicians who stood at their head. Whilst it could take a minister months to understand the intricacies of a diplomatic problem, the civil servant would have followed the difficulty since its inception. Even so, key politicians within the British Government, specifically Winston Churchill, Anthony Eden and Oliver Stanley, unashamedly promoted imperial interests. Working together, key civil servants and politicians exerted a significant, and sometimes decisive, control over British imperial policy.

The Whitehall bureaucracy

Whitehall was a hierarchy like any other bureaucracy. At its summit was the Cabinet which included leading politicians selected for political and meritocratic reasons, each representing various government offices. The Cabinet itself was headed by the Prime Minister whose position became increasingly influential in the extremities of war. Indeed, there were in effect two Cabinets during the hostilities; the growth of government and urgency of the situation meant that decisions had to be made quickly. A select few ministers were therefore included in a War Cabinet which masterminded Britain's war effort.

Beneath the Cabinet were various offices representing all things bright and not so beautiful. For example, the Board of Trade managed commerce, the Treasury held the purse strings of government, the Foreign Office dealt with diplomacy, and the Colonial Office organised the administration of British colonies. However, the principal offices that concerned themselves with Hong Kong were the Foreign and Colonial Offices.

The Foreign and Colonial Offices

The Foreign Office was regarded as the most prestigious office at Cabinet, a hangover from Britain's imperial heyday. This fact was augmented by Anthony Eden's tenure since he was also the acknowledged heir to Winston Churchill during the war. The office had a long tradition of considering diplomacy a sophisticated art form and was unaccustomed to outside interference: what it said usually went in Whitehall.

The Colonial Office, however, was never considered a first-class appointment for politicians. Administering the colonies was mundane compared to the dashing, international deal-making pursued at the Foreign Office. Once the Empire had passed its zenith, the office gathered the image of a place where time stood still and where a prolonged stay would spell the wilderness for a political career. It was, perhaps, symbolic that the Colonial Office was situated in particularly cramped offices in Downing Street.

Cooperation between the two offices was fundamental to the formation of Whitehall's Hong Kong policy, but it was an uneasy relationship. There was an inherent tendency towards conflict because they were interdependent. The Foreign Office controlled Britain's China policy while the Colonial Office controlled the administration of Hong Kong, an issue which could not readily be divorced from the diplomatic minefield of relations with China and America. To an extent, the imperial consensus moderated bureaucratic friction but it could not remove personal and departmental animosities rooted in human nature. Retrospectively, the existence of the Colonial Office as a separate entity is surprising. It added an extra layer of bureaucracy to an already complex situation, even ignoring the issue of cost. The administration of colonies could quite easily have been performed by a department within the Foreign Office, but this was not to be.

Instead, the Colonial Office continued to exist as the Foreign Office's poor relation within Whitehall. Even diplomats within the Foreign Office occasionally lamented its lowly status. Anthony Eden's private secretary, dismayed at the appointment of Oliver Stanley as Colonial Secretary, remarked: 'The Colonial Office is one of the most important and venerable of our Government departments; yet it is always a Cinderella.'[31] Things had changed little in the 100 years of the Colonial Office's existence. It was always a step to somewhere else, a brief stop in government in preparation for higher office. Rarely did anyone choose to become Colonial Secretary. A comparison of Colonial and Foreign Secretaries illustrates that ministerial 'turnover' was twice as rapid at the Colonial Office. Even if the Colonial Secretary wanted to take an active policy role, the nature of the office's organisation and the huge variety of colonies stood in his way. Much of the office's decision making remained with 'the man on the spot' which meant that the Colonial Secretary or the permanent under-secretary were not automatically informed of important policy dilemmas. The variety of colonies also mitigated against general principles being applied willy-nilly across the Empire, making a tight grasp on colonial policy difficult. Lord Cranborne, Colonial Secretary, told the Chinese Ambassador in September 1942, that 'It was almost impossible to lay down a cut and dried policy for all colonies alike.'[32]

Institutionally, the Colonial Office's Achilles heel was that its policies largely rested on the machinations of the Foreign Office: colonial policy could not exist in opposition to (the Foreign Office's) foreign policy, although the reverse was not true. This state of affairs may have been unproblematic in more peaceful times, but the Second World War profoundly affected both Britain's colonies and her position in the world. In the case of Hong Kong this sometimes brought foreign and colonial policies into open conflict, particularly as the Foreign Office often took a more sympathetic approach to Anglo-American relations.

Ashley Clarke, head of the Far Eastern department within the Foreign Office, expressed what he saw as the Colonial Office's narrow viewpoint over Hong Kong: They 'are very anxious that any settlement in regard to Hong Kong should be an Anglo-Chinese affair and that the Americans shall not come into it'.[33] International relations, however, made it increasingly hard for the Foreign Office to pursue an independent foreign policy as openly as the Colonial Office would have liked. Britain had grown increasingly dependent on American military and financial aid during the war. The resolution of this dilemma remained a constant anxiety in relations between the Colonial Office and the Foreign Office.

Other Whitehall offices

There were few government offices outside the triangle of the Prime Minister, Foreign Office and Colonial Office which affected Hong Kong policy directly or conspicuously. This select grouping, however, could not always act in bureaucratic isolation and there were several other offices which on occasion helped influence and define Hong Kong policy.

It has been said that the Treasury was, and remains, a graveyard for aspiring politicians. Although it is a hugely prestigious post, the incumbent Chancellor of the Exchequer has always found it hard to please anyone, never mind everyone. They either stand accused of the policies of their predecessors, or of their own profligacy and short-termism. Nearly all Whitehall offices dislike the Treasury for curtailing their spending targets. Britain's bankruptcy during the war did not, however, result in a marked enlargement of the Treasury's power to influence foreign policy. This should perhaps not be surprising considering the Empire's traditional disregard for financial factors. Nonetheless, the Treasury's insistence that Britain could not afford political loans to China or post-war credits did define the Foreign Office and Board of Trade's stance at certain times, with implications for Hong Kong.

The Board of Trade, which aimed to promote British commerce around the world, also assumed a peripheral role in the formation of Hong Kong policy. It was a minor office and therefore frequently found itself limited by the Treasury's stringent budget cuts. The office was, though, a keen supporter of Hong Kong as a trading base for British interests in China, and the Colonial Office was quick to see the advantage of using such ideas to justify Hong Kong retention post-war.

The Chiefs of Staff committee representing the three main services – the army, the navy and the airforce – was more successful in influencing the Whitehall triumvirate of Hong Kong policy offices. The Chiefs of Staff held within their grasp Britain's military potential to recapture Hong Kong. They acted as the liaison between Cabinet and the military, operating under Cabinet direction. This explains why Winston Churchill spent so much time with the Chiefs of Staff (much to their chagrin), following the military minutiae which he loved so much. Although their point of view was primarily military and logistical, with passing reference to political consequences, they came under constant political pressure to steer British military policy towards political ends. In the Far East that meant pushing imperial forces towards the recapture of her lost colonies: Burma, Malaya, Singapore and Borneo. Hong Kong, however, presented a particular problem. The geographical and strategic position of the colony made Hong Kong's recapture by British forces a logistical nightmare: it was thousands of miles from a British base, and was included in the American-dominated Chinese theatre of operations.

With Britain's marginalisation in the China theatre by American and Chinese interests, the importance of the newly created Ministry of Economic Warfare, commonly known as Special Operations Executive (SOE), was dramatically illustrated. In past histories of the Far East its significance has been overlooked, partly due to the restricted nature of its documents. SOE was a thinly veiled cover for clandestine and subversive operations against Axis forces. Set up in 1939, SOE operated, among other places, in the Far East. Although the Ministry had an uncertain position within Whitehall, SOE was a bastion of imperial thinking and a prime mover in devising schemes to resurrect British rule in Hong Kong. SOE agents were the only British personnel who had access to the Hong Kong area and provided invaluable intelligence on the colony. It was no wonder that the Colonial Office became strong sponsors of SOE. Some of SOE's schemes, however, were justifiably criticised. For example, an effort to exfiltrate Chinese dock labour from Hong Kong with the promise of new jobs and higher wages was a complete waste of time and money. It cost several million dollars to achieve a negligible effect on Japanese shipbuilding capacity in the colony, while it removed skilled labour from where it was most needed post-war. Appropriately, this was codenamed Operation Nonchalant![34] Other SOE strategies, though, were vital in retaining Britain's toehold in the colony. Working through the British Army Aid Group (BAAG) which operated around the Hong Kong area rescuing POWs, a direct link with the British prisoners in the colony was maintained. This link potentially offered the only opportunity that Britain had to seize the colony by force at the end of the war. This was a practical counterpoise to the bureaucratic hypothesising which dominated much of London's planning.

Regardless of how accurate or useful SOE reports were, its voice was limited within Whitehall. Hugh Dalton, its first minister, was a difficult man to work with and did little to endear the new ministry to other established offices. A seconded Foreign Office official sent to keep an eye on him called him 'the reverse of easy'. In a ridiculous demarcation dispute with Brendan Bracken at the Ministry of Information which degenerated into personal insults, little was done to boost his credibility, and ultimately led to his transfer to the Board of Trade in early 1942.[35] Dalton's replacement, Lord Selborne, although possessed of more diplomacy than his predecessor, could do little to prevent SOE's marginalisation from real power and had to appeal to his personal friendship with Churchill to save the ministry on several occasions. The Foreign Office was extremely suspicious of SOE and thought it was encroaching on its jurisdiction. Anthony Eden told Churchill: 'It is incongruous that the Ministry of Economic Warfare should control SOE. The minister is neither a member of the War Cabinet, nor the Defence Committee. He cannot therefore be aware of our secret policies and purposes.'[36]

Personality and Empire

Any analysis of Whitehall policy making cannot be divorced from the personalities that stood behind it. The role of Winston Churchill, in particular, remained pivotal. Other less well-known figures also contributed to the rebuilding of imperial confidence which had been destroyed by the events of 1941. Gerard Gent, in charge of Hong Kong policy at the Colonial Office, was unrelenting in his lobbying for British sovereignty; Sir Maurice Peterson, former ambassador to Franco's Spain, remained a pillar of imperial mindedness at the Foreign Office. Whatever military strength Britain lacked in the Far Eastern war was more than countered by the imperial commitment of so many of these civil servants, politicians and servicemen.

Leading by example: Winston Churchill

Winston Churchill's role in resuscitating imperial confidence, and the resultant drive to recapture and retain her lost colonies, should not be underestimated. He stood at the helm of British government throughout the Far Eastern war, save for a month at its end. While he could not keep up with the day to day minutiae of policy, Churchill took a particular interest in broad policy affecting diplomatic and colonial matters. Only Anthony Eden was regarded as equally competent in the sphere of foreign affairs. After an uncertain start to his premiership, by the time the Pacific war broke out he appeared an almost indispensable component to the smooth running of British government. It would be an exaggeration to assert that foreign and colonial policy could not be made in opposition to Churchill, but it was undoubtedly difficult. By nature he was not a committee man or a party man, despite his heavy involvement with both. Instead, he held certain deep-rooted beliefs that were forcibly articulated to his Cabinet colleagues and the general public. Perhaps inevitably, therefore, Whitehall found itself dominated by his strategic thinking. The beliefs Churchill held are therefore invariably important.

In many ways he shared the Victorian imperial outlook, believing that it was Britain's mission to civilise and rule lesser peoples. On 10 November 1942 he delivered his celebrated Mansion House speech outlining British colonial policy. He told his audience:

> Let me, however, make this clear, in case there should be any mistake about it in any quarter. We mean to hold our own. I have not become the King's First Minister in order to preside over the liquidation of the British Empire. (Loud cheers.) For that task, if it ever were presented, someone else would have to be found . . .

He continued, reaffirming his faith:

> I am proud to be a member of that vast commonwealth and society of nations and communities gathered in and around the ancient British monarchy, without which the good cause might well have perished from the face of the earth. Here we are, and here we stand, a veritable rock of salvation in a drifting world . . . we have no need to make excuses or apologies.[37]

This was not an atypical speech, and like all his major speeches, it was carefully written for its particular audience, whether present or an ocean away. Neither was it mere rhetoric; the Prime Minister was persuaded that with the victory at El Alamein in late 1942, the time had come to reaffirm what Britain stood for in the peace. The impact of this speech can be measured by the numerous references to it made by government departments, setting the direction of policy from which practical plans could be developed. It was clear above all else that Empire would remain at the heart of British foreign policy. The similar beliefs held by the civil servants made them predisposed to agree.

Anthony Eden at the Foreign Office

At Churchill's right hand stood Anthony Eden, his Foreign Secretary. He was a very able and industrious lieutenant who shared his Prime Minister's colonial viewpoint, if not his temper. Relations between the two were of the utmost importance in efforts to preserve the Empire and, despite stormy patches, were based on mutual affection. Eden remained at King Charles Street, home of the Foreign Office, for the period of the Pacific war, allowing a consistent and stable foreign policy to develop in close consultation with the Prime Minister. Indeed, Churchill insisted that Eden remain at the Foreign Office despite his immense workload because he had become so dependent upon his heir apparent.

While there was mutual understanding on the need to prevent American isolationism and defend the Empire, there was also room for disagreement. For example, Eden took a more sympathetic view of Chinese aspirations. Whereas Churchill was quick to castigate Chiang Kai-shek's pseudo-totalitarian regime as a 'faggot vote' on behalf of America, the Foreign Secretary attempted to mollify Chinese claims over Hong Kong through cooperation rather than confrontation.[38] Indeed, it was Eden who later urged Churchill not to sign the secret Yalta agreement between America and Russia which conceded Chinese territory to the Soviets without consulting the Chinese. He called it 'discreditable'; 'It was unjust to take decisions affecting the future of China without consulting her and in the absence of her representatives.'[39]

Eden's alternative approach to the colonial issue, however, did not necessarily go down well with more ardent imperialists within the government. The accusation from Leo Amery, Secretary of State at the India Office, and Oliver Stanley, Colonial Secretary, that Eden was soft on the Empire never quite left him. On the other hand, there was little for all that to separate Eden and the more fervent imperialists over Hong Kong's future. After receiving a request from the British Ambassador in China to consider negotiating away the colony's leased territory, the Foreign Secretary minuted (original emphasis): 'Certainly not. We are only yielding *extraterritorial* rights. Hong Kong is British territory whether leased or not.'[40] Personal enmity frequently explained such misconceptions.

Foreign Office civil servants and junior ministers also played an important role advising Eden on the development of Hong Kong policy. Gladwyn Jebb, estranged within the Foreign Office after a sojourn with SOE, thought that Eden had 'antennae in all directions, but no brain. He doesn't read papers, he only sniffs them.'[41] Although this view was incited by resentment, it holds a certain truth since both Churchill and Eden only read (what were thought to be) the most important papers. Necessarily, this meant that much of the foreign affairs workload fell back onto the professional diplomats. The permanent under-secretary during the period, Sir Alexander Cadogan, managed the civil servants regardless of political changes in government. Cadogan's relationship with Eden was especially important. A weak secretary of state would have been dependent on his under-secretary for advice and expertise. A strong-minded and knowledgeable secretary would have used the under-secretary to translate his ideas into action. More often, the reality was somewhere between these extremes. Alexander Cadogan exemplified this: he was at the same time councillor and delegate for Eden. With both of them having considerable Far Eastern experience, they swiftly built up a healthy respect for each other's abilities. For Cadogan this often meant taking the lead on Hong Kong policy. His under-secretary regularly recorded 'Masses of paper and . . . files from A[nthony Eden] marked "A[lexander] C[adogan] please speak".'[42]

Eden was also assisted by a deputy under-secretary from the House of Commons, Richard Law MP. Below Law and Cadogan were assistant under-secretaries like Sir Maurice Peterson, who often decided what was shown to Eden and Cadogan. Peterson's other duty was writing the many letters on Eden's behalf concerning Hong Kong. Heads of department were the next rank down on the seniority ladder. Ashley Clarke was head of the Far Eastern department in the Foreign Office in 1941. His job was to flesh out the choices facing his superiors, and possibly suggest favoured alternatives. Councillors, such as Sir John Brenan, assisted in this task.

Lord Cranborne and Oliver Stanley at the Colonial Office

Personal relations were never more in evidence than in dealings between the Foreign Office and the Colonial Office. When Lord Cranborne was Colonial Secretary for a brief interlude during Britain's Far Eastern setbacks of 1942, the two offices worked well together. The key reason was that Cranborne, or 'Bobbety' as he was affectionately known, was a close friend to Anthony Eden. The two men and their respective wives met socially, and knew each other's opinions without having to set foot inside Whitehall. This brief honeymoon did not last long, however. Traditional Foreign Office–Colonial Office rivalries quickly resurfaced with Cranborne's departure in November 1942 for the Dominions Office. His successor, Oliver Stanley, lacked the close personal friendship with Eden which offered to moderate the natural antagonisms between the two offices. Although Eden and Stanley shared very similar social backgrounds (both were old Etonians) and imperial views, their political rivalry exacerbated prejudices between their respective offices over Hong Kong policy.

The appointment of Oliver Stanley to the Colonial Office was, in fact, partly a conciliatory gesture at Churchill's behest, as well as a political manoeuvre. The Foreign Office realised that it would reduce Eden's political power base and thus his ability to stand up to Churchill. Eden's private secretary recorded in his diary negative thoughts which were no doubt shared by his superior: 'The appointment of Stanley is an appeasement. He is a disgruntled and disloyal critic outside; inside he will prove a flabby and timid Colonial Secretary.'[43] According to Hugh Dalton, an important member of the Labour Party, Stanley reciprocated these feelings. When Dalton dined with Stanley the latter proceeded to bad-mouth both the Prime Minister and his Foreign Secretary. Stanley thought that '[Eden] was the sort of man who ought [not] to be close to the Prime Minister. He was, he added, vain, weak and unreliable.'[44]

When the Churchill coalition was formed Oliver Stanley had been offered the Dominions office but, being a loyal Chamberlainite, had turned it down. Stanley's letter of refusal to Churchill made it perfectly clear that there was little love lost between himself and the new Prime Minister:

I have felt from the beginning that the obvious antipathy of minds and outlook, which has led to increasing tensions between the two of us during the last few months, would make a proper relationship between a minister and his chief almost impossible. You have made it abundantly clear on many occasions that you mistrust my capacity . . . The contemptuous, if frank way in which the appointment was offered revealed the position only too clearly. You may be quite right when you say that I lack drive and initiative, but, if I do, I ought not to be a minister and, if you think I do, then you ought not to ask me to be one.[45]

Stanley, however, could not be ignored. He was very much a member of the Tory hierarchy, and as such, someone Churchill felt he ought to placate. In 1941 Churchill was persuaded to offer him the Colonial Office, and Stanley's temper having cooled, he accepted. But privately the Prime Minister still disliked Stanley. Churchill thought that he was 'really suited to be a Dean of a Cathedral, walking round the monastic fish-ponds and contemplating some academic "mot" which he could bring out next time he was invited to dine with the Fellows of his old College'.[46]

Despite rampant personal egos and backbiting within Whitehall, imperial consensus and the civil service structure ameliorated the most destructive aspects of human foibles. For example, notwithstanding political enmity, Oliver Stanley remained emphatically supportive of Churchill's uncompromising brand of colonialism. Under Stanley, the Colonial Office became unyielding in its determination not to surrender Hong Kong to China. Speaking at Oxford in March 1943, Stanley dismissed American interference in the Empire, and reaffirmed that the British colonies would remain the sole responsibility of Great Britain.[47] Remaining in office until the end of the war, he ensured that a consistent Colonial Office voice was heard within Whitehall, augmented by his staff of civil servants. Most important was Sir George Gater, permanent under-secretary, and under-secretary Gerard Gent, in charge of Hong Kong policy.[48]

Clement Attlee and the questioning of Empire

The all-embracing nature of the imperial consensus was demonstrated by the fact that Clement Attlee, the Labour Party leader, remained the only significant critic of British imperialism within the London Establishment. As an avid supporter of American-sponsored internationalism and the concept of the United Nations, he challenged the continued need for British imperial bases. In one of his first memoranda as Prime Minister in 1945, he argued that the old concepts of imperial sovereignty were outdated and unnecessary:

> If the new organisation [of the United Nations] is a reality, it does not matter who holds Cyrenaica or Somalia or controls the Suez Canal. If it is not a reality we had better be thinking of the defence of England, for unless we can protect the home country no strategic position elsewhere will avail.

The establishment of trusteeships (where Britain renounced her sovereignty over her colonies but temporarily retained control) was also rejected by Attlee not because it was appeasement of American anti-colonialism, but because of its economic costs. He thought it would 'involve us in immediate [financial] loss. There is no prospect of their paying for themselves. The more we do for them the quicker shall we be faced with the premature claims of self-government. We have quite enough of these awkward problems already.'[49] Despite the radical agenda which these questions suggested, however, the Labour leader provided little real opposition to the old imperial thinking. Although he was highly intelligent, Attlee was also a weak and vacillating leader of the Labour Party; a compromise candidate arrived at by default precisely because other contenders were too divisive.[50] Behind his romantic yearning for international socialism, lay a preoccupation with domestic social reform. Foreign affairs was of interest only to the extent that it would drain money from those reforms.[51] Furthermore, while his influence within the coalition government was undermined by his own party, Attlee also found it difficult to resist calls for government unity. Despite his initial misgivings he agreed to put his name to Lord Cranborne's colonial paper which committed Britain to returning to the Far East. It stressed the benefits of imperialism where only defeat had 'blotted out . . . our long record of positive and beneficial achievements', with future 'British participation in the management of Asia . . . essential to its stability and welfare in the future'.[52] In such circumstances, there was no real alternative propounded within Whitehall to Britain's imperial role.

An explanation of British policy must look beyond tangible interests. The retention of Hong Kong was a reflex action of a deeply ingrained imperialist instinct; an attempt to preserve British Imperial power when it was ebbing away. Porter and Stockwell conclude that:

No one seriously questioned the costs of reoccupying the South East Asian colonies and Hong Kong. No government has ever found it easy to reduce significant engagements inherited from the past; only a few have found it possible. In the absence of that careful planning which might have produced accurate or convincing analysis of imperial expenditure, and amid the tangle of existing commitments to imperial mission, colonial self-government and developments, material shortages and financial costs alone rarely provided conclusive arguments against Empire.[53]

3
The Anglo-American Relationship at War, 1941–45

[T]he British Empire, certain of its destiny must take long views
. . . Experience shows that foreign traders and others including
the Americans would only be too pleased to see 'British
Imperialism' serve as the lightning conductor in a storm of
hatred which would otherwise involve them . . . [I have] the
faith that under God the British Commonwealth of Nations is
the greatest power on earth for good.[1]

Sir George Moss, 1944

The British want to recapture Burma. It's the first time they've
shown any real interest in the Pacific War, and why? For their
colonial Empire! . . . It's all part of the British colonial question. Burma – that affects India, and French Indo-China, and
Indonesia – they're all interrelated. If one gets freedom, the
others get ideas.[2]

President Roosevelt, Casablanca Conference, 1942

During the Second World War, Britain and America stood against
tyranny, supported 'democracy' and had the military strength to change
the world. Such collective values were a rarity in those desperate times.
Nonetheless, the most surprising aspect of Anglo-American relations
during the war were the strains placed upon them. These two Great
Powers, once subject and master, fought a diplomatic and military battle
which was in some senses as bloody and bitter as those fought against
the Axis powers. Overlooking their mutual understandings, they preferred to wallow in petty squabbles, one of which was the future status
of Hong Kong. It was only towards the end of the war that relations
began to heal.

The Anglo-American relationship dominated British thinking during the Second World War but not Washington's. Where London saw one true ally, America saw several. President Roosevelt split the world into regional alliances, using Russia in eastern Europe, Britain in Western Europe, and China in the Far East. Britain, however, preferred to cast herself as Washington's sole global ally, in a world where Britain and America could divide up the post-war spoils between themselves. Such notions flattered Britain's imperial ego and offered to protect Britain's empire for a while longer. The realities of the Far Eastern war, though, began to pick apart this misleading assumption.

In many respects the Anglo-American alliance was geographically restricted to Europe. In the Far East, America hoped to build a special relationship with the Chinese leader, Chiang Kai-shek, in the process displacing the old imperial powers. London's refusal to acknowledge this, combined with her decision to reconquer the lost Asian possessions, set her on collision course with America. Whatever the British did it would not be enough to appease innate American anti-colonialism. London tried to present its struggle for Empire as compatible with American ideas of democracy, internationalism and sovereign rights but to no avail. London was acutely aware of Washington's imperial hypocrisy with its implicit ideology of materialism and free trade, but this was of little comfort. The British Empire could not afford the Second World War and was held materially and economically hostage to Washington's benevolence. From the heady heights of imperial glory, it was a humiliating climbdown for Britain.

The recapture of Hong Kong became a test case between British imperial intransigence and America's new found military and economic might. If Britain had difficulty coming to terms with her descent from power, America had problems exercising her strength responsibly. The reality of global war was that neither of them could fight it alone. Considering Washington's antipathy, it was remarkable that Britain's Far Eastern empire emerged largely intact out of the Second World War.

The many faces of the Anglo-American relationship

Bad marriages can suffer from agonising silences and passionate arguments. The Anglo-American relationship had its share of both. The first and most important disagreement, however, stemmed from the fact that neither Britain nor America was prepared to concede the pre-eminence of the other. They were too used to acting independently. Each country considered itself to be a world power in its own right and wanted to do things their own way. The collapse of the British Empire in the Far East allowed Americans to believe that the Empire was a spent force while Washington's breezy rhetoric concerning Chinese democracy and trade allowed London to believe that the Americans were 'children playing with bricks'.[3] Neither was necessarily true. Although strategically the Empire had been stretched and snapped, Britain retained a strong influence in the Far East. Many indigenous peoples still looked to Britain for leadership while it is often forgotten that India fielded the largest volunteer army of the Second World War. At the same time, Britain's dismissal of American 'universalism', a vision of free trade and democracy, overlooked the power of trade to improve standards of living, including her own. The freeing of trade was in some way related to the widening of democracy. It is arguable that London's system of imperial preference had retarded the British economy by sheltering her industry from foreign competition and innovation. Taken together, the fundamental misconceptions held by London and Washington meant that compromise usually resulted in resentment. Unable to puddle their own canoe, the British had to share with a grudging American ally who questioned the necessity of having them on board at all. Pragmatism, then, was an early casualty. It was only the growing threat of Russia which made the Americans accept that two paddles were better than one.

The second difficulty in the Anglo-American relationship was presentational. Americans were uncultured, boisterous and simplistic upstarts. The British were stuffy, class-ridden snobs who pretended they still had an empire. Caricatures, perhaps, but politicians and soldiers on both sides could find numerous examples to fit. The fact that English and American language were easily interchangeable papered over many fundamental differences and misled many into thinking that the British and Americans were one and the same people. Winston Churchill was particularly prone to this affliction, one suspects because he himself was half American. On other occasions, the simple utterance of an American or British accent automatically attached the sins of national stereotype. Foreign travel was much more limited in those days and very few people had met many foreign nationals prior to the war. Such a clash of cultures exacerbated problems. General Wedemeyer, America's commander in China from 1944, recalled meeting a British major general in New Delhi. The British officer was reserved and sported a 'bristly moustache, immaculate uniform, and rows of campaign ribbons. During the course of our conference, we had occasion to use the word "schedule" frequently. Each time, he would pronounce it "shed-u-al". I had never heard such pronunciation and decided he was pulling my leg. Therefore, whenever I had to use the word, I pronounced it "ske-doo-ley." ' Several weeks later the British officer asked him whether Americans really pronounced it 'ske-doo-ley'![4]

Contrasting government structures in Washington and London also hindered joint policymaking. The American system of government was designed to balance power between Congress and the President. This might have been fine in principle but during the war it frequently resulted in bureaucratic duplication and disjointed policymaking. In the middle of this muddle, FDR consolidated his own imperial presidency and began to run the war single handedly. His colleagues, never mind his political opponents, were lucky to be informed of any decision Roosevelt made. The British parliamentary system, on the other hand, was simpler and in many respects more suited to war making. A bipartisan government of national unity was quickly forged, including the leaders of the two main political parties. Under this system the watch words were consultation and continuity. Whenever Churchill started to expand his power base he was given a sharp reminder that his position rested on the support of parliament and not President Roosevelt. The Prime Minister's attempt to monopolise the London end of the Anglo-American relationship was attacked by Anthony Eden. He told his private secretary, 'we can't have a dictatorship here, whatever he [Churchill] could imagine'.[5]

The personalised nature of the Anglo-American relationship that developed between Churchill and Roosevelt distorted policymaking. By cultivating a private relationship with FDR, the Prime Minister witnessed only a very narrow side of American policymaking. While good relations with the President were undoubtedly helpful, it cut out of the equation other British policymakers who proposed a more level-headed approach. Roosevelt was a secretive and manipulative politician and a dangerous person on whom to place the hopes of Empire, especially since there was no guarantee how long he would remain in power. Churchill, moreover, was hardly the ideal representative of British interests. His frequent emotional outbursts on the future of the Empire did little to allay American fears that London's policy was anything but reactionary and self-serving.

Pre-eminence: the eclipse of Britannia

In 1942 Britain's whim could no longer impose her political will upon the rest of the world. Retreat from the Far East vividly illustrated Britain's new reliance on Allies and international cooperation to secure her own interests; a role reversal not easily accepted within Whitehall. Indeed, British planners could have drawn the conclusion that Japanese aggression in 1941 became inevitable precisely because of Britain's pre-war reliance on America. Ever since Britain had terminated the Anglo-Japanese alliance in 1921 – largely under American pressure – and conceded naval parity to the USA, Britain's empire in the Far East had depended precariously on Washington's perception that British interests were American ones. Frequently, however, they were not: America had no significant territorial stake in the Far East, and consequently felt less urgency to stand firm against the Japanese.[6] The conflict between British aspirations for an independent foreign policy and the realities that suggested an alliance-led one, therefore, commanded British thinking throughout the war. How far London was prepared to go to resuscitate her imperial position against Allied opposition was a telling sign of Britain's inability to come to terms with her waning world status. Equally, it stressed the importance that the Empire still played in British politics. Hong Kong became a microcosm of this dilemma during the Second World War.

The ejection of Britain from Hong Kong in 1941 and London's demand that she should return there after the hostilities posed many questions that had not been asked when Britain seized the colony in 1841. Principally, because the international scene had changed so fundamentally, London was now called on to justify her claim to her Far Eastern colonies. With the war in the Pacific cast by many American politicians as a war against imperialism, Britain's empire was placed in a difficult position. Hong Kong provided a focus for this debate because both China and America were Britain's Far Eastern allies, and both insisted that China should resume sovereignty over her lost territory. Britain refuted this argument. At first quietly and then, as British self-confidence returned in late 1942, more vehemently. The differing roles cast for China by Britain and America illustrated that neither side would accept the supremacy of the other in Asia.

The battle for China: Sino-Anglo-American relations

Although China was still a weak power, there was a growing awareness in the Western world that China would one day be great, if not by her industrial might, then by the huge size of her population. China had also been fighting the Japanese since 1937, after years of Japanese encroachment into northern China. The Japanese argued that what they were doing in China was no different from previous Western powers who had carved out their own area of influence. The drastic means employed by the Japanese to enforce their rule, however, went far beyond other foreign annexations; murdering and brutalising hundreds of thousands of Chinese civilians. It was from this perspective that China's war effort increasingly came to rest on a moral basis. China was cast as fighting a heroic struggle against a heinous enemy, with few resources to sustain her in her battle. This was the view that many British, and particularly American, politicians subscribed to without further scrutiny of China's own conduct. China's 'halo' added international force to her plea for the return of Hong Kong.

And yet, for all China's newly acquired international standing, she remained a weak, unindustrialised country ruled by a corrupt Nationalist Party under Chiang Kai-shek. Even Chiang's legitimacy was openly undermined by his arch-rival Mao and the Chinese Communist Party who pursued an ongoing civil war, compounding China's misery. The reality of China's status, therefore, offered an ideal opportunity for the British to argue that Hong Kong should not be handed back to the chaos and corruption of Chinese rule. While the British were not against China's development into a world power per se, they remained suspicious of Chinese imperialism which held claims on other British Far Eastern possessions, including Malaya, Singapore and Burma. It was not, however, Chinese calls for the retrocession of Hong Kong that made the British take the issue so seriously. Without American support for Chinese claims, London's deliberations over the colony would have amounted to barely a footnote.

The Second World War clearly marked the coming of age for American military and political might. In no other theatre was this so apparent as in the Pacific. At the news of Japan's strike against Pearl Harbour, Winston Churchill was quick to concede American *military control* of the Far Eastern war. In fact, he was merely stating the obvious. British military strength was directed largely against Hitler, and resources would not allow an equally vigorous two-fronted war. America's huge industrial base and geographical proximity, on the other hand, provided the capacity to fight two extended wars simultaneously. Moreover, British resources were so depleted that America armed and supplied Britain on a huge scale under the terms of so-called 'lend-lease'. The scale of British dependency on Washington's generosity was striking. Lacking the *matériel* to fight the Far Eastern war, Britain attempted to use the sword of diplomacy to protect the Empire.

America's traditional anti-colonialism found its true voice in the Pacific war. No longer would America support the old imperial order; instead, she would sponsor independence and self-determination.

China, especially, captured the popular imagination in the United States as a country struggling to throw off the shackles of imperialism, just as America had done 170 years before. China's predicament was also exploited by Washington as a means of preparing the American public for a world role after the war. Anthony Eden reported to Churchill during his trip to Washington in March 1943 that 'We have a strong impression that it is through [American] feeling for China that the President is seeking to lead his people to accept international responsibilities.'[7] The issue of Hong Kong was held up as an educational example for the American people: here was a piece of territory extracted from the Chinese under duress which they now wanted returned. As far as America was concerned, China had a moral right to Hong Kong that the British ought to acknowledge. It was the equivalent of a foreign power possessing Manhattan.

America's idealistic and sanctimonious sermons, unsurprisingly, came in for harsh criticism in London, particularly as they were open to accusations of hypocrisy, for example over America's treatment of Mexico. Lord Cranborne, Colonial Secretary in the summer of 1942 argued that:

> It is most important that we should not allow ourselves to be manoeuvred into the position of having been alone responsible for what has happened in the Far East. In fact, I feel that the responsibility of the United States is far heavier than ours. If they had been willing to collaborate with the League of Nations in the early days of the China incident, all that has happened since might, and probably would, have been averted. In fact, they hung back not only till it was too late to save the situation, but until they were actually attacked. By all means, let us shoulder our share of the blame. But do not let us shoulder theirs too.[8]

President Roosevelt was aware of these disagreements and the deep-rooted imperial basis behind London's foreign policy. He told his advisers that 'the British would take land anywhere in the world, even if it were only a rock or sand bar'.[9] He indicted British imperialism on moral and economic grounds as self-interested and repressive. And of course he was right in a way, which explains why Winston Churchill was so utterly opposed to any concessions over Hong Kong. He believed that retroceding the colony to China might prove to be the thin end of a very large wedge as far as the Empire was concerned.

From the first, China appeared the perfect regional ally for America. She was weak, a victim of external aggression, and superficially compliant with American policy. Traditionally a soft spot on the American conscience, China quickly assumed an honorary sainthood. In retrospect, Washington had backed a particularly truculent horse of limited ability. As far as the British were concerned there was no bidding competition for China's friendship. London had little in the way of financial or military carrots to offer the Chinese government in Chungking, and remained convinced that China was a threat to British interests in the region.

China makes a play for America

Following Japan's initial attacks in the Far East, the Chinese Nationalists attempted to separate British Far Eastern policy from America's. During 1942 the evidence confirmed London's fear of a united Sino-American front. When the Chinese asked for an enormous soft loan, the Americans acceded without batting an eyelid; Washington pushed Chinese claims for the abolition of extraterritoriality; Chinese and American delegates belittled the British at the quasi-official Pacific Relations Conference, and an American general, without precedence, became commander in chief of the Chinese army. All these events were detrimental to British interests. Richard Law MP, under-secretary of state at the Foreign Office, found it all 'most disheartening'.[10]

First out of the block was China's request for a huge financial loan from Britain and America. Officially this was to sustain Chinese resistance whilst Allied military assistance was unavailable; unofficially it was America's first instalment to buy Chinese allegiance. This incident set a precedent for trilateral negotiations between the three countries. With deep pockets, Washington could afford the promise of a large sum of money with no strings attached. Very quickly the British, trying desperately to keep in step with Washington, were manoeuvred into accepting the American position. British diplomats fumed, unable to understand that it was both America's and China's wish to exclude Britain from the Far East. Washington enjoyed the spectacle of Britain's anguished lobbying to no avail.

Chinese hostility towards Britain came from the highest level. Madame Chiang Kai-shek was the most outspoken and visible Chinese critic of British imperialism. She wrote cryptically in April 1942 (appropriately in the American *New York Times* magazine): 'The old Chinese commander at Taku, now in the Elysian shades, if he still retains an interest in mundane matters, can be pardoned if he gave vent to a Jovian guffaw at the manner of the fall of Hong Kong and Singapore.'[11] Of course this was expected to offend the British, and it did so, especially since it came from China's first lady. John Keswick, descendant and head of the large Hong Kong merchant, Jardine Matheson and Co., realised that the Chinese were going to seize their opportunity to kick the British whilst they were down. Working for SOE in Chungking he observed a change in the Chinese attitude 'since the loss of Hong Kong and Singapore. It is only here that one realises how sad and how bitter is the feeling about Hong Kong where all the Chinese that count had their money, their wives and quite a few sweethearts.'[12] All defeats were blamed on the British regardless of the antecedents that led to them, neatly excusing American pre-war vacillation in the Pacific. This was symbolic and significant because it indicated the choices that the Chinese Government had already made regarding their policies for the Pacific war.

After America's entry into the war, the Chinese Government was unstinting in its attempts to ally America to the Chinese Nationalist cause. A conscious calculation by Chiang Kai-shek, the Nationalist leader, placed Sino-American cooperation above all other issues, except the eradication of Chinese communism. This decision was based on what the Chinese regarded as a community of interests between the two countries: the destruction of Western imperialism in the Far East; the elevation of China into a strong and democratic ally of America; and China's peace-keeping role in the Pacific region. No other country, particularly an old imperial power like Britain which was associated with exploiting China in the nineteenth century, would be allowed a look in.

The exclusivity of the Sino-American special relationship suited both America and China, although each had different reasons for encouraging it. China was attempting to consolidate and assert itself as a Great Power after decades of humiliation in the face of Western imperialism. Its leaders also held less worthy motivations. The Soong dynasty that ruled China, which included Chiang Kai-shek, Madame Chiang, T.V. Soong and the wealthy Kung family, became increasingly focused on one goal: to squeeze the largest amounts of money and armaments out of America as was humanly possible. Indeed, Sterling Seagrave argues that the Chiang regime spent hundreds of millions of dollars each year 'to guarantee its image in America, and, thus, the continuance of the regime'.[13] The Americans, on the other hand, preferred to view their support of China in terms of lofty idealism. The American romantic attachment to China dated back to nineteenth-century American missionaries, and allowed many in Washington to consider China as a worthy and malleable junior ally.

America's alliance with China was historically rooted. Since the Hay Note at the turn of the century, Washington had posed as the protector of the Orient, preventing the carve-up of China by the 'selfish' imperial powers. Imaginatively using the Boxer indemnity, the Americans had embarked upon a cultural exchange programme, followed (symbolically) by missionaries in an attempt to Christianise China. The Soong dynasty, however, made it easier for the Americans to believe in the China they envisaged: Madame Chiang Kai-shek and T.V. Soong were both educated in America and were comfortable in a westernised environment. Even Chiang Kai-shek's public Christian baptism was partly aimed at putting a more lacquered veneer on his regime for American policymakers.[14] Both countries, therefore, had significant reasons to overlook any differences and cooperate.

As part and parcel of China's ensnarement of Washington, Hong Kong played a significant role. For political and prestige reasons, the Chungking Government wanted the colony back at the end of the war, along with the abolition of all unequal treaties. America, too, wanted Hong Kong returned, but their reasoning was often driven by different objectives. From London's standpoint, however, it was hard to differentiate American and Chinese policies: both pointed to the loss of British sovereignty. For all of the Allies, the diplomacy of Hong Kong was never a simple triangle, but from Britain's perspective it certainly did not appear to be an equal one either.

The battle for American friendship

The British reaction to Madame Chiang Kai-shek's article in April 1942 illustrated London's limited room to manoeuvre in the Far East. Although it was grossly insulting, the Foreign Office was incapable of responding to the article without the disapproval of the United States. At a time when Britain was dependent upon America for supplies as the battle of the Atlantic raged, nothing could be done to imperil Anglo-American relations. Typically the Chinese drew the comparison with a benevolent Washington and the selfish British regardless of widely divergent resources.[15] It was, instead, left to the Foreign Secretary to write a fawning letter to Madame Chiang Kai-shek explaining why Britain was not doing anything more in the Pacific:

> I beg you not to measure our intention of standing by China by the very diminished volume of assistance that we are or have been able to give ... I am sure that you will accept the fact that my presence

in the British Government is an assurance that the case of China will always be well to the fore.[16]

In the same month, Sir Horace Seymour, Britain's Ambassador to China, reported that American attempts to increase the prestige of the Chinese regime was making cooperation 'increasingly difficult' since the Chinese now had a superiority complex towards Britain. The facts, he went on to state, however, showed that there was much for the Chinese to be modest about. The survival of the Chinese army was 'due fundamentally to the fact that they have had unlimited room to retreat', while her military apathy 'has allowed the Japanese to withdraw with impunity considerable forces for service elsewhere'.[17] His plea for a leading article in *The Times* outlining the need for Sino-British cooperation was his only answer. At this point in the war, though, the British press shared many of the American delusions about the Chinese regime.

While it is commonly known that American press articles written by Pearl Buck, the daughter of an American missionary,[18] romanticised China, it is not so well known that the British press also followed this line in early 1942. A.L. Scott of the Foreign Office had harsh words for the British press. He criticised them for 'praising China to the skies and beyond', creating an 'unreal impression' in need of a 'douche of cold common sense'.[19] There were even articles on the Chinese army entering Nanking when there was no offensive ongoing![20] The unreality that was contaminating the British press threatened to damage the Allied war effort by raising unwarranted hopes. Since the Chinese Government was doing little to smother these stories and much to foster them, there was a dangerous vacuum developing where criticism of the Chinese Government was beyond the pale. The need to 'debunk the Chinese, – certainly to Cabinet and by negative methods to British public opinion' was put to Anthony Eden. Once again, the supremacy of the Anglo-American relationship meant no action was taken.[21] It was ironic that with every Allied defeat, China's diplomatic position became stronger.

In a Gallup opinion poll from July 1943 which asked who was winning the war for the Allies, the British survey ranked China ahead of America in importance. Churchill, however, failed to see the funny side of successful Chinese propaganda to inflate their war effort. Instead, he erupted to Eden because in his mind it offered ammunition to American critics of the Anglo-American alliance:

You should see this and my letter. Something should surely be done to regulate this foolish process as far as Great Britain is concerned. If the United States takes a bad view of the British effort, that will do very little harm; but great harm is done if the British rank the United States effort below that of China. Moreover it is rubbish.[22]

The Atlantic Charter and the Anglo-American alliance

British imperialism was increasingly caught in a pincer of Chinese and American criticism which the British could not answer. The only solution was to relinquish the Empire, which was to deny the ideological straitjacket of imperial consensus. London became increasingly despondent at the return of American idealism which they held responsible for World War II and which now seemed determined to destroy the British Empire. The clear blue water that separated the two countries was plainly illustrated in their differing interpretations of the First World War. This 'war to end all wars' continued to stalk both Britain and America, and was now viewed as a mere stop-gap to unfinished business. The failure of the Versailles peace treaty was attributed by the British to its overly idealistic basis, while the Americans believed it to be short-sighted and reactionary. In truth, it was probably a mixture of both. This clash of idealism and reaction (or tradition) resurfaced with the Atlantic Charter in August 1941.

The charter agreed at Roosevelt's and Churchill's first wartime meeting symbolised the continuing gulf between the old world and the new. When the two leaders met, they did not greet each other on equal terms. Churchill was desperate to gain an American commitment to enter the war on Britain's side, knowing that without the help of America, Britain could not win the war. It was therefore President Roosevelt who held the upper hand. Motivated by idealism, FDR forced the British to agree to loosely-termed principles which were at odds with the continued existence of the British Empire. It was agreed that Britain and America would not seek territorial aggrandisement, that territorial changes would have to accord with the wishes of the inhabitants, and that there would be freedom of trade and access to raw materials. Most controversially, the two countries would 'respect the right of all peoples to choose the form of government under which they live', with the 'wish to see sovereign rights and self-government restored to those who have been forcibly deprived of them'.

Unsurprisingly, this agreement caused considerable discord throughout the war. Churchill saw these points only as 'an interim and partial statement of war aims'; in no respect could 'self-government' be applied to the British Empire.[23] In fact, he told Roosevelt this personally, reinforcing these views with a speech in the House of Commons during early September 1941.[24] But such was the confusion of British policymakers that the Foreign Office did not immediately realise that Churchill had refused point blank to extend the Atlantic Charter to her colonies. Restrained by Britain's weakened military situation even Churchill found it necessary to moderate his public defence of the British Empire while attempting to woo American friendship. This element of ambiguity in Britain's public stance towards her colonies during 1942 was largely responsible for the uncertainty within the Foreign Office over the future of Hong Kong.

Fundamentally, however, British policymakers had not modified their contempt for what they saw as America's predilection for woolly moralising. When the famous American columnist Walter Lippmann wrote that imperialism ought to be abolished in favour of mutual cooperation, the Foreign Office was unanimous in its opposition. Ashley Clarke stressed that 'the problem of post-war settlement in the Far East is not going to be resolved simply by reference to high principles any more than perpetual peace was brought to Europe by President Wilson's Fourteen Points'. And although Anthony Eden did not blame the Americans for their idealism, he still thought them 'hopelessly ill-informed of world politics'. However, he warned that British policy had to offer a viable alternative or '*we* should certainly be to blame if we were once again to allow American sentiment and emotionalism to plan the future of the world' (original emphasis). What was he advocating be put in its place? He had no answer yet, but as Richard Law said, 'something constructive' had to be done that could safeguard the Empire whilst making it more acceptable to her Allies.[25] It was not so much a search for a new policy as new clothes for the old one.

The origins of Britain's Hong Kong policy were therefore already in place; it was to be a reactive one, and even though some junior diplomats were under the misapprehension that they were grappling for a new policy, it would point towards the retention of Hong Kong. It is important to understand that regardless of what some British diplomats implied, on closer inspection differences of opinion were usually a case of semantics. One example was Leo Amery's assertion that the Foreign Office should stop dithering and tell the Chinese to 'mind their own business' over Hong Kong: 'To haver about the future of Hong Kong seems to me only to invite demands by Chiang Kai-shek who will probably next want to have a word about the future government of Burma or even India.' Sir John Brenan of the Foreign Office, however, reacted strongly. He admitted Amery's fears might be true 'but it would be interesting to know how he thinks that these territories are to be defended against a revival of Japanese aggression when he and his school of thought have finally alienated the Chinese and driven the Americans back to isolationism'.[26] Although they could not see it, in their own individual ways they were both 'thinking imperially'.

Churchill, Empire and America: 'The best of both worlds'?

In a series of speeches to the House of Commons, Churchill attempted to rally support for his government around the issue of Empire, and define its meaning. On its future he saw that there was 'an all-party agreement on most fundamentals'. 'Here, after our failures . . . here, amid the wreck of empires, states, nations and institutions of every kind, we find the British Commonwealth and Empire more strongly united than ever before. In a world of confusion and ruin, the old flag flies.' Its basis, he suggested to the House of Commons, rested on more than just material well-being and 'enlightened self-interest'. Beyond such motives, he argued, were 'deeper and more mysterious influences which cause human beings to do the most incalculable, improvident, and, from the narrow point of view, profitless things'. What is more, he refused to believe that there was any inherent incompatibility between the continuing existence of the Empire and a projected American-sponsored United Nations organisation:

> I have never conceived that a fraternal association with the United States would militate in any way against the unity of the British Commonwealth and Empire . . . I do not think we need choose this or that. With wisdom, and patience, and vigour and courage, we may get the best of both worlds.[27]

Churchill's specific view on Hong Kong was equally reactionary and fitted into his general world view: he refused to contemplate any discussion with the Americans and Chinese over the colony's future. Caught up in other matters, Churchill still found time regularly to reflect on Hong Kong policy, indicating the importance that he, personally, placed on the colony's recapture. As late as the run-up to the Yalta conference in 1944, he was lecturing the Chiefs of Staff on the benefits of Soviet imperialism in the Far East as a counter-balance to Britain's continued possession of Hong Kong.[28] Indeed, at times the Prime Minister's infatuation with the Hong Kong issue became so great that it threatened to destabilise the Anglo-American alliance and disguise the incipient dangers of Soviet imperialism in Asia. Churchill encapsulated all the contradictions of British imperialism. While he maintained a persistent interest in Hong Kong's future out of all proportion to its size and strategic importance, he also held China and its leader, Chiang Kai-shek in utter contempt. It appeared of little concern to him that Hong Kong's economic and political prospects remained tied to the Chinese mainland. Churchill's indifference to Anglo-Chinese relations was vividly illustrated by the appointment of Lieutenant General Carton de Wiart as his personal representative to Chiang Kai-shek in October 1943, where he remained until the end of hostilities. De Wiart was a relatively junior officer and knew nothing of Chinese affairs. In fact, he had spent the early part of the war cooped up in an Italian POW camp!

It was also supremely ironic that the one person who placed the least trust in a British imperial consensus was Churchill himself. He frequently accused his closest colleagues of undermining his imperial policy despite all evidence to the contrary. In a private letter to his Foreign Secretary, he argued that:

> There must be no question of our being hustled or seduced into declarations affecting British sovereignty in any Dominions or Colonies. Pray remember my declaration against liquidating the British Empire. If the Americans want to take Japanese islands which they have conquered, let them do so with our blessing and any form of words that may be agreeable to them. But 'Hands off the British Empire' is our maxim and it must not be weakened or smirched to please sob-stuff merchants at home or foreigners of any hue.[29]

There was undoubtedly an egocentric streak in Churchill which inflated his own importance. At times, he hinted, as he did in the Mansion House speech of 1942, that his continued tenure as Prime Minister was the only obstacle that stood between himself and the dissolution of the British Empire. This was, though, a self-serving distortion of the truth. Not many people expressed their imperial sentiments as vehemently as Churchill, but few in the British Government held contrary opinions of the Empire.

Different forms of government: London and Washington

Despite British weakness in the Far East, her system of government provided coherence and continuity lacking from the Washington bureaucracy. On both sides of the Atlantic, however, the onset of war did not mean a cessation in domestic political intriguing. In London, Anthony Eden remained highly sensitive to the idea of Oliver Stanley leading the House of Commons and possibly usurping some of his own authority within the Conservative Party. For all the Foreign Secretary's assertions that he was not 'a Party man', it was difficult in British politics to exert influence outside the confines of a party. Churchill, in turn, was also a skilled political juggler, appointing Stanley as Colonial Secretary specifically to balance Eden's supporters within the government.[30] Political backbiting remained as prevalent as ever. The death of the Chancellor, Sir Kingsley Wood, in September 1943, illustrated the inability of many to put the national good before personal feeling. Whereas Leo Amery described him as a 'great success and with a wider outlook than most Chancellors', Oliver Harvey considered him no 'great loss to progress'.[31]

The British system of government, however, for all the personal animosities that inevitably arose, was always more cohesive than the American one. The shared values of Empire and deference were a great counter-balance to political infighting. There is a tendency to see the Conservative and Labour parties of the period as being diametrically opposed, something encouraged by the confrontational nature of the House of Commons with one side sitting opposite the other. Underneath this verbal sparring, however, was an implicit understanding between the opposing parties on foreign policy. British politics in this period was already moving towards the 'politics of consensus' which would dominate the post-war political landscape. The American system of government, on the other hand, was not only an unwieldy conglomeration of checks and balances because of its sheer size, but also a fizz of partisan politics. The Republicans, excluded from high office, became adept at using the China issue to beat their bête noire, the Democratic President. Walking over this broken glass, Roosevelt began to dominate foreign relations even if he could not always lead it.

The White House's domination of American foreign policy was sustainable because Roosevelt faced little opposition within government. His foreign secretary was a timid man. Despite his personal popularity in Congress and with the American people, Secretary of State Hull had long been removed from FDR's inner policymaking.[32] He admitted to Morgenthau, Secretary of the US Treasury, in July 1943 that Roosevelt had not consulted him on any major foreign policy issues since Pearl Harbour, 'and I don't know what's going on and the President won't let me help him'.[33] The replacement of Sumner Welles, Hull's deputy, with Stettinius, whom Hull had no say in appointing, did little to counteract the President's personal diplomacy, being a political lightweight and a novice to diplomatic affairs.

Cordell Hull, furthermore, compounded the State Department's impotency by sidelining the one diplomat who had influence with Roosevelt. Hull's personal loathing for Sumner Welles was so intense that it knew no bounds. Although bedridden with TB at the time, Hull forced the homosexual Welles from office in the summer of 1943. With the dismissal of the under-secretary of state for foreign affairs, the last tenuous link between the State Department and the White House was broken. A situation now existed where America's foreign office had no idea what its leader was planning or what he had negotiated; a scenario unthinkable in London. Roosevelt had so successfully divorced himself from Washington's established policymaking offices that it was not an exaggeration to talk of a government within a government.

The contrast between the position of Churchill and Roosevelt was never clearer than at the Cairo conference in 1943 when the Prime Minister arrived with innumerable Foreign and Cabinet Office representatives in tow. The President, on the other hand, turned up without any State Department officials or even his own Secretary of State! The British were lucky to have Churchill's egoism firmly integrated into the traditional parliamentary system. On almost every formal diplomatic occasion during the war, Churchill could be found sending back to London a telex of the agreement or communiqué for Cabinet approval. In the case of the Atlantic Charter, Clement Attlee wanted alterations and forced them. America had no such safeguard.

The President's dictatorship of foreign affairs had extremely damaging repercussions for America, eliminating the basis for bipartisan foreign policymaking when it was most needed. Irwin Gellman concludes that three men's incapacity to put the benefit of the nation before their own private demons was:

> a tragic weakness [that] destroyed much of what they had hoped to leave as their legacy. Roosevelt, even though he knew his health was failing, never explained his major foreign policy objectives to Vice-President Harry Truman or anyone else. Although Hull was bedridden at the end of his tenure, he never groomed a successor. [While] Welles kept his foreign assignations as classified as his sexual orientation.[34]

The British, however, were blissfully unaware of the divisions which racked American foreign relations. Had they realised, many sleepless nights would have been saved.

The limitations of American consensus

The Americans regarded British implicit assumptions of Empire jealously because of their own heterogeneous and insecure heritage. Roosevelt characterised the purposefulness of British foreign policy as being 'too much Eton and Oxford',[35] while his Chief of Staff, Admiral Leahy remained under no illusions about the single voice with which the British spoke. When he heard the British Foreign Secretary speak at the National Press Club during his visit to Washington in March 1943, Leahy wrote:

> Eden, like other British political officials in high position that I came to know, seemed to have a better understanding of the general political policy of his country than was the case with many of our own leaders. Anthony Eden knew what Britain wanted. I felt that if I could find anybody except Roosevelt who knew what America wanted, it would be an astonishing discovery.[36]

This partly explains why the Americans were so keen to specify the principles, if not the aims, that would mould the post-war peace: they lacked Britain's 'comfortable' consensus of restoring a formal empire. An important factor militating against the establishment of such mutual understanding within Washington, however, was the problems inherent in Rooseveltian government.

The American Cabinet had little of the collective decision-making responsibilities of its opposite in London, with nothing comparable to the integrated system of committees and secretariats that formulated British policy. The cohesion of Washington's government, therefore, relied heavily upon guidance and supervision from the White House. With its small staff and a President who frequently saw himself as a spokesman for, rather than the determiner of, the national will, the White House's ability to coordinate the Washington bureaucracy was strictly limited. Roosevelt's preference to divide and rule rather than promote bureaucratic harmony meant that coherence and decisiveness was not a dominant characteristic of American government. David Reynolds has described FDR as being

> the supreme exponent of consensus building, keeping his goals flexible and vague, constantly modifying them to accommodate powerful pressure groups in the bureaucracy, Congress or country, often opting for messy, short term compromises in the confidence

that changing events and his own powers of persuasion would eventually ensure the desired outcome.

This vagueness in Roosevelt's foreign policy consensus, moreover, was delimited by the very diversity of the American people and their history. To be all-embracing of the American people, it helped if policy aims were driven by idealistic sentiments rather than 'sordid' realpolitik which threatened to inflame sectional interests at the expense of a broad consensus. For example, the post-war treatment of Poland, Germany and Italy all had significant repercussions within America because of the large percentages of the democratic vote which these sectional ethnic groups held. Of course, such woolly sentiments became increasingly difficult to maintain as the post-war settlement came into view, and demanded a pragmatic approach to peace making which the American people had not been prepared for. 'You can't always get what you want', was not a common refrain in American foreign policy. The fact that the President had to be so careful in presenting his policy aims illustrated the frailty of any American consensus in comparison with entrenched British values.[37]

The hidden precariousness of Rooseveltian foreign policy, however, had great repercussions for British Far East strategy during 1944. Through the Churchill–Roosevelt relationship London tended to see a consensus of American foreign policy which did not exist. The British Foreign Office were frequently convinced that the Americans knew exactly what they wanted, when in fact, Admiral Nimitz and General MacArthur violently disagreed with one another over military strategy. This was also the reason why many British personnel feared American troops recapturing British colonies and refusing to hand them back to Britain. The vehemence of American anti-imperialist arguments was often interpreted as agreement upon American post-war plans. Churchill and Roosevelt must share responsibility for this state of affairs. The Prime Minister covetously channelled Anglo-American relations through his close personal relationship with Roosevelt, in the process concealing the conflicts of American policy. Anthony Eden could not help because he did not enjoy an intimate relationship with his opposite number, Cordell Hull, who was in turn sidelined by Roosevelt. The President encouraged Churchill to believe in Roosevelt's own omnipotence, and thereby promoted a climate of fear within London which held that FDR, if he chose, could confiscate the entire British Empire. This skewed reading of the President's powers encouraged a strong counter-reaction from Churchill and others within the British Government. There was never any real chance that America could dictate a post-war peace and ignore British interests, but British misconceptions were so great that it was deemed a possibility.

Preparing for peace

Notwithstanding the rigours of war, Eden and Churchill recovered from their near exhaustion of early 1944, buoyed up by the anticipation of the cross-Channel attack into France. This huge logistical undertaking absorbed much of their time; its failure would have meant a potential prolongation of the war in Europe for another year. Its success, though, cleared the way for the early defeat of Germany, allowing the British to move more vigorously in planning for the post-war world and define their (hitherto neglected) strategy in the Far East. The Colonial Office even managed to reverse the Foreign Office's exclusion of Hong Kong from interdepartmental talks the preceding year now that the Far Eastern war was back on the agenda. Fear of Washington dictating a Far Eastern peace was instrumental in pushing British strategy forward with added urgency. The Americans, ironically, could not be credited with a similar purposefulness.

The looming final victory appeared to unsettle the Americans much more than it did the British. Their sunny optimism for planning a new world order in 1942 had been stripped of much of its varnish by the realities of war. The American leadership was also ailing. Roosevelt held weakly to his health whilst Cordell Hull, suffering from tuberculosis, remained bedridden much of the time, and was eventually to resign in late 1944. Perhaps a greater loss was FDR's closest confidant, Harry Hopkins, who fell seriously ill, leaving the President isolated and without a trusted friend. American foreign policy relied increasingly upon a waning enthusiasm and a negative consensus rather than the clear, if idealistic, aims espoused earlier in the war. The shake-up of the Far Eastern section of the State Department in March was one of many problems. Stanley Hornbeck, the head of department, was shunted sideways for withholding information with which he disagreed from Cordell Hull, and also because his subordinates refused to work with him any more, believing his ideas to be 'obsolete'. But rather than being sacked, Hornbeck was put in charge of post-war planning. Sir Alexander Blackburn at the Foreign Office found it hard to fathom what was going on in the State Department; for him it was all rather 'bewildering'. The same may be said of American foreign policy in general.[38]

Towards the end

The Anglo-American alliance was ultimately a means to an end, rather than an end in itself, and trouble arose when people confused the two. In the Far East this meant that the British expected too much from American cooperation; this had been given in the European and Mediterranean theatres, but the Far East was different. If London suffered from an over rigid interpretation of Anglo-American rules, Washington was having difficulty defining any at all. The Americans began to act as if they could run the Pacific theatre alone while preaching about internationalism. Beyond the crucial aim of defeating Japan, there were only vague aspirations towards universal peace and freedom. General Wedemeyer, concerned by what he saw as America's lack of statecraft characterised Roosevelt's advisers as 'drugstore strategists' with little grasp of what was at stake:

> More dangerous than our loose organisation was our lack of unanimity. We had no national agreement on the objectives for which we were fighting, no specifically American aims. There were of course, the Four Freedoms. But these were extremely nebulous objectives upon which to base military strategy. Finally, we Americans were not closely knit in our negotiations and contacts with other nations. It was not unusual for Americans to differ in the presence of foreigners. This practically never happened with the British in peace or wartime. They always presented a united front; apparently their differences of opinion ended at the water's edge.[39]

Anglo-American cooperation in Asia was, in many respects, replaced by unnecessary conflict. The results pleased neither ally and set America on a road that would end in Vietnam. American hostility to British involvement in Asia merely reinforced Britain's determination to hold her place in the Far East, expending scarce resources on a faltering empire which would shortly be abdicated. Unable or unwilling to think clearly about the longer-term political goals of the peace, Washington succeeded in creating the Asia she feared.

4
An Empire Brought into Question, 1942

Where our relations with China are important is in the very great potentiality to affect, for better or worse, our relations with America. The Americans are pathological about China, and keenly suspicious of any possible unfriendliness towards her on the part of others.[1]

Foreign Office minute, 1942

Making the Empire compliant with President Roosevelt's Ten Freedoms was a conjuring trick which the British never quite mastered. The conundrum was to define Britain's colonial policy and find some way of presenting it to her Allies. During 1942 and into early 1943, Britain's imperial confidence slowly began to recover, partly because it could get no lower. With it came a growing determination to avoid any concessions to her Allies over colonial matters, including Hong Kong. Britain's weakened state; financially, militarily, psychologically and ideologically, however, made it far from easy for London to state this belief explicitly. Britain's defence of her imperial colonies would, for the moment, have to be conducted with circumspection.

In the international arena, the London Foreign Office faced an inescapable dilemma regarding Hong Kong. Diplomatically it would have been far easier if the colony had never existed, but as Sir Alexander Cadogan pointed out, 'right or wrong . . . there it is'.[2] The fall of Hong Kong went deeper than wounding imperial pride; it seriously raised doubts about the long-established legitimacy of Britain's right to rule, and provided a ready barrel over which Washington and Chungking could place British colonialism. Both the Chinese and Americans saw the Japanese advances across South-East Asia as an opportunity to redraw the map according to their own ideas and aspirations, which held no place for the British. Of course their ideas were nothing new, but the failure of Britain's Far Eastern policy had done much to level the playing field of international politics. It was much harder, now, for London arrogantly to ignore claims from China that the colony should be returned. The Americans on the whole supported these claims, exhibiting their anti-colonial heritage and their own agenda for China. The terms 'international supervision', 'collective security' and 'trusteeship' which littered American declarations were clearly aimed at the British Empire. The real question for London was not what concessions she would have to make in the Far East, but what she could escape with.

It was perverse that the real danger to Hong Kong came from Britain's own Allies once the Pacific war was underway. As early as January 1942 a meeting of American academics and Far Eastern interest groups readily agreed that Hong Kong would return to Chinese jurisdiction at the peace conference.[3] This was merely the beginning of an avalanche of opinion and sniping at British sovereignty over Hong Kong. It ranged from the heights of the presidency to the lowly Ohio petrol station owner.[4] All were united in wishing to see British imperialism extinguished once and for all in the Far East. Militarily, as the British well knew, the Pacific war would rest largely with the Americans even though the British had larger interests in the region. The conjunction of American idealism with British military weakness left the British leadership frustrated. Eden remembered how in late February 1942 Churchill sat stricken, devastated by the loss of Singapore. 'He was most depressed now, sat with his head in his hands, talked of lasting only a few weeks etc.'[5]

From the outset, the Americans and Chinese were keen to define the peace aims for the Far East. This was despite the Allies being in no position to dictate such terms, and the emphasis already having been placed on a Germany first policy. A holding operation was the best that could initially be envisaged in the Pacific. For the Americans and Chinese, however, defining peace aims early on had several advantages. Washington was particularly anxious to know what it was fighting for, unlike in the First World War, which meant that America was in no mood to defend the reactionary agendas of imperial powers. Generous concessions, furthermore, promised to forestall a threatened Chinese collapse. Keeping the Chinese in the war was a concern common to London and Washington: the guilt of allowing the Chinese to fight on alone since 1937 weighed heavily, whilst racially the Chinese offered the opportunity to neutralise Japan's effort to call their own imperialistic war a racial one. Understanding their own internal disabilities, the Chinese saw their opportunity, utilising American help, to dispel uninvited foreign influence from their country once and for all. Early commitments were anything but ideal for the British. The Empire had been struck a blow that had stunned even the strongest imperialists. The territorial gains collected over a century had not only been overrun, but were now threatened with liquidation by her own Allies. Crucially, Britain had to revive her own imperial confidence.

Britain's crisis of imperial confidence

If British imperial troops defending the colonies against the Japanese in 1941–42 had momentarily ceased to believe in Empire, the same could also be said of their governing elite. Initial feelings of arrogance and supremacy were quickly stripped away by defeat to reveal inner doubts about Britain and her wider role in the world. Back in Whitehall the defeats were taken badly, with the loss of Singapore coming as a bombshell to the general public and politicians alike. The Prime Minister, 'one evening, months later, when he was sitting in his bathroom enveloped in a towel . . . stopped drying himself and gloomily surveyed the floor: "I cannot get over Singapore," he said sadly' to his doctor.[6] Gerard Gent, under-secretary at the Colonial Office and a key Hong Kong policymaker was 'very, very defensive'.[7] People found it incredibly hard to understand what had happened and why.

Winston Churchill's role in rebuilding British imperial confidence was fundamental, requiring all of his eloquence and faith. In a series of public speeches he attempted to rationalise the Empire's setbacks. Facing 'a vast, measureless array of disasters' in January 1942, the Prime Minister urged the House of Commons:

> Not to allow ourselves to get rattled because this or that place has been captured, because, once the ultimate power of the United Nations has been brought to bear, the opposite process will be brought into play, and will move forward remorselessly to the final conclusion, provided that we persevere, provided that we fight with the utmost vigour and tenacity, and provided, above all, that we remain united.[8]

The crisis of confidence within Whitehall in early 1942, however, needed more than honeyed words of reassurance. In the face of what appeared inexplicable defeats, the British bureaucracy threatened to descend into a state of mutual recrimination. Gerard Gent at the Colonial Office told his Secretary of State that the Foreign Office 'suffer[ed] from what to my mind is quite a fatal lack of belief and confidence in our position in the colonies'.[9] In the face of these inner doubts, the British were also confronted with withering public and private criticism from Britain's Allies.

Different ways of thinking imperially: Foreign and Colonial Office conflict

With the defeats of early 1942 Hong Kong increasingly became mixed up in an inter-Allied propaganda war which provided more comfort to the Japanese than to her enemies. While the Foreign Office was frequently sympathetic to China's previous suffering at the hands of the Japanese, the Colonial Office was more concerned with China's territorial claims against the British Empire.

Despite the failings of China as an ally, the Foreign Office held a genuine desire to help China and its people. Foreign Office personnel like Sir Horace Seymour, the British Ambassador to China, might describe the China front in all its misery but he still had a deep respect for its people. The same may be said of Anthony Eden. For numerous reasons, none of them wanted China knocked out of the war even if Chiang Kai-shek's Nationalists were corrupt and quasi-fascist. Indeed, many members of the China department in the Foreign Office had considerable experience of the Far East which accentuated these feelings. Sir Alexander Cadogan had been ambassador to China in the 1930s, Sir John Brenan vice-consul in Shanghai and Sir Maurice Peterson First Secretary at the Tokyo embassy. In their eyes, Chinese virtue had been established since the Marco Polo bridge incident in 1937.

The Colonial Office, however, was not used to such understanding and patience: they had been accustomed to dictating their wishes to colonial peoples. Although the war meant this could no longer happen, the instinct was hard to suppress. Gladwyn Jebb, a senior official in the Foreign Office, accepted this intellectual conflict between the Foreign and Colonial Offices. He argued that the Foreign Office

> should be uninfluenced by the views of the Colonial Office [regarding Hong Kong]. After all the primary objective of the Colonial Office – entirely rightly – is to defend the rights and interests of the British colonial Empire. The primary objective of the Foreign Office, on the other hand, is to ensure that, if possible, America comes into the peace.[10]

It was the hope of British foreign policy that these two contradictory strands could be resolved. The first object of British foreign policy was to re-establish Anglo-Chinese relations on an even keel. This was easier said than done. The Chinese Ambassador in London, Wellington Koo, lunching with Eden at the end of May admitted 'misunderstandings and seemed sincerely anxious to improve matters'.[11] However, the Chinese Ambassador held little real power. Diplomatic niceties counted for little unless there were concrete improvements in relations, and mutual distrust between the two countries was deeply ingrained. British suspicions were amply illustrated by their rejection of the offer of Chinese troops to defend both Hong Kong and Burma.[12] The dismissal of Chinese overtures in some ways increased the likelihood of Hong Kong's capture by the Japanese. As one of the defenders of Hong Kong pointed out:

> It was a forlorn hope (as some had been pointing out for many months) to attempt to defend Hong Kong in 1940 and 1941 without a long record of close and mutually frank Anglo-Chinese joint planning for defence behind us . . . The feeling was that Britain would rather have lost the colony than accept Chinese help. For my own part, I agree with them.[13]

However, the British Parliamentary Mission to China discovered in November 1942 that a promised Chinese offensive to assist the defenders of Hong Kong in December 1941 never existed.[14] Such incidents reinforced the bad blood which remained between China and Britain. Nevertheless, after December 1941 the British were more predisposed to let bygones be bygones. Unfortunately, the Chungking Government did not feel the same way. They had already decided that with American help British influence would be forced out of China.

The first mention from within the Foreign Office of Hong Kong's future came in April 1942. Reacting to a report from David MacDougall that the Chinese lower and middle civil servants in Chungking expected to receive Hong Kong back at the end of the war, the Foreign Office found it hard to muster any enthusiasm to counter Chinese claims. A.L. Scott thought the proposition unpalatable but saw little alternative now that China was being sponsored by the Americans. He did, however, anticipate the dissension of the Colonial Office in the matter:

> I can see every objection to the Chinese taking it for granted that Hong Kong will fall into their laps like a ripe plum after the war. But

as we shall have to reward China in some way after the war there is much to be said for a straightforward statement now that it is our ultimate intention, no date being mentioned; this might be especially desirable if the Americans steal our thunder over the renunciation of extraterritorial rights. But I can't exactly see the Colonial Office welcoming the idea, and after all they are the people concerned.[15]

His departmental head, Ashley Clarke, a man deeply involved in later policy, simply commented that the view of the Colonial Office should be ascertained. One thing was certain, Britain would not push ahead with a renunciation of extraterritoriality in a moment of weakness. Ashley Clarke, moreover, was still prevaricating come July, reiterating that 'we had better wait and see what the Colonial Office have to say about Hong Kong'.[16] At times it appeared as if the Foreign Office wanted to delegate responsibility for the colony altogether to the Colonial Office, even though it was strictly their jurisdiction. The collapse of imperial confidence within the Foreign Office had paralysed its ability to think clearly about the future of Hong Kong. The Colonial Office, however, felt less uncertain. Gerard Gent, under-secretary at the Colonial Office, realised that it was not his office's job to formulate Hong Kong policy but felt driven to do so, exasperated by the Foreign Office. 'It is certain', he wrote,

> that the Foreign Office need stimulating in order that their phobia in these urgent practical questions of the formulation of post war policy in the Far East, including the restoration of British authority in Malaya and Hong Kong, may be removed. I told Sir John Brenan [of the Foreign Office], when I saw him yesterday, that it seems to me that it may be necessary for the Colonial Office to start the ball rolling by convening an interdepartmental meeting if it was impossible for the Foreign Office (whose function it ought to be) to do so, since *any plans we make in the Colonial Office must envisage our restoration in Malaya and Hong Kong* whatever changes might thereafter result from negotiations with China or other of our present allies.[17] (emphasis added)

The realisation within the Foreign Office that Britain's diplomatic position in the Far East was on the back foot was reinforced by the prospect of attending the Institute of Pacific Relations (IPR) conference. The conference was a favourite for American academics and interested parties, and was set for September 1942, at Mount Tremblant in Quebec.

The expectation of a British delegation being pilloried by American and Chinese delegates was not an appealing one within the Foreign Office. There was a fear 'that the trend of the discussion at the Conference would inevitably be favourable to the early renunciation of extra-territoriality and possibly even the eventual return of Hong Kong to China'.[18] Sir Maurice Peterson, superintending under-secretary at the Foreign Office, even contemplated trying to cancel the conference altogether through pressure on the American State Department.

It was a sign of how rattled the Foreign Office had become; the destruction of all their peacetime diplomatic efforts had left deep scars. In some respects, there was a feeling that they had failed in their job to preserve peace in the Far East and were finding it hard to pick up the pieces. The IPR conference, however, was hardly worthy of such trepidation: did it really matter what foreign academics and international busybodies thought? Richard Law, writing for Eden, sympathised with Sir Maurice Peterson but felt the conference must go ahead despite 'the risk of washing a lot of dirty linen in public' for the sake of Allied relations and America in particular. Their conclusion would be to send a well chosen British delegation who could put 'on a good show'. It was clear that the Foreign Office placed Anglo-American relations above anything else. During what was a crucial period for Britain, playing down American failings in the Pacific was a painful exercise in self-control for Whitehall.[19]

The spectre of the Foreign Office having to define Britain's Far Eastern policy so early on for the Americans and Chinese was at the root of this considerable discomfort. Sir John Brenan was deeply pessimistic at the whole scenario. 'So far as the Pacific is concerned', he wrote, 'it looks as though the "UN" will mean the US. For the Americans this is a "war of liberation", and if we are not careful we shall be told bluntly enough that they are not fighting to preserve the British colonial empire.' He perceptively enunciated the key problem facing the British over Hong Kong. His warning particularly applied to places which the Chinese or Americans might recapture, and the location of the colony made this more than likely. The question of where Britain should try to conciliate, and when she should follow her own star, was not easily solved. Brenan warned:

> Any suggestion on our part that we expect to resume full possession of these territories on the old footing will be badly received. We might provoke an opposition that would have a serious repercussion on the whole American attitude towards collaboration with ourselves

for post-war reconstruction . . . Whatever our future policy may be, short of putting the clock back to 1937, it will require difficult decisions at the highest level.[20]

Instead, he advocated finding some method of preserving the valuable bits of the Empire, particularly raw materials and trade, and yet at the same time appeasing the Americans; perhaps a squaring of the illusive circle, securing Britain's imperial interests and preventing America's return to isolationism. Logically this meant that Hong Kong, along with all other British colonial possessions, would have to be assessed in some shape or form to see whether or not it was a key British asset. However, this was totally against the imperial thinking which underpinned the Empire. Indeed, Oliver Stanley mocked the Foreign Office for being 'horrified that a colonial policy should be directed in the first place to the benefit of the colonies and only after that to the appeasement of the USA'.[21] Brenan's consideration that a joint mandatory system might be workable, especially with American guarantees, would no doubt have reinforced this prejudice.

In the event, the IPR conference was postponed until December 1942. As expected the Hong Kong question was broached by both the Chinese and Americans with unsatisfactory consequences for Britain.

The question of the Chinese loan

Parallel with the British diplomatic rearguard action in early 1942, there was a further issue which threatened Sino-British relations. The Chinese pleaded with America and Britain for a large war loan at the end of 1941. The loan was asked for when the Allies were at a low ebb and least likely to resist. It is worth elaborating and investigating this saga for the reason that it rehearsed many of the problems that London would later face over extraterritoriality and Hong Kong: Britain was to be entwined in triangular negotiations with American and China which proved how difficult it would be to seek equal partnership with her Far Eastern Allies. The disturbing messages that the Foreign Office could have learnt from during these negotiations were, however, ignored. The natural cynicism which tainted Britain's relations with China was tempered by a modicum of genuine goodwill and understanding.

The loan negotiations also shed light on the nature of the Anglo-American relationship. The British found it hard to accept that from the American point of view the relationship was circumscribed according to region. In many respects, these discussions were the first real indications that America and China expected to expel British interests from the Orient.

The loan

Chiang Kai-shek approached Britain on 28 December 1941 with a request for a loan totalling $400 m ($6.3 billion at 1993 prices). The request to America followed two days later for $500 m ($7.8 billion at 1993 prices), giving a grand total of almost $1 billion.[22] For a bankrupt country like Britain the amount was incredibly large, although for the Americans the figure was a drop in the ocean. The Generalissimo's reasoning for these enormous loans was the apparent need for a tangible sign of the Allied commitment to the Chinese cause. Wellington Koo spoke cryptically, admitting 'that what he wanted was a picture on the wall which he could display to his people and he did not much care whether he could use it or not'.[23] But use it they certainly would. The unspoken assumption by Britain and America was that China's rotten financial system needed propping up, if it were not to collapse completely, drained by incessant KMT (Nationalist Party) corruption. The talk of a loan was completely misleading as the likelihood of the Allies ever seeing their money again was negligible. Nonetheless, this did not prevent the ever-optimistic British initially contemplating interest on their money![24]

British reaction to Chiang's approach was colourfully expressed by Sir Frederick Phillips of the British Purchasing Mission in Washington DC. In a letter to Morgenthau, the American Secretary of the Treasury, Phillips informed him that the British thought the sums 'enormous' and that 'it was the reverse of obvious how far large dollar credits could enable China to face her real problem, which is to check the enormous inflation of Chinese currency resulting from the war. It appears that the Chinese budget is being met 90% or more by printing notes.'[25] Sir Otto Niemeyer, head of the British economic mission to China, furthermore, wrote to Anthony Eden cautioning him about deteriorating relations with China. The loan would not solve this problem:

> Whatever may have been the danger of economics leading to political collapse during China's previous state of resistance to Japan, she is now committed to the Allied cause . . . Their hopes of America, combined with Fox's [the American member of the Chinese stabilisation board] negative attitude make them less and less willing to collaborate, and I am sensible that I am wearing out my welcome . . . The last thing I wish to do is to fall out, but I definitely do not believe

that given the nature and the attitude of the Chinese Government my staying is anything but a pure waste of time.[26]

The Americans, in China and Washington, however, viewed the loan in a very positive light. They refused to accept any shortcomings in the Chinese regime and instead saw it as an opportunity to reinforce the Sino-American relationship.[27] The only American with serious misgivings was Clarence Gauss, the ambassador in Chungking.[28] He carried little weight in Washington and only remained in place because of Congressional pressure.

The British Treasury quickly decided that in no circumstances could it afford to offer China a $400 million 'loan', and responded with a diminished offer tied to stringent conditions that it must be spent in the sterling area (so that British goods were bought when available): political considerations were to be subjugated to financial necessity. The Foreign Office negotiating position was to be defined by the Treasury. Kingsley Wood, the Chancellor, also saw the issue in terms of the Empire and its future reconstruction. He told Cabinet that 'After the war we shall have to face the very difficult task of paying out of our current exports for our imports . . . and we cannot afford to give China a first call on those exports . . . It would be impossible to defend having let China "in on the ground floor" to this extent, in priority to our own Dominions and Colonies.'[29] The defence of the sterling area was a cornerstone of British economic power and yet political necessity meant that American cooperation was still sought. Nonetheless, Britain refused to cave in to Chinese demands.

London appeared oblivious to the American desire to pillory Britain's China policy. Even before the real negotiations had started, Hornbeck, head of the State Department's Far Eastern section told Cordell Hull not to wait for the British. Hornbeck 'suggested that frequently one of the best ways to get the British to act is to take action and expect them to act in order to save themselves from being left behind'.[30] Laughlin Currie, Roosevelt's aide, was also 'vigorously opposed' to a joint Anglo-American loan in the belief that America was in a 'better position to do the job' alone.[31] Secretary of the Treasury, Morgenthau, even claimed to his colleagues that he had obtained Churchill's agreement to dismiss Sir Otto Niemeyer for his negative approach to the loan![32]

This policy of recrimination was at odds with the goodwill emanating from London despite her financial problems. The destructive nature of America's China policy was set on course during the loan negotiations. China was to be solely an American ally, a position that temporarily suited both countries' purposes: the Nationalist Chinese could milk the philanthropy of the American Treasury, while Washington bureaucrats could cling to romantic dreams of the Chinese and anticipate the political and economic leverage they thought their money had bought. Stanley Hornbeck believed that while the war was in its defensive stages America 'could gain great present advantage' if they were generous.[33] Of course, this would be at the expense of Sino-British relations. Ultimately, however, no one would gain except Mao and his communists. The more America gave the Chinese, the less incentive they had to mend their corrupt system, and the more it would tie Washington to supporting Chiang Kai-shek.

An act authorising an unconditional loan was steamrollered through Congress, ready for signing on 21 March 1942. Hornbeck's last minute doubts came to nothing as the Americans had already capitulated to Chinese demands. The momentum of Washington's China policy was building up a head of steam that would take more than casual rethinking to stop.[34]

Britain refuses to agree to the loan

With the signing of the American loan, Britain was left out in the cold. Anthony Eden's hands were tied by the Treasury demands as he reiterated to Wellington Koo on 20 April; Britain simply could not afford the loan.[35] Feeling understandably disappointed with both their Allies, the British soldiered on, refusing to give what Hornbeck now described as a 'gift' to the Chinese. Moreover, British hesitation over the loan appeared increasingly well founded. In Washington, Luthringer, the American Assistant Chief of the Financial Division, soon listed endless problems with the Chinese:

> In part these difficulties arise from what appears to be an increasing impatience of China with respect to any form of outside control. As evidence of this attitude I would cite . . . [t]he attitude of [T.V.] Soong and his Government that our recent financial aid to China was completely without conditions and control by this Government of the uses to which the funds were to be put.[36]

And by July even the Sinophile Henry Morgenthau was 'perturbed at the magnitude and rapidity of Chinese drawings upon American credit'.[37] However, the Americans increasingly saw what they wanted to see in China, which was typified by Cordell Hull's admiration for China's 'brilliant resistance' against the Japanese.[38]

Not all Americans, though, proved so unhelpful to Britain's position. Luthringer of the Treasury courageously proposed what the British desired: a compromise position. He defended Britain's reasoning behind the conditions of the loan, noting 'that in general the conditions imposed by the British should be regarded as arising from the financial necessities of the British situation rather than any difference in attitude towards China of the British Government and this Government'.[39] But he was swimming against the tide: Hamilton, Hornbeck and Berle (Assistant Secretary of State) found little reason to support the British position. As Hornbeck annotated, 'The Chinese are becoming constantly more impatient of the British attitude, methods and performance.'[40] The thought that Washington diplomats were actively fostering this belief did not occur to him.

Chinese blackmail

By the beginning of May 1942, British patience was beginning to run out. Foreign Office attitudes began to harden; P. Broad argued that 'if we give way to what is really tantamount to blackmailing threat, we should gain neither credit nor respect'. The ever forthright Sir Maurice Peterson readily agreed, laying some of the blame with Sir Horace Seymour in Chungking who seemed reluctant to take a hard line. In spite of all this provocation, however, Anthony Eden refused to allow British patience to snap; London would continue politely to refuse Chinese overtures. After all, Seymour ('the poor man'), had 'little enough to take a strong line with'. Until Britain's military performance moved on to the offensive, that is the way it would have to stay.[41]

The loan saga, in fact, dragged on into early January 1943 when it was effectively shelved by the Chinese.[42] Surprisingly, despite Eden's initial misgivings, the British ultimately stood firm against American and Chinese pressure thanks to the uncompromising stance of the Treasury. The success of British resolve, when exercised, was shown by the fact that a Sino-British loan was not signed until 2 May 1944, and it was the Chinese who gave way to British conditions.

'The most absolute reserve': British Hong Kong policy begins to crystallise[43]

> A[lexander] Cadogan is no doubt right to sound a note of caution but I should have thought that we could draw a distinction in our treatment of Hong Kong and Shanghai.[44]
>
> Anthony Eden, July 1942

Although the loan negotiations offered a warning of the resistance Britain would encounter if she tried to reassemble her Far East empire, London began to think about how this could be achieved. It was with some reluctance that the Foreign Office came to contemplate colonial concessions in the Far East. The colonial system itself had not failed, only Britain's ability to check the aggressive actions of others. Sir John Brenan and A.L. Scott at the Foreign Office both believed that Hong Kong might have to be given back as part of a post-war settlement because of the hammering that had been inflicted on Britain in 1941 and 1942. The shock of these defeats was not just confined to junior civil servants, as we have seen, but there was certainly a stronger inclination within the middle ranks of the Foreign Office to contemplate colonial concessions. Their Secretary of State was less willing to compromise. In July, the British Ambassador in China had telexed London informing them that the Chinese were inquiring about Britain's attitude towards the Far Eastern peace, no doubt hoping to hear that the colony would be retroceded. Despite the reluctance of the Far Eastern department to commit itself to retaining Hong Kong (its head, Ashley Clarke, only wanted to ask the Colonial Office's opinion), Sir Maurice Peterson, Alexander Cadogan and Anthony Eden felt more confident that the colony's capture in no way jeopardised its Crown status. However, as Brenan had pointed out the difficulty in stating such a policy openly, a compromise was reached whereby the Hong Kong issue was effectively silenced outside Whitehall. Seymour was instructed that 'the most absolute reserve about our own attitude towards the future of Hong Kong' must be maintained.[45] In the circumstances, and as the loan negotiations illustrated, silence appeared the best way to keep Hong Kong off the international agenda. At this stage of the war even Churchill was reluctant to speak openly beyond winning the war, realising that the Allies would inevitably disagree about the far-off peace.

The reaction to a suggested broadcast by Churchill to China at this time was revealing. Due to China's desperate situation (Allied supplies through the Burma road cut; no Allied offensives possible) the Foreign Office's Far Eastern department was unanimously behind anything 'we possibly can [do] to maintain Chinese morale and will to resist'.[46] The outcome of this was that the entire department favoured a speech by the Prime Minister eulogising the Chinese on their national day (7 July). The Foreign Secretary, however, thought that this was most unwise, believing 'material help is better than speeches, which are apt to cheapen the orator and swell the heads of the audience'.[47] No doubt,

Eden had in mind the recent troublesome loan negotiations with the Chinese.

Like his counterpart in the Foreign Office, the Colonial Secretary, Lord Cranborne, began to grapple with Hong Kong in the context of Britain's Far Eastern empire. He shared Eden's great pride in the achievements of British rule:

> It seems to me that what we must first decide is where, if anywhere, we have failed. Is it in the administration of our territories or merely their defence? It may be said that our administration has not been perfect, that it was too rigid, that it did not show itself capable of adapting itself to the conditions of war, that it was too little inspired by a high spiritual outlook, and so on. But, taken by and large, our record of administration is not one of which we need be ashamed. We created Singapore and Hong Kong, two of the greatest ports in the Pacific, out of nothing. We made of Malaya one of the richest and most vital producing areas of the world. These are not mean achievements. Where we did fail was in giving them protection from Japan, and this criticism may equally be levelled at the Dutch and the Americans.[48]

Where there was disagreement between the Foreign and Colonial Offices was over the specifics, in particular Hong Kong. In late June, Gerard Gent and David MacDougall had spoken with Sir John Brenan of the Foreign Office who advised that Hong Kong might have to be retroceded back to China at the end of the war. Gent was by inclination vehemently opposed to any concessions, as he told his permanent under-secretary, Sir George Gater. What Gent failed to realise, however, was that the people he spoke to within the Far Eastern department at the Foreign Office were not representative of senior thinking. At this stage of the war, Hong Kong planning was left at a relatively junior level while Anthony Eden and Alexander Cadogan attempted to stem the defeats and win the war.

Lord Cranborne listened to Sir George Gater's and Gerard Gent's opinions regarding Hong Kong. He strongly agreed that 'we should not decide now to lower our flag there after the war. To put it on a higher plane, that would be to surrender one of our main bargaining counters before the negotiations begin.'[49] If negotiations had to take place, they would not be from weakness.

A paper by G.F. Hudson stimulated further discussion within the Foreign Office, including lengthy analysis from Sir John Brenan on the nature of the colony, its future, and the British position.[50] As the first detailed consideration of the problem within the Foreign Office, it is worth quoting extensively. Brenan wrote:

The points to be remembered in regard to this colony are (a) that it can no longer be regarded as a naval base or military strong point from our side in the event of war; it is a hostage to fortune. (b) It is not a source of raw materials. (c) Its chief importance in recent years has been as an entrepôt for trade with China. (d) In keeping it under British administration *we cannot allege that we are training a backward native people for the duty of self-government.* The population is Chinese, and it could not and would not want to maintain its independence of the Mother land which has been self-governing from the dawn of history.

. . . I understand that the Colonial Office are thinking in terms of an Anglo-Chinese condominium. I feel convinced from a long experience in that part of the world that this would be a most unhappy and unprofitable arrangement from the British point of view. The Chinese nationalists and party authorities would work unceasingly to get us out, and with the help of the local Chinese population could soon make our precarious foothold in the administration quite untenable.

. . . *We should either insist on governing Hong Kong by ourselves, because it has been ceded to us by treaty and we intend to keep it for frankly imperial reasons, or we should give it back to China.* In giving it back, however, there is no reason why we should not obtain economic safeguards for British commercial interests.[51] (emphasis added)

This minute was perhaps the clearest analysis of British interests in Hong Kong during the entire war. It graphically illustrated the stark choice confronting British policy between imperial thinking and tangible British interests. That Sir John Brenan could actually identify the emotional basis behind British foreign policy from superficial economic arguments made him exceptional within the British Establishment. This fact in itself, however, meant that his views would never be widely accepted in London because most politicians and civil servants saw no separation between imperial mindedness and British interests.

Sir John Brenan's analysis of the Hong Kong dilemma made it clear that there were few remaining justifications that Britain could use with her Allies for the continuation of British rule. The standard argument that British colonialism was preparing backward people for self-government did not exist in this case. Regardless of that, Brenan knew from experience the stranglehold that China could exert over the colony. On another level, it is interesting to note Brenan's paternalistic tendencies. He urged that any plans for the Far East should focus on 'the welfare of the local populations . . . and improvements of the conditions essential to their spiritual and material prosperity'![52] Brenan's liberal views, though, met considerable opposition from his superiors who were by inclination more conservative. Sir Maurice Peterson 'disagreed entirely with argument that, to placate United States opinion or any other reason, we shall have to cede Hong Kong to China'.[53] It was increasingly evident that the length of internal Foreign Office minutes were quite unrelated to their importance; Brenan and others in the Far Eastern department could merrily write lengthy synopses on how Britain ought to retrocede Hong Kong but, again and again, Eden, Cadogan or Sir Maurice Peterson would scribble a few words and the process would be halted.

Lord Cranborne's Far Eastern paper, August 1942

With America and China pressing hard, it became increasingly difficult for Britain to prevaricate on her future Far Eastern policy. Throughout August, Lord Cranborne attempted to synchronise both Colonial and Foreign Office viewpoints. Under the Colonial Secretary's direction, a paper was prepared by his private secretary which discussed Britain's future role in the Far East. This paper reached Cabinet in early September.

At high level, Eden and Cranborne agreed on the basic aims of Far Eastern policy, and on Hong Kong. This was no doubt helped by their close personal friendship. In the background, Sino-British relations continued to deteriorate with Chiang Kai-shek's interference in Indian affairs greatly antagonising Churchill and Amery (then Secretary of State for India).[54] Leo Amery remained a persistent vigilante for the Empire. As Cranborne's paper was being drawn up, the Indian Secretary wrote a personal letter to Anthony Eden:

> I am sorry if I misheard you at the Cabinet yesterday evening. But you certainly used the word 'going back', and not 'backward', and I confess I had been made anxious by a telegram which I had seen about Hong Kong . . . I should have thought that the only possible line to take is that if the Chinese raise questions about Hong Kong to tell them to mind their own business. Hong Kong was created by us, and the bulk of its population, at any rate of its permanent

population, are British subjects – the fact that they may be of Chinese origin has nothing to do with it.[55]

However, Eden never showed any predilection to return Hong Kong to China. What Amery seemed to misunderstand was the Foreign Secretary's attempt to conciliate the Americans with the illusion of compromise. Eden's private minutes, which would never have been seen by the Americans (although perhaps by the Soviets considering their infiltration within the Foreign Office) proved his determination to retain British sovereignty and obtain American partnership in the peace. To him, and to many other important British politicians, the two were not incompatible.

'Strongly divergent views'?

Prior to the completion of Lord Cranborne's paper, a meeting was convened between the two offices. Richard Law, Ashley Clarke and Sir David Scott represented the Foreign Office while Lord Cranborne, Gerard Gent and Sir George Gater represented the Colonial Office. It was now that the Foreign Office attempted to take back the reins for Far Eastern planning. Ashley Clarke suggested that 'since there appeared no marked divergence of view between the departments . . . the Foreign Office should attempt to produce a paper into which the Colonial Office memorandum could be embodied'. This could then be presented to Cabinet. However, there was one issue on which there were 'strongly divergent views': Hong Kong.[56] Sir Maurice Peterson and Leo Amery were in sharp disagreement with Lord Cranborne and the rest of the Foreign Office who viewed the colony's future pragmatically. Gerard Gent attempted to explained Lord Cranborne's position:

> It was agreed that Hong Kong was a special case, and that any matter about our sovereignty there was primarily for negotiation between ourselves and China. The memorandum explained that the maintenance of British sovereignty was not indispensable to us in Hong Kong, and that we should be prepared, at a suitable time, to discuss the whole position with China, not even excepting the question of sovereignty.

It was clear that these views were those of the Colonial Secretary himself, and were not representative of the more reactionary elements within the Colonial Office. Privately, Gerard Gent was horrified at the thought of relinquishing the colony, but kept silent for now. Cranborne appeared to have thought that the colony could prove to be more trouble than it was worth. He explained that Hong Kong

need not in the new conditions be regarded as a cardinal point of British policy. If there were advantages to us as well as general advantages in the post-war settlement, its sovereignty should revert to China. We must, however, be ourselves the judges of our action vis-à-vis China in respect to Hong Kong, and we should avoid being placed in a position of acting, or appearing to act, under the pressure of American criticism in any discussion we had on the matter with the Chinese Government.[57] (emphasis added)

From this meeting, Ashley Clarke concluded (controversially) that opinion within the two offices 'certainly seems to point to the rendition of Hong Kong'.[58]

The Colonial Office paper on Hong Kong

When the weighty Colonial Office paper finally arrived on Anthony Eden's desk on 24 August, it added little to previous discussions; Hong Kong remained a negotiable factor in any future Far Eastern settlement. It was unlikely that Eden read any further than the Colonial Secretary's covering letter which he found 'cheerfully robust'.[59] Cranborne made it clear that he was firmly committed to preserving Britain's empire in the Far East.

Hong Kong was an exception because it was an exceptional colony. The Colonial Office admitted that Britain had failed to integrate the colony into the Empire beyond its outward trappings because the colony remained 'geographically an integral part of China'. Hong Kong's long-term security was also undermined by China's territorial claims. The New Territories lease, which had 50 years remaining, was too short for significant investments and its loss to China come 1997 would expose Hong Kong to Chinese extortion. The anticipated loss of extraterritoriality in the near future added a further twist. Rather than lose the colony with no guarantees, the Colonial Office began to consider the option to negotiate whilst Britain still held the initiative.

Predictably, perhaps, whatever reassurances Cranborne offered, the mere thought of contemplating the retrocession of the colony was too much for some. Sir Maurice Peterson once more railed against any sign of flexibility over Hong Kong. He believed that abolition of extraterritoriality was more than enough for the Chinese. 'No doubt there will have to be changes and concessions but if we are going to make them in watertight compartments we shall get very near appeasement or even scuttle. I am against restoring Hong Kong to China.'[60] He even admitted that he might be 'in a minority of one' in refusing to contemplate any possibility of the retrocession of Hong Kong, although this was exaggerated: with Leo Amery it made two.[61] Such resolute talk, though, was unnecessary.

It was acknowledged that the colony was something of a special case. The disagreements within Whitehall were the inevitable product of exploratory or 'think-tank' discussions. It would be wrong to read too much into these inter-office exchanges at such an early stage in the war. Ashley Clarke sounded a conciliatory note to Sir Maurice Peterson, attempting to place the colony in its broader context. He asked people not to attach

> too great importance to the issue of Hong Kong, on which views will inevitably be divergent. Hong Kong is an issue entirely to itself and though in my humble opinion the line proposed by the Colonial Office is the right one, it need not affect fundamentally the main contribution of the paper . . . [that] Anglo-American co-operation is essential.[62]

Hong Kong: a concession to Anglo-American relations?

When eventually Ashley Clarke produced the joint Foreign and Colonial Office paper which Lord Cranborne wished for, it reiterated much of what had already been discussed. Wisely, perhaps, the caveat was now added that the suggestions were 'to be regarded as the barest outline and highly tentative'. Nonetheless, the paper suggested that 'the key to obtaining American support may . . . be found in our attitude towards Hong Kong'.

The Foreign Office saw Hong Kong as an opportunity to shore up the Anglo-American relationship, not as a means of furthering Sino-British relations. Indeed, the Chinese were believed to be the 'chief opponent' of British colonialism in the Far East, where they were already 'dreaming of pan-Asiatic leadership'! The chimera of Chinese nationalism was an unfailing standby for the British wishing to defend their Far Eastern colonies.[63] In fact, SOE argued in late 1942 that the Chinese were hell bent 'on aggressive nationalism', with Hong Kong a 'legitimate prize . . . As Chinese expansion is only possible in the face of a weakened Britain, there is an anti-British policy and meddling with Indian affairs.'[64] In reality, however, America was the real danger. This fact would slowly dawn upon London as American post-war plans became more fixed, but first Whitehall would try conciliation.

In retrospect, the idea of collective defence, which stood at the heart of the paper, suggested the imminent disappearance of Britain as an imperial power. Incapable of defending her own colonies, Britain would work in partnership with America and other suitable countries. Leaving aside the point that this was a concealed admission of Britain's weakness, it was also an idea completely at odds with the concept of Empire. Empires existed when one country had supreme power, not when it had to rely on allies to prop it up. London wished to remain in charge and contract out the defence. The paper explicitly stated that 'From the administrative point of view it is essential that we should resume the fullest measure of internal responsibility [within the colonies] and that we should not be called upon to share such responsibilities with one or more outside powers (i.e. no condominiums).'[65] Washington, though, would settle for nothing less than Britain's capitulation on this point. London's difficulty in contemplating the token retrocession of Hong Kong indicated that there was never any real possibility of Britain and America agreeing to a joint defence of their Far Eastern interests.

It should be noted that no other British colony in the Far East was being offered for negotiation besides Hong Kong: not Singapore, Malaya, Burma or Borneo. Why was this? Hong Kong appeared the most opportune sacrifice to American and Chinese opinion. The other colonies had larger potential markets and raw materials (especially the tin and rubber of Malaya, and the oil of Borneo). Hong Kong, furthermore, had been a persistent thorn in the British side. British sovereignty had long been disputed by the Chinese, and certain British administrations had even accepted the fairness of China's claims. Indeed, after the First World War, Sir John Jordan, British Ambassador to China, had suggested that the New Territories be returned to China, for without such a sacrifice 'no solution of the problem seems possible'. Once again, the Far Eastern section of the Foreign Office responded favourably to this idea. The then Foreign Secretary, Lord Curzon, however, dismissed the idea as 'idealistic and impractical'; senior politicians remained highly sensitive to accusations of selling off the imperial silver.[66]

Cabinet discussion of the Foreign Office–Colonial Office paper, September 1942

On 10 September, a Cabinet meeting was held at the Foreign Office to discuss the joint Foreign Office–Colonial Office paper. Clement Attlee, as Secretary of State for Dominions, chaired the meeting of Eden,

Amery and Cranborne. This was the first senior interdepartmental discussion concerning future British policy in the Pacific war. There was considerable agreement that the overall aim was to encourage American cooperation in the region after the war. Eden led the way, stating that a 'mere restoration of the status quo with all concerned clinging rigidly to their pre-war rights and policies would not attract the Americans to incur any obligations' for future Pacific defence. He continued: 'Our principal object must be to establish a system in the . . . region in which the US will not only consent to participate, but will be definitely anxious to participate.' However, the question of Hong Kong was dragged up again. Leo Amery repeated his argument that Britain should not retrocede the colony, or at least not without 'considering what essential desiderata we could obtain in return'. He even wanted to swap Britain's existing trade base at Hainan for a better strategic site elsewhere in China! As usual, however, the differences of opinion were by degree and resolvable. Lord Cranborne reiterated that Britain would obviously not act unilaterally:

> What we gave up was contingent on what other Powers were prepared to do in the common interest. It was only proposed that we should declare our readiness to discuss Hong Kong in return for certain advantages. *If conditions in China were not favourable to such discussions or if such advantages were not forthcoming, the proposal would naturally fall to the ground.* (emphasis added)

Even so, the Colonial Secretary was making an important concession to the Foreign Office by suggesting that the Colonial Office would not stand in the way of any post-war peace settlement. The Colonial Office had most to lose from the abandonment of any colonies which were in effect its lifeblood and job base. Against Amery's narrow reactionary opinion, Cranborne and Eden understood that Allied cooperation in defence of the Far East was of the greatest importance. After all, its earlier breakdown had allowed Japan the freedom to contemplate her attacks throughout the region. Perhaps less explicitly, the design for Far East cooperation assumed that Britain would have something to defend there.[67]

For all the cosiness of the Whitehall atmosphere, Clement Attlee remained a voice apart in questioning the assumptions of Empire. He opposed the Far Eastern strategy on the grounds that it seemed to return to pre-war ideas (which it did) and untrammelled free trade. Who was going to pay for the defence, he asked, which was the last question for the imperially minded. Of course, Attlee had his own reasons for wanting to cut overseas defence expenditure post-war since he was chasing his dream of building a socialist 'New Jerusalem' at home. This was about as radical as any internal challenge to British Far East policy was allowed to get for British imperialists. Even then the Labour leader was regarded as a harmless eccentric by his colleagues. Nobody, except Amery, took his internationalist posturing seriously.[68] Attlee's desire that 'the economic implications of a settlement in the Far East should be carefully examined' were brushed off with complacency by the economist, F.G. Coultas:

> I had a word with Mr Norman Young of the Treasury off the record. His view was that in the past we unquestionably gained through the administration of our Far Eastern possessions. The Malay States, for instance, were self-supporting and we not only profited by the trade of the territories, but also by the position which control of world markets created for us financially. [As regards the future of existing investments under any trustworthy international administration] it ought not to make any difference whether we administer them ourselves or not from the economic point of view. My own view is that it would be almost impossible for any international administration to be trusted by this country. *I hope therefore, we may regard Mr Attlee's suggestions as a 'red herring'.*[69] (emphasis added)

The period around September 1942 was the closest that Hong Kong came to being retroceded to China, and even then it was not very close. Much of the debate within Whitehall was academic, driven by the shock of Japanese defeats and the pressure of American and Chinese post-war planning almost to desperation. As Britain recovered her imperial verve with military victories, the motivation to contemplate territorial concessions evaporated. When had Britain ever been on a winning side and lost British possessions? To do such a thing was unthinkable for the ruling elite. The Americans, moreover, would not be conciliated by piecemeal concessions; Washington desired the dismantling of the entire British Empire, not just the occasional colony.[70] This much was painfully obvious when Richard Law visited Washington in September.

American colonial policy: 'children playing with bricks'

Richard Law's top secret report on his meetings with all the senior American officials in Washington (except Roosevelt) made for disturbing reading back in London. He recognised that the Anglo-American relationship was shifting, and to the disadvantage of London:

> It will be necessary, I think, for us to realise that we can't have it both ways. We can't have a confident and assured United States, looking outwards, eager to assume responsibility and eager to help, and at the same time, a United States without a mind of its own, ready to accept our leadership and to follow meekly in our paths. We can only work with the Americans upon a basis of partnership. And we must realise, that on paper we shall not appear as the senior partnership.

This was a particularly painful realignment for the British who were reluctant to admit that the Empire was fading before their very eyes. Perhaps more worrying for the British, though, was the policymaking shambles on display to Law in Washington. He sensed increasing dissatisfaction with Roosevelt's laissez-faire attitude towards post-war planning. Law wrote a damning indictment of American policymakers, arguing that:

> Washington sees world problems through a telescope where we look at them through a microscope. Washington is thinking in terms of centuries and continents when we are thinking of question time next Wednesday and the Free Austria movement. It is easy to understand what critics of the Administration mean when they speak of the 'lunatic fringe' at Washington. For these people are not men of the world. They are children, playing with bricks and 'making the world over'.[71]

Law's encounter with the administrative chaos of Washington was nothing new to the disillusioned William Bullitt, sometime associate of Roosevelt. Speaking in London, where he was working as a naval attaché, Bullitt described how Roosevelt himself accentuated the American policymaking muddle and had never 'made a record of a conversation in his life'. Apparently, the President's dislike of the State Department had reached such a low that he was using naval codes to cut them out of signals traffic. Even allowing for the disagreements within Whitehall, the British Government's Far Eastern planning (for all its worry of being left behind), was in comparison to the Americans a machine of efficiency and cooperation.[72] The fractured nature of American policymaking, though, served as an opportunity and a danger for the British in the Far East. The question of who was really speaking for American foreign policy was a recurring mystery during the Pacific war, although the vehemence with which it was spoken often gave the impression of a unity of purpose it intrinsically lacked. The divisions between American policymakers, however, were their undoing. Ominously, though, Britain was no nearer being able to state her imperial policies to her Allies. Law warned of the consequences if Britain openly advertised her policy of colonial retrenchment to America:

> It is difficult to know how we are to deal with the United States on these great questions of imperial and world policy. When I left England I thought that we ought to begin to formulate our own views and then state them clearly and fearlessly. I do not think now that this will be good enough. For one thing it is likely to end us in open controversy with the United States Administration. The evil consequences of such a situation would be immeasurably disastrous. It would be far better I think, to discuss these problems informally with the Americans before we make any public statements.[73]

Anthony Eden's request to Sir Horace Seymour in China that he maintain the utmost reserve on the issue of Hong Kong was, perhaps, wise at this crossroads.

5
China Claims Hong Kong, 1942–43

Strictly speaking the Chinese have no grounds for attempting to couple Hong Kong and Kowloon or even, it seems, the New Territories, with the negotiation of our [extraterritoriality] Treaty . . . The cession of Hong Kong and Kowloon may have been right or wrong, but there it is.[1]

Sir Alexander Cadogan, Foreign Office, 1942

China's claim to Hong Kong was historic and geographic, something which even the British would not deny. It was through the complicated nature of the colony's cession to Britain in the nineteenth century, however, that China attempted to regain its lost territory. During the Second World War and up until 1997, the Chinese argued that the treaties of cession were 'unequal' and, consequently, unlawful.

Hong Kong island and the adjoining coastal area of Kowloon were ceded in perpetuity. The 365 square miles of New Territories, however, were leased for a 99 year period, expiring in July 1997. Initially the lease was to provide a defensible perimeter to the colony but advances in modern warfare soon bankrupted such thinking. By the outbreak of war with Japan the ceded colony had also effectively merged into the New Territories making the two areas mutually dependent: the urban centre of Kowloon had spread into the leased territories and the overspill population was fast establishing new settlement. As the colony grew, so did its reliance on the New Territories for its water and food supplies. The economic and military realities of the colony in 1941 meant that the classification of leased and permanently ceded territory was academic; Hong Kong was now indivisible.

China's only explicit official (and serious) request for the return of Hong Kong during the war came in late 1942 when extraterritoriality negotiations restarted between America, Britain and China. Extraterritoriality, which dealt with foreign concessions on the mainland, was extended by Chungking to include Hong Kong's New Territories. Following the track of the loan negotiations, Britain was bumped down a road she had no wish to go; concessions only encouraged further Chinese claims. It was clear to Ashley Clarke that 'their plan is no doubt one of prising us out of Hong Kong step by step'.[2]

The extraterritoriality negotiations

Retrospectively

For over a century Western powers had exacted privileges and possessions from a weak and disunited China, exemplified by the International Settlement in Shanghai. With the establishment of a Chinese National Government over a unified China at Nanking in 1928, the move to renegotiate these 'unequal treaties' began in earnest. By the summer of 1931 a position was reached where both Britain and America were completing final drafts of their treaties to abolish extraterritoriality and remove their claims to exemption from Chinese law. Instead of the expected natural evolution of these negotiations, however, the Japanese invaded Manchuria in September 1931 bringing all negotiations to a halt. It was now the Chinese who had reason to preserve the vestiges of extraterritoriality as it offered the one sanctuary against the advancing Japanese army. In answer to American inquiries on procedure concerning the negotiations, the British replied that their policy was 'to wait until the Chinese raised the question', and there it remained until the outbreak of the Pacific war.[3]

Considering the trouble it would later cause him, it was ironic that Anthony Eden chose to resuscitate the negotiations in March 1942. His suggestion was to push ahead with the abolition of extraterritoriality, doing 'it in such a manner that China knows the initiative is ours, not American'. At a time when Britain was militarily impotent in the Far East, the unilateral abolition of extraterritoriality appeared to provide a painless symbolic gesture indicating that Britain was seriously concerned with equalising relations with China.[4] Britain had little else with which to strengthen Chinese morale and much to apologise for: the fall of British Burma had cut the main artery of supplies into China via the Burma road. The loss of this route meant that most China-designated lend-lease *matériel* never reached her, being requisitioned for other theatres because China was 'the most difficult supply operation of the entire war'.[5] More cynically, the abolition of extraterritoriality was inevitable; Britain was going to give up very few rights that it could have kept after the war. Empty gesture or not, Eden's attempt at a pre-emptive strike was not universally welcomed in the Foreign Office.

The permanent under-secretary, Sir Alexander Cadogan, was insistent that the Chinese would construe any unilateral renunciation of extraterritoriality as British weakness. If he needed grounds for this, Chinese blackmail over the loan provided a recent example. Cadogan received widespread support for his view, causing Eden to reconsider. In the end, the Foreign Secretary wavered at the prospect of overruling Cadogan and shelved the idea of pressing ahead without American consultation. Eden's comments concerning the Sino-British loan seem particularly appropriate for explaining his decision. He wrote that, 'I cannot resist the considered judgement of men who know far more about the Far East than I.'[6] In keeping with British policy, however, an agreement was reached with the Americans that London and Washington would consult with each other before either decided to act over extraterritoriality.[7]

Interestingly, there was little pressure in Washington for abolishing extraterritoriality at this time. The large Sino-American loan, in its last stages of negotiation, had given some within the State Department pause for thought. Walter Adams noted that the recent 'credit extended by the US to China was too easily obtained to be appreciated or for its most effective use to be insured'. The same, he thought, would happen with the abolition of extraterritoriality. Exhibiting a caution that would later desert America's China policy, Adam's superior, Stanley Hornbeck, agreed: 'In any case we do not need to "play the card" now, and we may need for a card to play at a later date.'[8]

With hindsight, Alexander Cadogan's recommendation not to push ahead with the unilateral abolition of extraterritoriality must be viewed as unfortunate for British policy. As the State Department files show, the Americans were not keen to move at this time and it would have allowed London to take the lead in Far Eastern affairs – one of the few opportunities that was ever presented to London during the war. Eden's wish to pursue a more proactive foreign policy, however, was not widely shared in senior circles. Such ideas were often placed in the same league as post-war planning. Sir Alexander Cadogan characterised this as 'crystal gazing', something 'as incomprehensible as it is futile'.[9] The Prime Minister, moreover, was equally extreme. He told Anthony Eden in October 1942 that the post-war 'Four Power Plan' was irrelevant:

Any conclusions drawn now are sure to have little relation to what will happen. It is even dangerous to discuss some aspects of the problem, for instance the position of Russia . . . We should aid the United States to the utmost in this great American interest and a successful joint war against Japan would form a very good background for collaboration about the settlement of Europe, the British Empire, India and other things like that. Meanwhile I hope that these speculative studies will be entrusted mainly to those on whose hands time hangs heavy, and that we shall not overlook Mrs. Glass's Cookery Book recipe for Jugged Hare – 'First you catch your hare'.[10]

Eden was disappointed with these sentiments. He told Churchill that:

My desire is to have the basis of a foreign policy now, which, if the basis is sound to-day, should carry us over into the peace. It is from every point of view bad business to have to live from hand to mouth where we can avoid it, and the only consequence of so doing is that the US makes a policy and we follow, which I do not regard as a satisfactory role for the British Empire.[11]

Nevertheless, unable to break free from Britain's reactionary inertia, Eden found himself, along with British Far East policy, captive to American designs.

America reopens extraterritoriality negotiations, September 1942

On 1 September, the Americans informed London that they had decided to conclude the abolition of extraterritoriality with China. Although Washington advised London before approaching Chungking, the initiative had been wrestled from the British. The reaction in London was a perplexed one; they had assumed that negotiations would be frozen for the foreseeable future. Ashley Clarke approached America's London Ambassador, John Winant, for an explanation. Winant reiterated the official reason given by the American Secretary of State, that 'an ideal moment to take an affirmative step in the matter is not likely to arise, the present [being] probably as good as any, especially as the initiative still lies with us'. Privately, in a secret annex to Winant, Cordell Hull explained a hidden motive; he hoped that the immediate renunciation of extraterritoriality might oust Britain from Hong Kong and Shanghai.[12] It brought back unhappy memories of Hull's reaction to the temporary closure of the Burma road in June 1940 by the British. Privately,

Hull had expressed his understanding to London but when the announcement was made he publicly criticised the action. Unwilling to take their own lead on extraterritoriality, the British were once more reduced to pursuing a joint Anglo-American approach with little enthusiasm from their ally.[13]

In contrast to deliberations within the Foreign Office, a more cautious approach to the future of Hong Kong was presented to the outside world. Following Richard Law's advice on the dangers of stating British post-wars aims, Ashley Clarke behaved most circumspectly with the American commentator, Walter Lippmann. The columnist was told that there were many reasons why there could be 'no formal attitude in regard to Hong Kong until the end of the war'.[14] This type of response became increasingly typical of the Foreign Office when they were dealing with sensitive Far Eastern issues. The persistence of such quiet diplomacy did, though, eventually pay a dividend of sorts. In October, the British persuaded the Americans to ditch their preferred policy of confidentially informing China of the extraterritoriality proposals afoot. Instead, Washington was persuaded to pursue a joint Anglo-American public declaration of intent, at least offering some hope to London of preserving the pretence of an equal partnership in world eyes. The Chinese as usual, however, refused to acquiesce and chose to contrast British and American policies. In the London *Times*, Chiang Kai-shek's messages of appreciation to Roosevelt and Churchill were couched in very different terms for the more perceptive reader: while Churchill was credited for his 'far sighted statesmanship', Chiang thanked the President 'from the bottom of my heart' for 'your superb and inspired leadership'.[15]

Anglo-American cooperation at odds

Through October to December the minutiae of the extraterritoriality treaties were hammered out. Initially the negotiations focused on trade and commercial interests, which Britain was more sensitive about, having more to lose than the Americans. The American Ambassador to China, however, believed that the British were right to insist on comprehensive safeguards for trading within China. He cabled Washington that 'an over generous policy at this time of first surrendering extraterritorial and related rights and expecting later fair and just treatment in general and trade relations would in my opinion be fatal'.[16] He was, though, out of step with American policy; Roosevelt was more interested in grand gestures than safeguarding America's small financial interests in China.

For the Foreign Office, the abolition of extraterritoriality was an exercise in damage limitation. Ashley Clarke wanted to ensure that 'the loss of extraterritorial rights shall not produce new inequalities to our detriment'. Although it was solely the Foreign Office who were negotiating on Britain's behalf, they were under pressure from the China Association and the Federation of British Industries to defend British privileges. Particularly important to British trading interests was the national treatment of commerce, which was a provision whereby British nationals would be granted reciprocal terms for carrying out trade within China. In their intransigent mood, the Chinese stubbornly resisted any concessions on their part. It was only after considerable talking that the Chinese agreed to insert this into the treaty, only to find that American federal and state legislation made it hard to promise reciprocal treatment.[17] The Foreign Office were livid.[18]

Eden attempted to reassure British businesses at a meeting on 19 November that the abolition of extraterritoriality would be in their own interests. In this he was slightly economical with facts, musing a few days later, 'I hope I haven't made things look too good for them.' (The spirit of enlightened imperialism had seemingly passed many of the delegation by, as they proposed that China be put on 'probation' for a trial period after the treaty was signed!) Nevertheless, with the Americans pushing for a quick treaty, the British had little support from Washington to negotiate hard with the Chinese. The Americans believed that a comprehensive commercial treaty would have to be negotiated at the end of the war, and so that was that.[19]

The first crack in the British facade came in the beginning of December. British diplomats were at last becoming disenchanted with American behaviour in what was still ostensibly a joint approach to the Chinese. Washington had now allowed China to win three issues to which London attached considerable importance; namely national treatment of trade, coastal trade and inland navigation (which allowed for the use of British pilots). The normally sympathetic Sir John Brenan exploded:

> By their rush tactics they have deprived us of any opportunity of real negotiations with the Chinese. *We could hardly have done worse for ourselves if we had acted alone.* It now remains to be seen if the Chinese, having got all they want from the US, will hold up our treaty over the Kowloon question. (emphasis added)

Such was the strength of feeling within the Foreign Office that an official 'remonstrance' was sent to Ambassador Winant by Cadogan on 7 December.[20] To compound British troubles with the Americans, in the middle of November the Chinese had chosen to raise the subject of Hong Kong. Of course, they were too circumspect to ask outright for the retrocession of the colony and staked their claims through the lease of the New Territories (or as Brenan referred to it incorrectly, Kowloon). Chinese demands for the leased territories to be included in the extra-territoriality negotiations were seen by Ashley Clarke for what they were. He realised that 'their plan is no doubt one of prising us out of Hong Kong step by step'.[21]

Enter Hong Kong

From day one of the extraterritoriality negotiations the British had set themselves against placing Hong Kong on the agenda. Richard Law explicitly stated in the House of Commons that the two issues were quite separate.[22] Sir Horace Seymour in Chungking, however, was not happy about such a hardline policy, and telexed Eden immediately. He argued that 'It would be most unfortunate if we should appear to be toning down our gesture and you may consider it desirable to let the public know immediately that rendition of settlements and concessions are included in our offer.' The Foreign Secretary, however, curtly told Seymour (original emphasis), 'Certainly not. We are only yielding *extraterritorial* rights. Hong Kong is British territory whether leased or otherwise.'[23] This was the definitive stance by Eden during the negotiations, and would lead Britain to the precipice of terminating diplomatic relations with China.

Chinese claims on the lease of the New Territories presented British policymakers with the dilemma that they had been seeking to avoid. On 13 November, Seymour met the Chinese Premier, T.V. Soong, who asked for the leased territory to be discussed. Soong disingenuously claimed that 'the Chinese Government had not raised the question of Hong Kong, but that they felt that the 1898 Convention ought certainly to be dealt with in the present treaty'. It was now clear that China wanted a clean sweep of all rights resulting from so-called 'unequal treaties'. More worrying for the British, however, in the words of Seymour, was the fact that 'the points the Chinese are now pushing are of little relevance to the Americans who will be likely to agree with them'. London's negotiating position was being undermined so badly by Washington that it left her dangerously exposed to Chinese threats if Britain insisted on continuing her joint approach with the Americans.[24]

The American reaction to Richard Law's statement in the House was symptomatic of London's problems. *Time* magazine's article entitled 'Bitter Tea' trod the familiar path of American obsession and fantasy with regard to China, adding a personal attack on Law himself:

> The Chinese, who had just given Wendell Wilkie[25] one of the warmest receptions in Oriental history, cheered themselves hoarse. The Western press scarcely noticed that presently big, bland Richard Kidston Law, Parliamentary Under Secretary of Foreign Affairs, rose in the House of Commons to say that Britain's intentions did not include surrendering Hong Kong. The Chinese noticed it.

Surprisingly, the article did not disagree with Eden's argument that Hong Kong was not technically part of the extraterritoriality negotiations. Instead, its argument for the retrocession of the colony rested on moral grounds:

> The question of Hong Kong was not one of extraterritoriality, which concerns the legal rights of foreigners in Chinese territory; the great seaport was legally owned by the British and possessed pro tem by the Japanese. But the Chinese could scarcely help regarding Hong Kong as Chinese, whether it was in charge of British or Japs. And the Chinese had taken hope that foreign sovereignty as well as foreign privileges were about to disappear in China.[26]

Considering American articles like *Time* magazine's, London could be excused for thinking that the Americans had incited the Chinese to proceed along this path.

When the news about the lease reached London, Anthony Eden was furious and refused to contemplate negotiations over Hong Kong. Seymour's advice that Britain should accept discussions over the New Territories while the rest of Hong Kong was not mentioned met a chilly response; the component parts of the colony were seen as inseparable. Everyone within the Foreign Office realised that without the New Territories the colony was worthless. The Governor of Hong Kong, way back in 1931, had come to this same conclusion. It was his opinion that 'not only Kowloon, but the greater part of the New Territories are absolutely necessary to Hong Kong, both on economic and strategic grounds'.[27] Ashley Clarke could see three possibilities for action, although only one that was acceptable. London could acquiesce to the Chinese demand and risk losing the colony; it could refuse 'point-blank' and lose the backing of Washington; or it could postpone the question altogether. For Ashley Clarke, the only option was the last one; Britain could not afford to lose either American or Chinese goodwill at this time. He suggested resuscitating Lord Cranborne's formula from the August Foreign and Colonial Office paper, namely that when the United Nations had won the war and were cooperating for the good of all, then 'in such circumstances we should be ready to consider with the Chinese Government the future position of Hong Kong'. The idea was that this formula would do more than temporarily solve the issue; it could form a 'locus classicus' which Britain could refer to whenever the Chinese or the Americans raised the question. It would also save London from acute embarrassment if the Chinese recaptured the territory.[28]

The differences within the Foreign Office were never more explicit than at this moment. Ashley Clarke, representing his Far Eastern department, stood for compromise in the face of Sino-American intransigence. Anthony Eden, however, had by this stage had enough of pandering to Chinese demands. He rejected Ashley Clarke's idea, believing that 'It seems to go too far, and I don't see why we should indicate a readiness to consider the surrender of Hong Kong now. I should prefer to say that the New Territory is outside the scope of this agreement but that we are prepared to discuss this question when victory is won.' Ashley Clarke's argument that the Chinese 'have us in a cleft stick because they know that we shall not receive US support in resisting their demand and are capable of refusing to sign the treaty', brought an incisive 'so are we' from the Foreign Secretary. Alexander Cadogan went further noting that 'ultimately . . . we shall have to stand firm on this, and if the Chinese break the Treaty negotiations on it, they must do so'. Another meeting took place at Eden's insistence the next day (23 November) to try and resolve the situation as time was running out for London if the British were to sign simultaneously with the Americans.[29] Indeed, China was applying pressure on Washington to sign immediately, ostensibly because they wanted to announce the treaty at the last session of their Central Executive Committee on 27 November. At the same time, it is not beyond comprehension that the Chinese were consciously rushing the Americans to squeeze the British on Hong Kong as they struggled to maintain the illusion of Anglo-American cooperation.[30]

The outcome of the Foreign Secretary's meeting on the leased territories was the resolve to stand firm against Chinese claims, albeit offering the compromise of the Colonial Office formula (restricted solely to

the New Territories) if Chungking persisted. The latter was warmly sponsored by Richard Law. If the Chinese did not agree, however, the talks
would collapse. Eden told Cadogan, 'You have always told me that [the]
Chinese invariably try to stretch any concessions offered. In this case I
would prefer to offer none.' Even now, however, the Foreign Office was
concerned with American opinion and how the British would be perceived. The amended Colonial Office formula was accepted 'to make the
Chinese more ready to acquiesce in dropping the subject for now and
to forestall any US criticism which may later arise'.[31]

Lord Halifax, Britain's Ambassador to America, was also taking an
interest in British policy from Washington. When he enquired about
Hong Kong's future once more at the end of November, Eden himself
now sent a resolute response, replacing his previous instructions from
August to 'maintain the most absolute reserve'. According to Halifax,
Richard Law's statement in parliament that Hong Kong and extraterritoriality were unconnected was 'understood by the well-informed [in
Washington] but the general public has been inclined to interpret it as
a statement of intention to retain Hong Kong'. This time, however, Eden
was less concerned with American sensibilities:

> If recent statements in Parliament and the Prime Minister's declara-
> tion [at the Mansion House] that what we have we hold are inter-
> preted as statements of our intention to retain Hong Kong, I see no
> disadvantages.
>
> I suggest that the line to take with enquiries is to say that our
> objective is to defeat Japan and reconquer Hong Kong.[32]

The last month of negotiations exemplified the logistical difficulty
of synchronising British policy with their ambassador in Chungking,
thousands of miles away. The history of Hong Kong owed much to 'the
man on the spot', and the same applied to Sir Horace Seymour who
effectively came to represent the colony's interests in China. Perhaps
most worrying from the Colonial Office's point of view was his less than
robust attitude to defending British sovereignty. He was, however, kept
in ignorance of much of London's discussions including the fact that
as a last resort, China would be offered a compromise. While London
was prepared to drive a hard bargain with the Chinese, Seymour was
not. On 7 December, he telexed Eden:

> I feel sure that the Chinese will not willingly acquiesce on continu-
> ance of the lease after the war. I agree that the best course would be

to stand if we can on a simple refusal to include New Territories . . .
I doubt however whether the Chinese in their present mood will be
satisfied with anything but an assurance that the question of the lease
will be reviewed after the war.

Chungking's aggressive approach to the whole question only served to
reassure Eden that there could be no compromise with the Chinese.
'Every development', he wrote, 'shows that we are on a slippery slope
once we admit discussion even later of [the] future of [the] New
Territories. I should prefer to stick to the plain statement of the fact that
these territories are outside the scope of the treaty. It is time and I don't
see why we shouldn't say so.'[33]

Towards a compromise

With the leased territories seemingly within their grasp the Chinese
proved as intransigent as London had become. T.V. Soong, supported
by Dr Wu, the new Chinese Minister of Foreign Affairs, insisted on
discussing the New Territories and now, preferably, the colony as a
whole with the British.[34] These sentiments were conveyed again when
Han Li-wu, another Chinese diplomat, called on Sir Eric Teichman at
the Chungking embassy. This time, however, he brought with him a
suggested compromise.

The Chinese proposal was uncannily similar to previous British
thinking. The Nationalist Government's offer would recognise that
the New Territories were not relevant to the extraterritoriality negotiations but would insist that the lease be discussed later on; the same idea
that the British were already prepared to fall back on if needed. How
the Chinese came to this conclusion is unclear, but it is possible that
they had picked up London's stance from the Americans or even,
perhaps, from Seymour himself. However the Chinese reached their
final position, London remained disappointed by events. Ashley Clarke
noted that the whole idea was to make the offer to the Chinese, not
vice-versa! Once again, it was going to appear to the world (as surely
the Chinese would make it known) that Britain was ungracious and
uncompromising.

The hope of salvaging some credit from these seemingly doomed
negotiations caused Ashley Clarke to propose acceptance of Han Li-wu's
compromise, rather than risk a showdown with Chungking. Sir
John Brenan and Alexander Cadogan agreed, the latter adding that
'I imagine we shall not in practice be prepared after the war to
maintain a refusal to discuss the matter'. However, as was becoming a

habit, the Foreign Secretary refused to accept this inevitability and called for another meeting the next day. 'Mr Ashley Clarke's reasoning is incomprehensible to me. I have always been taught [that] the more we give [the] Chinese [the] more they ask.'[35] Eden was prepared to seek the War Cabinet's approval for his policy when it met on 28 December, which was achieved unanimously. The Cabinet paper stated that 'Dr Wellington Koo [the Chinese ambassador, then back in Chungking] had told Seymour that he thought that the Chinese Government would not sign unless it was clearly indicated that we return the leased territory to China . . . This would be very awkward since we should have abandoned our extraterritoriality privileges and no Treaty would have been signed to put anything in their place.' Nevertheless, the Foreign Secretary insisted that Britain should stand firm because she had given way on several important issues to the Americans. Britain would reiterate her willingness to discuss the lease and its terms, but only post-war.[36] At this pivotal meeting, Eden's tough stance elicited warm Cabinet approval. Alexander Cadogan agreed that the British were 'on perfectly firm ground' in resisting Chinese demands. This fact did not, however, stop Churchill from launching into a tirade against the Cabinet. He gave an 'impassioned speech (which cheered him up) on those people who got up each morning asking themselves how much more of the Empire they could give away'![37]

The gravity of the situation should not be understated. Eden was ultimately countenancing the complete breakdown of Sino-British relations during the war if Chiang Kai-shek refused to back down, a move which would have appalled the Americans and done untold damage to the Allied alliance. The Foreign Secretary wrote to his American counterpart, Cordell Hull, and explained Britain's point of view, leaving no doubt that Eden held the Americans partly responsible for the situation:

> We are unable to admit that this question [of Hong Kong] falls under the head of the abrogation of extraterritoriality and we are unable to withdraw from the position which we have taken up. To do so would be to lay ourselves open to further Chinese pressure on other matters the extent of which cannot be foretold.
>
> If as a result of this we are unable to reach the agreement with the Chinese Government on a treaty abolishing extraterritoriality it will obviously be highly regrettable. But we have faced this eventuality in taking our decision which is final . . . We should be grateful if [the

American Government] felt able to use their influence with the Chinese Government to prevent this occurring.[38]

Despite Anthony Eden's firm policy not everyone in Britain agreed that his was the right path. David Ewer, writing for the socialist *Daily Herald*, opposed Britain's policy towards a colony where 'our title is dubious and which is no value to us'.[39]

American pressure on China forces a compromise

If patience is a virtue, the British were rewarded in late December. During a press conference Cordell Hull told American journalists that the New Territories were outside the scope of the present discussions. Foreseeing that the talks would soon collapse, the Americans privately told the Chinese temporarily to drop their claim to Hong Kong. Lord Halifax, who was closest to the Washington bureaucracy, reported that the

> State Department . . . had been prepared to indicate to the Chinese Government that they were displeased by the frequent introduction of extraneous issues and that although the question of the leased territory was one between China and the UK it was of concern to the US Government in so far as its introduction might impair the smooth settlement of extraterritorial question. [Eden annotated, 'good', to the script.]

Without the support of their sponsor, the Chinese suddenly dropped the issue like a stone. Still, Halifax's understanding of American actions were at best naive. Reading through the story of the extraterritoriality negotiations it is hardly credible to conclude, as he does, that 'it was evident [that the Americans] would have done their best to help us on general grounds'. On the contrary, the Americans could have coerced Chungking from a very early stage into dropping the Hong Kong issue on the grounds that it was destructive to the Allied alliance. Instead, they did not and, if anything, encouraged Chinese claims, restraining Chungking only after Anthony Eden had secured Cabinet support for a breakdown of the negotiations.[40] Indeed, the State Department had insisted when the issue of the Hong Kong lease was first raised, that 'the sympathy of the American public would lie almost entirely with China and would be strongly critical of the Government' if they had supported Britain.[41]

Regardless of American duplicity, the reaction within the Foreign Office was one of overflowing appreciation for Washington's intervention. L.H. Foulds found it 'gratifying', while Ashley Clarke thought there were 'satisfactory points in the treaty which should be placed on the credit side of the Anglo-American co-operation ledger and on balance I am sure we have scored'. Even Alexander Cadogan believed the Americans had 'shown a good disposition'.[42] If anyone had their image tarnished in British eyes it was the Chinese, who became increasingly dispensable. As the treaty proved, it was American cooperation which counted. Eden confided to his diary on 31 December that he was 'Greatly cheered by news that Chinese would after all sign Treaty without Kowloon. So . . . we shall get our Treaty after all and firmness be rewarded.'[43]

London's muted criticism of the Americans was driven by necessity. On completion of the extraterritoriality treaties Ashley Clarke wrote to Stanley Hornbeck on Eden's behalf reiterating the importance of an Anglo-American understanding:

> This attempt to sail in convoy meant, it is true, that the faster ship had to drop some of its speed and the slower had to jettison some of its valuable cargo. But I hope you do not feel that anything of substantial or permanent value was lost in the additional weeks required for negotiating the passage . . . However we made port. That is what matters: and we can take counsel from such vicissitudes as we may have encountered on the voyage for the purpose of making out of this experiment a regular practice in approaching the problems with which you, the Chinese and we will be confronted in the future.[44]

Signing of the treaty

With the dropping of the lease issue, the extraterritoriality negotiations had almost reached their full stop. The Chinese, however, were unsure how far to pursue Hong Kong. In his memoirs, Wellington Koo claimed responsibility for convincing Chiang Kai-shek to accept the compromise.[45] Koo also stated that it was Sir Horace Seymour who suggested the compromise and told him privately that he believed that after the end of the war Britain would return Hong Kong. After an anxious meeting at K.C. Wu's on the afternoon of 25 December, Chinese officials visited Chiang arguing that China was faced with the option of breaking relations with London and ruining the Allied alliance or accepting a compromised treaty. But it was not only American pressure that made the Chinese stop and think; the looming threat of Russia was also instrumental. It was well known in Chinese circles that Stalin held it within his power to destroy the Nationalist Party by sponsoring Mao and his Chinese communists. For once, the Generalissimo listened and agreed with the proviso that Britain should merely 'claim' she would return the leased territories.[46]

The joint extraterritoriality treaties were not actually signed until 11 January because of American translation difficulties. After all the pressure Washington had exerted on London to reach a speedy settlement, the Foreign Office could be forgiven for a wry smile. One last drama, though, remained to complicate the signing ceremony.

The day after the signing ceremony in Chungking on 12 January 1943, Sir Horace Seymour received a note from the Chinese Foreign Minister, dated 11 January. It stated 'that the Chinese Government reserve[d] its right to propose [Hong Kong's leased territories] for discussion at a later date'. The final component of the compromise was now in place. This was no surprise to Seymour, who had after all suggested the formula. He counselled a simple note of acknowledgement, believing a dispute over Hong Kong to 'be inevitable at some stage, but it seems better to defer the dispute as long as possible and to leave the matter as it stands unless the Chinese raise it again'. This was accepted by London.[47]

In keeping with their previous behaviour, the Chinese broke their promise to keep their note to Seymour secret. At a Chinese press conference on 12 January, T.V. Soong explained how China reserved the right to raise the lease of the New Territories at any point. The Foreign Office, now used to dampening fires over the Hong Kong issue, treated the incident to large doses of cold water and chose to ignore the Chinese note. Sir Maurice Peterson was grateful that Britain had actually escaped any explicit claim to Hong Kong itself. He remembered that Britain had taken the lead in renouncing her lease to Weihaiwie (a British concession from China) at the Washington conference of 1921–22, so far as he could remember for three reasons: '(a) we were not using it effectively (b) we *thought* we had got the lion to lie down with the lamb (c) we got away from Washington *without* extraterritoriality being raised' (original emphasis).[48] In January 1943, the British had lost the privilege of extraterritoriality but had escaped any explicit discussion on the future of Hong Kong. For this small mercy, the Foreign Office was grateful.

Emotional rescue: British imperial confidence at the end of 1942

The problem of Sino-British relations

Whether or not the signing of the extraterritoriality treaty deserves to be called 'an epoch-making event, the greatest treaty of which China had been a party in the century' is contentious.[49] The Chinese did not give the appearance of being satiated by their gains despite their public fanfare. From the British point of view it was a difficult question to know how to handle Sino-British relations. Should they be used, as some within the Foreign Office suggested, to ingratiate themselves with the Americans, or should Britain attempt to establish a new basis for a Sino-British understanding. Both paths had great pitfalls and shared a common problem: the enmity with which the Chinese viewed Britain. There appeared little Britain could do to challenge this view. Chiang Kai-shek's ghosted book on China's post-war aspirations, *China's Destiny* (written in 1943), was aggressively nationalistic causing Sir Maurice Peterson to suggest that 'large parts of [*China's Destiny*] might have been written by Hitler or at least Franco'.[50] The book laid the blame for China's failings and the many humiliating concessions extracted from her firmly at the feet of imperialist powers. Of course, the British were at the forefront of such foes. Chiang's thinking, though, was not a radical departure. Even in 1990, the Chinese Prime Minister, Li Peng, was inciting his people to 'expose the crime committed by imperialists in their aggression against China . . . so as to heighten their vigilance against the imperialist strategy of peaceful evolution'. He was not, of course, talking about the Western sanctions imposed after the Tiananmen Square massacre, but the first opium war of 1842.[51]

Despite London's genuine desire for a united and strong China, the British still clung to the past as the Chinese and Americans believed. A hundred years of British colonialism in China would not disappear overnight. This revival of emotional investment in the concept of Empire would remain central to Britain's defence of her right to retain Hong Kong. The British, like the Chinese, were prisoners of their past.

The Mansion House speech

At the Battle of El Alamein in October 1942, which took place in an area of oasis in the Egyptian desert, Britain registered its first major land victory of the war against Rommel's outnumbered Africa Corps. It was not the decisive turning point that Churchill represented it as, but combined with the Soviet defence of Stalingrad it provided a useful platform for the Prime Minister to define his views on the British Empire and stoke the imperial spirit. For Churchill it was 'not even the beginning of the end. But it is, perhaps the end of the beginning'. In one of his most celebrated speeches he declared that he would 'not become the King's First Minister in order to preside over the liquidation of the British Empire. (Loud cheers). For that task, if ever it were presented, someone else would have to be found.'[52] This salvo across the bows of the gathering forces of anti-imperialism worldwide put the Prime Minister's unwavering resolve on record for the first time during the war. It was not only aimed abroad; its effect was equally powerful at home. Britain's defeats on the battlefield would not be transformed into weakness at the conference table. These defiant words, moreover, were used to justify Britain's increasingly uncompromising Hong Kong policy within the Colonial and Foreign Offices, particularly among senior office holders. This growing resolve was further strengthened by the appointment of a new Colonial Secretary, Major Oliver Stanley. He was on the right of the Conservative Party and pursued a much more unyielding line on colonial concessions, something the conservative Colonial Office welcomed after the flexibility of Lord Cranborne.

The Prime Minister's speech articulated what many within Whitehall felt, but which the defeats of earlier years cautioned against. He was providing the leadership of a premier, marshalling the collapsed confidence of British imperialism in an attempt for Britain to retake its place as one of the Great Powers. Anthony Eden, always happy for Churchill to handle the public relations side of the Anglo-American relationship, was also impressed by the Mansion House speech.[53] However, behind the defiant rhetoric of 'We mean to hold our own' (often corrupted to 'we hold what we have') more specific arguments were required to justify the retention of Hong Kong. The loss of extraterritoriality suggested a more selfish analysis of the colony's assets. Hong Kong's position as a British trading base received renewed attention from the China trade lobby and the Board of Trade, with the Colonial Office happy to tag along. The Treasury, though, was influential in resisting such arguments. Uninhibited by diplomatic agendas they denigrated the China market as unimportant and a high risk.

Trade and the Anglo-Chinese loan revisited

The misconception that China was still a lucrative and valuable emerging market coincided with Britain's need to increase exports post-war and justify her Far Eastern empire. The China Association gushed that 'if we are to continue to have valuable commercial assets in the Far East, it would appear highly desirable to keep Hong Kong under the British flag'.[54] Butterfield and Swire, a large China trader, readily agreed, calling to 'retain the substance [of extraterritorial rights] and give away only the shadow'.[55] Of course, the reality of the assumptions underpinning business in China were somewhat different. For example, Douglas Jay and Hugh Gaitskell calculated in 1938 that the dependent colonial empire produced only 1 per cent of Britain's GNP. UK exports to China as a percentage of total trade exports were a paltry 0.8 per cent on average before the war with reverse imports at 1.1 per cent.[56] In truth, the British traders had been privileged for decades in China, not that trade itself was at all easy. Nonetheless, the China Association line, already gospel in the Colonial Office, was accepted by the Foreign Office and incorporated into their arguments to retain the colony.

When the Sino-British loan remained deadlocked into late 1942, Ashley Clarke counselled his department to 'avoid a major row over this, exasperating though it is'.[57] But confidence was growing. Sir John Brenan thought the time was ripe for a change of policy. He argued that it was:

A mistake to go on encouraging the Chinese in the belief that the obligations are all on the side of their allies. Now that the tide has turned definitely against the Axis there is much less likelihood of a Chinese capitulation to Japan, and it will make for healthier relations between China and ourselves to slow down this one-way traffic in gifts and favours. I trust we shall stand firm on the loan question.[58]

Kingsley Wood made it clear that he subscribed to this no-nonsense approach in dealing with the Chinese. He wrote to the Board of Trade explaining that 'It is, I am afraid, easy to draw a contrast which will reveal us in many respects as less successful and apparently less generous to the Chinese than the US Government and the US people though that contrast is not entirely a matter of difference of goodwill.'[59] The problem of presenting British policy to her allies, however, remained. The Pacific Relations Conference at Mount Tremblant in late 1942 provided an understanding of the diplomatic minefield confronting Britain's Ambassador in Chungking.

Institute of Pacific Relations Conference, Mount Tremblant, December 1942

David McDougall, now working in propaganda for the Colonial Office in Washington, attended the conference held in Quebec between 4–14

December 1942. He characterised the gathering as little more than an academic talking shop, 'the sort of men . . . to whom the words "Well said!" have been addressed more often than "Well done!"'.[60] But the strength of the American delegation, which included people like Stanley Hornbeck and Owen Lattimore, added an official touch which forced London to take the conference seriously. Throughout the conference American reverence for China was all too evident. MacDougall wrote that 'the China I heard discussed at Mount Tremblant did not exist . . . it was improper to mention China without a slightly moist eyes and all but a breaking voice'. On the other hand, distrust of Britain was limitless. Even the Canadian and Australian delegates rallied with the Americans and Chinese against British imperialism. The embattled British delegation, led by Lord Hailey and including Arthur Creech Jones, Sir John Pratt, E.M. Gull from the China Association and Sir George Samson from the Washington embassy, reacted to this onslaught by standing together. Creech Jones, the Labour Party's colonial expert, was no friend of Tory imperialism but he had even less time for American criticism. At one point, looking red in the face and very angry, he lectured the other delegates on their hypocrisy. He would not accept 'basic and fundamental criticism of our imperial role' which was 'the adolescent questioning of concepts which had been discussed and settled years ago in England'.

One more point was clear from the debates: Churchill's Mansion House speech had certainly not settled the issue of Hong Kong. At the earliest opportunity, the official Chinese delegates from their Ministry of Foreign Affairs, clamoured for the colony's return. Lord Hailey's argument that it could be retained by Britain and used as an international defence base did not wash with the Chinese; they wanted it back 'no strings attached'. This was the clearest demand expressed by the Chinese so far during the war for the colony's return. Strangely, however, they based their claim on *moral rights* and agreed that it was outside the scope of the extraterritoriality treaties not yet signed. (This was certainly not the view being put forward by T.V. Soong during the parallel extra-territoriality negotiations.) Overwhelmed by the mobilised opinion against Britain's renewed sovereignty, even the loyal imperialist David MacDougall (who was to be a senior administrator of Hong Kong post-war) advised the retrocession of the colony:

> As no other nation (not even the Dutch) betrays the slightest sign of supporting an attempt to retain Hong Kong for any purpose what-soever, I think we ought to remember that we are likely to get better

terms as regards our interests in the colony if, sooner rather than later, we tell the Chinese the place is theirs.[61]

However, the only British delegate officially briefed by the Foreign Office on the question of Hong Kong was Sir John Pratt, an ex-Foreign Office official specialising in the Far East. This proved to be a contentious decision; he was a Sinophile, even believing the seizure of Kowloon in 1898 to have been unjustified. As a precaution, therefore, he was advised that if the subject were broached he should reply that it was a matter for discussion after hostilities had ended, in line with Cranborne's August paper.[62] Privately, though, Pratt told the Chinese that he was 'confident that when the time came to deal with Hong Kong, the Chinese would be completely satisfied'.[63] This statement went down like a lead balloon in the Foreign Office. Sir Maurice Peterson thought (emphasis original) that 'the best thing we can do is to get him home and *keep* him here'.[64]

Returning home, Sir John Pratt remained unrepentant at his indiscretion. At his London debrief Sir John noted, 'It was quite impossible to defend the Empire in America on the basis of "what we have we hold" theory, but only on the basis that the Empire is good for the world as a whole.' The retrocession of Hong Kong, according to him, presented 'an opportunity for a great gesture and this should be taken especially because there was no benefit to be gained from the retention of Hong Kong'. A scribe at the Foreign Office added, 'In his view, indeed, positive disadvantages.'[65] Pratt's outlook, however, was at best eccentric and underestimated imperial commitment within Whitehall.

Hong Kong crossroads

With the signing of the extraterritoriality treaties Lord Halifax sent his congratulations to Anthony Eden on 13 January 1943 for 'having got China to withdraw their last minute point about Kowloon'. His final question asking for 'personal advice' on the colony, however, set in motion a decisive debate which would leave Hong Kong's future within the British Empire increasingly assured.[66]

An evaluation of Hong Kong's assets?

In the light of Halifax's telex of 13 January it was left to the ever rational Sir John Brenan to suggest an accurate assessment of Hong Kong's military and commercial assets before deciding what to do with the colony. Still, the Far Eastern department felt they could say little to

Halifax until they had considered the matter in more detail. At this point, however, a curious breakdown in relations between the Foreign and Colonial Offices led Ashley Clarke to believe (wrongly) that the Colonial Office still adhered to Lord Cranborne's flexible policy of possible retrocession.[67] This prompted Neville Butler and Richard Law to consider how the Hong Kong dilemma could be liquidated. Butler, head of the North American department within the Foreign Office, saw little advantage in clinging to the colony:

> Is not Hong Kong, unless it is somehow sterilised, likely to contribute substantially to all Far East questions affecting China and indeed all questions brought before the prospective 'Four Powers', being approached in a diplomatic setting of Britain versus China and the US? Whereas if it were eliminated we should be in a strong position for getting America to support us against any manifestations of Chinese imperialism in Burma, Malaya or elsewhere.[68]

Richard Law mined a similar vein of pessimism, concluding that 'when the time comes, we shall conclude that Hong Kong is not worth putting up a fight for'. It only remained to consider when to announce the retrocession. He had little doubt that any examination of the economics of the colony would not 'invalidate the general argument'. For all this speculation, however, Oliver Stanley, the new Colonial Secretary, categorically opposed any concessions to China over the sovereignty of Hong Kong. This raises serious questions about the relationship between the Foreign and Colonial Offices. How the Foreign Office could have failed to realise that the Colonial Office was now clinging to the colony so tenaciously remains a mystery.[69]

Nevertheless, a crossroads was about to be reached. On 4 February, Anthony Eden halted further discussions on Hong Kong's future. After reading Richard Law's minute, the Foreign Secretary wrote:

> I have given further thought. I shall prefer to stand flat at the present and to maintain [the] attitude we have adopted in parliament about Hong Kong. Whilst the Americans are busy finding claims to determine the future of French islands in the Pacific, we shall, I think, keep our cards up.[70]

Halifax had his answer. It was further proof that the Foreign Office would make their own decision concerning Hong Kong, without reference to the Colonial Office.

As it happened, the Colonial Secretary happily supported Eden. At the end of January 1943, Stanley informed the House of Commons that there would be no change in the status of Hong Kong, despite the extraterritoriality treaties.[71] Now, Stanley's private secretary wrote to the Foreign Secretary repudiating Cranborne's August 1942 memorandum. The Colonial Secretary rejected the flexibility of Cranborne's paper which was 'compiled last year in quite different circumstances and before he himself became concerned in the matter'. On 16 February Eden and Stanley met to clear up this issue, agreeing that it was best 'to stand pat at present' on Stanley's recent reply given to the House of Commons; Lord Halifax was to defend Britain's right to re-establish Hong Kong as a Crown Colony.[72] Anthony Eden's neat sidestep had ameliorated the immediate question of Hong Kong for the foreseeable future.

Alexander Cadogan, wrote in his diary on the last day of 1942: 'We're certainly in a very different position from what we were a year ago. There's a light at the end of the tunnel, but I can't see the exit yet . . . God bless us all in 1943.'[73]

6
London's Hong Kong Planning, 1943–44

Both the Americans and the Chinese have a feeling that they hope to see British influence removed from Asia . . . Apart from the Prime Minister's pronouncement about his refusal to preside over the liquidation of the British Empire and our determination to carry the war into the Pacific until Japan is crushed, there has however been no considered statement about our views on our Far Eastern possessions.[1]

Assistant Director Operations, SOE, 1943

In early 1943, as the war in the Pacific reached its turning point and the Allies moved to the offensive, British intelligence units in the Far East were troubled. They were concerned that London's Far Eastern strategy, which included Hong Kong, was being submerged by European affairs closer to home and the interference of American politicians. The fact that the Commander in Chief of India controlled British Far Eastern military policy despite having his own serious internal difficulties appeared indicative.[2]

The traditional approach to peacemaking was to remain noncommittal until things became clearer, or as SOE's area commander put it, 'A policy of having no policy': the favoured approach of both Churchill and Alexander Cadogan. It was arguable that these problems would solve themselves in the light of military success but SOE also believed that it was becoming 'a fact that the interested nations take our silence as acquiescence in the theory that by our defeats we have forfeited our position'.[3] SOE's answer was to state explicitly that Britain would return to every single one of her Far Eastern colonies. There was a feeling that Churchill's recent Mansion House speech could be dismissed by Britain's Allies as the usual Churchillian rhetoric and bluster. A more thoughtful statement would remove any doubt. Anthony Eden had already put this point to Churchill in October 1942 and received the unhelpful reproach of 'first you catch the hare'.[4]

SOE, however, was under no illusion that words alone would suffice in shoring up Britain's position. The lack of direction and profile to Britain's Far Eastern war was blamed on a system of government that allowed such a state of affairs:

> Until one man of political authority . . . is charged with the responsibility of studying and co-ordinating all the many problems of the Far Eastern interests of the Empire as a whole, few, if any, of the [problems] will ever be brought to a successful conclusion. At present the permanent heads of the various Government departments, whose duties touch on the Orient, do much but the Far East is not their sole duty and when their recommendations have been made there is always the danger that European and American considerations will swamp those of the Far East merely because they are closer and sharper in perspective.[5]

The creation in mid-1943 of the new British command in South East Asia, South East Asia Command (SEAC), promised to rectify these problems and increase British standing in the Far Eastern war. SEAC's formation, however, did little in reality to break Washington's stranglehold on the Pacific war. The new command was in essence an American sop to British sensibilities. Militarily, the SEAC command area was irrelevant to the defeat of Japan, keeping the British at arm's length from the heart of the Japanese empire which the Americans wanted to keep for themselves. Washington had no inclination to taint its Pacific operations by combined campaigns against Japan with the reactionary British. SEAC's creation, moreover, was not even universally welcomed in London. When Lord Louis Mountbatten, as head of SEAC, proposed a second Foreign Office parliamentary under-secretary dealing specifically with the Pacific, Anthony Eden thought the suggestion 'nonsense'. Although the Foreign Secretary was not opposed to greater institutional planning per se, he resisted any encroachment upon his own power base, and was confident that the 'existing machinery is equal to the task' in the Far Eastern war.[6] America's ambition to distance itself from Britain in the Pacific did, however, have major unforeseen benefits from London's point of view.

SEAC was very important politically, if not militarily, to Britain. Its area of operations contained the lion's share of Britain's colonies in the

Far East, including India, Malaya, Burma and Sumatra. At least these colonies now had a high chance of being recaptured by British forces. Tellingly, however, Hong Kong was not included in SEAC and remained in the joint Sino-American theatre. This, though, was not necessarily a bad thing. It remains one of the supreme ironies of American policy that Hong Kong's exclusion from SEAC stimulated, rather than retarded, British planning to recapture the colony. The Colonial Office, in conjunction with the War Office, decided that British possessions outside of SEAC (Hong Kong, North Borneo and Sarawak) be prepared for the renewal of British rule.[7] Although the Colonial Office's attempt to lead Whitehall policy ended in frustration, they were able to develop an administrative blueprint for the colony.

Colonial Office planning

Gerard Gent was once more a key figure within Downing Street. He promptly began to draw economic interests into the Hong Kong equation by developing relations with the China Association. This reached its pinnacle in 1945 with the drafting of two China Association officials into the Hong Kong civil affairs unit. Never inclined to forego life's luxuries, Gent also realised the importance of retaining the New Territories for golf and horse racing, the loss of which 'would make [British expatriate] life unpleasant!'[8]

The China Association's primary concern was with the status of the leased territory. Monson, Gent's understudy, was a little surprised to hear this. He thought that the China traders were prepared to lose the New Territories if Hong Kong island were preserved as British territory. This was certainly not the case. The Association warned the Colonial Office in May 1943 that 'uninformed opinion may be misled by outside pressure . . . to cede the colony to China'. In spite of these misunderstandings, however, Monson remained unperturbed and believed that the Colonial Office could play a vital role in recovering the colony:

A final decision on the question [of Hong Kong] would of course be a Cabinet matter, but it is clear that in present circumstances little would be gained from our taking a determined public stand. The main line of policy at the moment is clearly that we must all concentrate on turning the Japs out of Hong Kong and during the period it is up to us in this department to work as we are doing at the necessary rehabilitation plans on the assumption that we will be allowed to put them into effect.[9]

His superior, Gent, readily agreed, pointing out that economic aspects alone were sufficient to justify the retention of the whole colony.[10] Here again was an assumption by a civil servant that British trade interests were important. It is interesting to contrast the view of the Foreign Office on post-war trade with China. The Foreign Office had cabled Sir Horace Seymour on 22 July:

> As far as we can foresee, post-war trade on any scale with China will necessarily have to be on a formal long-credit basis. Treasury have always made it clear (*vide* negotiations for the £50 million loan) that we cannot be committed now to permitting large scale long-term credits to China after the war . . . If this criterion were adopted China would figure low on the list of desirable destinations.[11]

The badgering of the China Association had revealed that the Colonial Office's own Hong Kong policy was less than clear. Monson's colleague, Paskin, felt that before interdepartmental talks could be approached the office would 'most certainly have to face up to the future of Hong Kong with greater precision than has previously been done'.[12] For Gerard Gent, though, there was not much to define: Hong Kong would be retained. On this basis he approached the permanent under-secretary of the Colonial Office, Sir George Gater, and persuaded him that coordination of Hong Kong policy could not wait. Gater had hoped that the issue could be approached in a more leisurely fashion when Oliver Stanley had returned from his imminent West African visit. But such was Gent's persistence that the Colonial Secretary was approached immediately.

The resultant series of minutes in which the office considered Hong Kong conformed rigidly with the established Colonial Office system of bureaucratic decision making. According to Norman Miners 'a file was never put before the Secretary of State without a definite recommendation on what action should be taken. If the relevant officials who had minuted earlier were in disagreement, the permanent under-secretary indicated which policy alternative was preferable, and on most occasions the Secretary of State acquiesced by initialling the file.'[13]

Sir George Gater informed Oliver Stanley that the Colonial Office must have a definite policy on Hong Kong before pushing ahead with Whitehall talks. 'Mr Gent suggests that our attitude should be to retain the lease of the New Territories, which runs for 99 years from 1898, if that course is found to be politically practicable in post-war conditions vis-à-vis China. I agree that this should be our objective.' The Colonial

Office, furthermore, would not encourage any future investigation into the implications of losing the New Territories.[14] Oliver Stanley, enthusiastic to restore British prestige, happily consented. However, he expressed concern at the Colonial Office's position within Whitehall: 'Whether we can finally maintain this position [of retaining British sovereignty over Hong Kong] is more doubtful. I should like the office to consider sometime whether our position in Hong Kong is tenable or at any rate valuable with a bitterly hostile China.'[15]

Despite Stanley's own vehement imperialism this was an enlightening admission of the Colonial Secretary's own insecurity *vis-à-vis* the Foreign Office. Stanley's fears, however, were ill-conceived. He was exaggerating the differences between the Foreign and Colonial Offices, possibly because of his dislike for Anthony Eden and Winston Churchill. Instead, the colony's continued existence symbolised the survival of the British Empire for many senior decision makers. This was not a trivial question of the Colonial Office asking for more colonial development money or the retention of the opium trade, but was a matter that touched upon the whole Whitehall Establishment. It was a recurring theme that the consensus of Empire was viewed most sceptically by those most deeply involved in its running.

Summer 1943: Colonial Office–Foreign Office interdependence

By the summer of 1943, the Colonial Office had settled its central dilemma: it was now expected that British sovereignty would be resumed and in practical terms the colony would be treated as an inseparable entity.[16] Other problems, however, remained. What would happen if Chinese forces reoccupied Hong Kong and if they then refused to leave? Questions such as these impinged upon other offices which meant that there would have to be inter-office collaboration. Following Gent's idea of synchronising policy, the Colonial Office set about arranging a meeting for interested parties.

In late August, the Colonial Office contacted the Foreign Office. Paskin's invitation to Ashley Clarke set out the Colonial Office position in no uncertain terms, believing that 'It is clear . . . that our intention and right to liberate Hong Kong and restore it as a British colony is quite uncompromised, and this includes the New Territories.'[17] The Colonial Office, though, was in for a rude awakening when the Foreign Office replied.

The limitations of the Colonial Office's power to determine Hong Kong policy were clearly illustrated by their failed attempt to coordinate policy. The Foreign Office, with the return of Ashley Clarke from leave, declined to participate in any meeting with a brusque explanation that raised more questions than it answered. G.P. Young, on behalf of Ashley Clarke, replied that 'We should be unable to make any addition to the official view point set out' by the Colonial Office (that Britain had every right to return to Hong Kong).[18] The issue appeared unimportant to King Charles Street. But the Colonial Office *did* require advice on whether the Hong Kong issue should be pursued to the detriment of Chinese and American relations, an important question hitherto shied away from. Evidently, the Colonial Office thought that Hong Kong *should* be pursued regardless of Sino-American animosity, but what was the Foreign Office thinking?

The Foreign Office reply was received with dismay in Downing Street. Gerard Gent found the Foreign Office response 'dismal' whilst Monson considered it 'pretty myopic'.[19] Regardless of the Foreign Office's rejection, however, Monson attempted to push ahead but his disappointment was compounded: other ministries refused to consider coordinating Hong Kong policy without Foreign Office agreement. King Charles Street was evidently the linchpin as refusals from the Board of Trade, Air Ministry, Admiralty and War Transport Ministry followed in quick succession. The Admiralty were not even tempted to participate by Monson's reference to the strategic value of Hong Kong for the navy. For there to be effective coordination the Foreign Office had to agree. As Monson asserted, 'they, not the Colonial Office, must be the experts from whom advice on that point should be sought'.[20]

The Colonial Office was undermined principally by its poor relationship with the powerful Foreign Office. Relations between the two offices were so distant that a formal reason for declining the Colonial Office's invitation was not even given by the Foreign Office, and the Colonial Office did not feel able to ask for one. The unequal basis of the relationship meant that Colonial Office initiatives were left dependent upon the whim of the Foreign Office. This point was vividly demonstrated when Monson and Paskin had to resort to cornering Ashley Clarke and Sir Alexander Blackburn to receive an explanation of Foreign Office actions. The real reason for the Foreign Office's refusal to consider interdepartmental talks was only discovered when Paskin and Monson met Ashley Clarke and Sir Alexander Blackburn informally when they called round to Downing Street on unrelated business. Apparently the Foreign Office's refusal to participate in any inter-office discussions derived from their understanding of Anthony Eden's view expressed in his February 1943 minute to 'keep our cards up'. This was taken literally by Ashley Clarke in the Far Eastern department of the

Foreign Office, and was stretched to preclude talks within Whitehall on Hong Kong despite A.L. Scott's belief that such a meeting would be 'useful'.[21] It was also, perhaps, indicative of Alexander Cadogan's aversion to planning: 'it is to me as incomprehensible as futile'.[22] Ashley Clarke, in fact, wanted to contribute to a general Hong Kong discussion. As his own internal Foreign Office minutes show, he argued for the need to assess 'on the basis of expert strategic and economic information, wherein our own advantage lies' regarding the colony. It was Eden's 'cards up' minute, however, which defined Ashley Clarke's response to the Colonial Office. Whatever Ashley Clarke's own thoughts on the subject, the Foreign Secretary's minute meant that 'there is nothing that we can be authorised to say along [these] lines'.[23]

It could, however, be unfair to blame the Foreign Office's non-cooperation on Eden despite Paskin's confession that any further inter-departmental talks would require the consent of the Foreign Secretary.[24] Although historian Steve Tsang assumes that the interdepartmental discussions 'were frustrated by the Foreign Secretary', an alternative explanation may exist for the collapse of the Colonial Office's coordination efforts.[25] It is possible that Anthony Eden was *never given* the option to participate by Alexander Cadogan or his subordinates. The Foreign Secretary, after all, showed a much greater disposition to encourage post-war planning than Churchill. There is no evidence, furthermore, that Eden saw the papers concerned with what may have appeared a (superficially) unimportant matter.

The Hong Kong Planning Unit (HKPU)

Despite the collapse of Whitehall coordination the Colonial Office continued along its own planning path without the Foreign Office. By December 1943 Gent was prepared to put the wider diplomatic angle on the institutional back burner, the Foreign Office's 'dismal response' having taken the wind out of his sails:

> I think no advantage would be gained by pursuing with other departments second or third lines of defence in our Hong Kong policy at present. The issue is bound to come up sooner or later and we can wait for it. In the meantime our planning for Hong Kong Civil Affairs will go ahead on the basis that British administration is to be resumed.[26]

The Colonial Office's civil affairs team was the key component in their developing policy.

The Hong Kong Planning Unit (HKPU) was formed in August 1943, under N.L. Smith, a retired Colonial Secretary of Hong Kong, although he was not expected to be appointed to the eventual team himself.[27] It was planned that a specially trained civil affairs unit would work under the cloak of a military government at the end of the war to restore British rule.[28] According to the official historian, F.S.V. Donnison, 'It was still quite uncertain how the re-occupation would actually be effected, but all planning was on the basis of an opposed landing, with Civil Affairs units attached to operational troops.'[29] Every possible topic for administration was considered, from Chinese policy to opium.

Under the supervision of Gerard Gent the mechanics of Britain's Hong Kong policy developed through 1943. At first the HKPU operated under the auspices of the Malayan Planning Unit until a permanent head and Chief Civil Affairs Officer were found. Initially the unit was small due to the detached nature of the planning; the end of the Pacific war still seemed a long way off. In February 1944 the unit's size was still only nine. With the appointment of David MacDougall as head of the HKPU in September 1944 the unit moved onto a more serious footing. MacDougall was a suitable choice, having great experience with the pre-war Hong Kong administration. He had also attended the Institute of Pacific Relations Conference at Mount Tremblant where, ironically, he had advocated the retrocession of the colony to China. Like many British personnel his confidence in the Empire had recovered with the turning tide of war.

It is arguable that traditional Colonial Office perceptions of its weak position within Whitehall had radically changed with war. Usually, in more peaceful times, when the Colonial Secretary directly approached his opposite number within other Whitehall offices for assistance, the result was failure. It was suspected that other ministers attached greater significance to wider British interests and public opinion than narrow colonial issues. An illustrative example was the Colonial Office's failure to apply for development grants for Hong Kong using the Colonial Development Act of 1929. On the other hand, in the same year, once the government had agreed to give the Boxer Indemnity Fund back to China, the Colonial Secretary was able to persuade Cabinet to allocate £250000 of the money to Hong Kong University.[30]

The Pacific war appeared to leave the situation unaltered. However, the truth was that wartime had strengthened and not undermined Oliver Stanley's position *vis-à-vis* other offices. The period was something of a renaissance as far as the Colonial Office was concerned as it scrambled to plan new colonial governments and breathe new life into the old Empire. It was no longer a case of peacetime lobbying for un-interesting improvements to colonies such as the banning of opium smoking or suppression of *mui-tsai* (child slavery); the British Empire was now under threat, and with it the existence of Hong Kong. What-ever indifference parliament usually held for colonial affairs, the danger posed to British colonies was of cross-party importance.

In this light, a direct approach by Oliver Stanley to Anthony Eden in an effort to coordinate Hong Kong policy may well have succeeded despite his own doubts. Stanley's success in passing the 1945 Colonial Development Bill with 'very little criticism' and enthusiastic coverage from *The Economist* was proof of the renewed importance colonial affairs now took in British imperial life.[31] Leo Amery, a former Colonial Secretary, watched bemused:

> Sat on the Bench for an hour and a half while Oliver Stanley got through the Committee stage and Third Reading of his Colonial Development Fund Bill, amid universal acclaim. What paradise I should have thought myself in if I could have secured in my day only a fraction of what he is now getting from the Treasury.[32]

The Colonial Office's continuing scepticism of the Foreign Office probably derived from traditional institutional animosities, and in particular the isolation of Oliver Stanley from Eden and Churchill.

Parliament returns to Hong Kong: 1944

In the summer of 1944, the time had come for Britain to reassert her sovereignty over Hong Kong in public as well in private. The Colonial Secretary asserted in parliament that Churchill's Mansion House speech defending the Empire still stood, needing 'no altera-tion or addition'. More significantly, in November Clement Attlee, the deputy Prime Minister and self-confessed 'internationalist', told the House of Commons that Hong Kong was not excluded from Churchill's Mansion House declaration. The influence of both of these statements on long-term British planning, although difficult to measure accurately, was considerable. Judging by the reactions from Whitehall offices and other interest groups, it is clear that these statements were received and accepted as signals of Britain's determination to return to her colony.[33]

With the Foreign Office sitting on the Hong Kong sideline, much of the running was left to the increasingly exhausted Colonial Office.

Although Gerard Gent had argued in late 1943 that the Hong Kong issue was 'bound to come up sooner or later, and we can wait for it', events were now shifting fast.[34] Britain's struggle to sort out a coherent Far Eastern strategy presented the Colonial Office with a new opportunity to throw the colony into the mix. In contrast to their previous snub of Colonial Office attempts to discuss the colony at interdepartmental level in 1943, this time the Foreign Office agreed.

The impetus to cajole, rather than follow the Foreign Office, was increased by the Prime Minister's and Oliver Stanley's uncompromising statements on Hong Kong. Into this fray came a reactionary memorandum from Sir George Moss, a veteran of the consular service in China and a member of the General Committee of the China Association. Moss's memo, addressed to the Colonial Office, discussed at length the problem of Hong Kong and advised that London ignore Chinese claims. Such sentiments were greeted with receptive ears by Gerard Gent, who wrote to Moss that his argument was 'a convincing one'. Gent's understudy, Monson, also effused that 'in view of the general refusal of departments to meet our invitation to consider the pros and cons of the matter, we may feel some satisfaction in Sir George Moss' conclusion that HMG – the Dominions should study the problem in all its aspects'.[35]

In itself the memorandum was relatively unimportant but reactions to it drew out several important points. Since it was distributed to all the relevant Whitehall offices it is possible to piece together a very clear picture of how these offices perceived the Hong Kong issue at this time. Most obvious was the divergence of opinion between the Colonial Office/SOE and the Foreign Office. Whereas Gent was keen that others should read a lengthy paraphrase of his own views (18 pages in all!) and distribute it to the Hong Kong Planning Unit, the Foreign Office read it with detached amusement. Sir Alexander Blackburn characterised it as 'a queer mixture of Kiplingesque idealised imperialism and reaction'[36] despite his opinion that in less lyrical language it was close to the official policy on Hong Kong. (He had, it seems, forgotten that Churchill had only a month before described Rudyard Kipling as 'that refreshing fountain of British imperial ideas'.)[37] Sir Horace Seymour's first concern in Chungking was the reaction of the Americans to such an undiluted piece of pro-imperialism; not the kind of evidence to convince them of a new progressive British foreign policy. He commented that 'the Americans would love this!'[38] SOE, on the other hand, were in league with the Colonial Office. Ideas from people like Sir George Moss were excellent ammunition to prepare for the return of British rule. Its importance was such that Lord Selborne, head of SOE, actually had a private meeting with Moss to discuss his ideas for the colony.[39] Moss's paper also had one further important use: to illustrate the strength of the imperial mindset amongst the British Establishment. While the Foreign Office was attuned to toning down espousals of British patriotism or self-interest, Sir George Moss wrote in unadulterated imperial prose which struck a chord with the Colonial service and SOE. He asked rhetorically what the case for holding Hong Kong was, answering that in the short term there was little substantial reason. But 'Appeasement is of no value in the long run and however disguised, the rendition of Hong Kong would, in truth, be appeasement and would crumble the foundations of the Empire which is sustained by British faith and morale.'[40] War had made such views unfashionable, particularly when dealing with the intricacies and sensitivities of the Allied coalition. The Americans and Chinese argued that the Second World War was against imperialism; was it not the case that the war was the product of the Allied denial of German and Japanese imperial aims. This atmosphere made many British politicians uneasy about openly articulating their belief in the Empire. The Foreign Office was particularly susceptible, being disinclined to take Churchill's speeches and Moss's unapologetic words at face value; to do so was in their view 'undiplomatic' and the equivalent of pouring petrol onto the flames. These differences, however, were frequently rhetorical rather than substantial. Churchill had stated a truism when he argued that there was 'an all-party agreement on most fundamentals' of Empire.

The Foreign Office: unenthusiastic (still)

When the Foreign Office finally agreed to Gerard Gent's suggestion that Hong Kong should be included in upcoming Far Eastern discussions, it was without enthusiasm. L.H. Foulds in the Far Eastern section overturned his department's previous interpretation of Eden's 'cards up' minute (which precluded talks) only on basis that 'as the principle of discussions of Far Eastern policy has been accepted, it seems impossible to exclude Hong Kong'.[41] Once again, there was no evidence that the issue was thought important enough to bother Eden with. There was a feeling within the Foreign Office that future events would dictate Hong Kong's status. While the Colonial Office was invigorated by Sir George Moss's paper on the future of the colony, the Foreign Office was restrained by continuing Chinese pressure for Hong Kong's retrocession. At the same time that Moss's paper was received at King Charles Street, the American edition of the *Shanghai Evening Post and*

Mercury carried an editorial which argued: 'Viewing the whole thing realistically, it is impossible to see anything but trouble ahead if Britain hangs onto Hong Kong.'[42] One person who was never convinced of the need to pander to American sentiments over Hong Kong, however, was Sir Maurice Peterson, superintending under-secretary at the Foreign Office. He readily seized on the hypocrisy of America's actions in the Pacific to justify Britain's hold on Hong Kong:

> But surely American plans do enter very much into the question of Hong Kong . . . If the Americans are going to keep the Japanese mandated Pacific islands so as to have a series of stepping stones across the Pacific into the heart of China, it is going to be even more difficult for us to relinquish Hong Kong.[43]

Peterson's sentiments closely echoed Eden's 'cards up' stance of letting the Americans undermine their own credibility on the colonial issue by annexing captured Japanese islands. This was an idea that particularly appealed to Winston Churchill.[44]

As midsummer approached in London, the pace quickened. The successful outcome of Operation Overlord in France meant that London policymakers were beginning to contemplate the shift in focus from the European war to the Pacific theatre. The exclusion of the colony from SEAC's operational sphere was also uppermost in the minds of the Colonial Office and SOE.

When the Colonial Office met with SOE in June to discuss their area of mutual concern, Hong Kong, it was evident that they were both awaiting detailed instructions from the Cabinet. Gent told SOE that regarding the colony, 'no policy has yet received Cabinet approval'.[45] Nonetheless, these joint meetings were constructive and by August Gent had received higher approval (presumably from Oliver Stanley) to form a shadow government in waiting, utilising the various planning directives drawn up by the Hong Kong Planning Unit. In many respects, SOE proved very useful to the aims of the Colonial Office: Gent saw the benefits of close cooperation with a paramilitary unit which had the capability to seize Hong Kong at the end of hostilities. Of course there were weak links: SOE was not solely responsible for British military operations in the south China theatre. They were frequently acting through the British Army Aid Group whose prerogative was ostensibly to obtain intelligence and rescue downed

American airmen. Their commander, Colonel Ride, reacted very ambivalently to outside pressures suggesting that his command should secretly prepare to reoccupy Hong Kong in an emergency. Ride was particularly piqued by the Hong Kong Planning Unit's secondment of his own personnel.

Gent still found it hard to put aside his own suspicions of the Foreign Office and British policy in general: here was a man who certainly did not mind putting a few American and Chinese noses out of joint in an unequivocal parliamentary announcement over Hong Kong. All the dithering in London was time lost in reasserting British sovereignty, according to the under-secretary. And meanwhile, American intelligence, which the British believed contained some virulently Anglophobic staff, was in danger of usurping what little British influence remained in south China. Gent told his colleagues in SOE that he was 'definitely in favour of any action which could be taken in the interval to bring home to our Allies that it was intended to re-instate Hong Kong as British territory'. Incidentally, he added that any actions that could 'stiffen the attitude of our own authorities' would also be most welcome.[46]

The Colonial Office was again finding itself frustrated by being one cog in a machine, when in effect it wanted to control Hong Kong policy. Who did control Hong Kong policy was a good question. It was not even clear to which operational command the responsibility for the ultimate liberation of Hong Kong would fall. While the BAAG was earmarked as the emergency civil affairs unit to seize the colony until David MacDougall arrived, Colonel Ride's attitude was not 100 per cent guaranteed.[47] This uncertainty, verging at times on futility, had however always been the case with British Far Eastern operations; the British had to use what little influence they had left remaining in the China theatre, even if that meant using the BAAG.

The embryonic negotiations for the formation of the United Nations Organisation also prised the bandages off British Hong Kong policy. Sir Hilton Poynton, the Colonial Office member of the British UN negotiating team wanted guidance on how to approach Hong Kong should it be raised as an issue at the Dumbarton Oaks Conference (August–October 1944). The British were expecting the colonial issue to be dragged centre-stage by the Americans in the guise of 'trusteeship', supported no doubt by the Chinese. After careful consideration Poynton was told by the Colonial Office that he should not make any initiative of his own on the subject; Hong Kong was not going to be bargained over. However, since during the extraterritoriality negotiations the question of the New Territories had been left open, 'care should be taken not to convey the impression that the door is bolted as well as shut'.[48] This advice was indicative of the tough Colonial Office stance on trusteeship in general at the conference.

At a high level Foreign Office–Colonial Office meeting in late July, Poynton and permanent under-secretary Sir George Gater met with Cadogan and Gladwyn Jebb to balance imperial interests against American cooperation. These were people who felt, unlike Churchill, that 'we need to choose this or that'. Cadogan bluntly stated that the Colonial Office's intransigence over trusteeship threatened future American financial aid that was vital to Britain. Gater, however, refused to concede, arguing that Oliver Stanley 'would see the strongest objections to any system which places the present Colonial Empire under any system of international supervision'. Indeed, the next day, after consulting the Colonial Secretary, Gater wrote to Cadogan that Stanley remained 'unable to suggest at the present time any concession which will not, in his opinion, be incompatible with our vital imperial interests'. Since the Colonial Office's position had indirectly been given previous Cabinet approval, the Foreign Office was temporarily checked, resentful at Colonial Office intransigence over issues it believed held much wider implications than they realised.[49] The Colonial Office, however, could justifiably refute this; its wider issues were merely different ones to the Foreign Office, namely the piecemeal attempt to chip away at the British Empire. Here was evidence that the Colonial Office could occasionally stand up to the Foreign Office on a topic which received, however inconsistently, the Prime Minister's support.

Unknown to the British, however, American military objections to the ideas of trusteeship had forced the State Department to strike the discussion from the Dumbarton Oaks agenda. British worries for the conference were unfounded.[50] Furthermore, however enthusiastically the Colonial Office lobbied on behalf of Hong Kong, the Foreign Office always attempted to remain detached. They were extremely wary of jumping through the Colonial Office's hoops. It did not matter to the Foreign Office either that most Chinese with interests in the colony wished to see British authority restored or whether future British business interests would be harmed.[51] The Foreign Office preferred to think that it could make policy on higher principles than money or persuasion from selfish British interest groups which they held the Colonial Office to be the agent of. They were, however, about to be proven wrong.

The green light at last: Attlee's parliamentary statement, November 1944

In early September, the Americans were informed of the existence of the Hong Kong Planning Unit which would be attached to any Allied operation aimed at recovering the colony.[52] Of greater importance, though, was the badgering by William Astor MP for a categorical parliamentary statement on Hong Kong.

During a parliamentary debate in June, William Astor, Conservative MP for East Fulham, effused to the point of tedium on the merits of Hong Kong as a British colony. He protested that he was 'not worried about the future of Hong Kong because it is undoubtedly British' although in this he was being disingenuous. In reality, he was a China trade lobbyist. His prime concern was to obtain a firm commitment from the government, or as he put it 'a definite declaration of policy', from which business interests could begin to plan post-war investments in the colony. Oliver Stanley, the Colonial Secretary, answered Astor's question in contrasting brevity, quietly ignoring comments by another MP, Mr Fraser, that the colony remained 'a thorn in the flesh of the Chinese': 'As regards [the] question about Hong Kong I can only refer him to the statement – to which he referred himself – made by the Prime Minister, which I think, needs no alteration or addition.'[53] Astor, like many people before him, was trying to expand upon Churchill's Mansion House speech. Since that speech in November 1942, however, Churchill had been careful not to be too explicit in what he meant regarding British colonies; his sentiment was clear, but greater explicitness threatened Anglo-American relations with disharmony. Even during the parliamentary debate on the future of the Empire prior to the first war-time meeting of Dominion Prime Ministers, Churchill remained reticent.[54] In the circumstances, therefore, William Astor was not completely reassured by Stanley's evasive answer, and would ask for a further categorical statement in November. It was clear that even Oliver Stanley remained cautious about inciting American public opinion when it was not essential to do so. Considering that the most important Anglo-American joint operation of the war was underway (the invasion of France), it was, perhaps, a sensible plan.

Unhappy with his previous answer in June and with the war in Europe now proceeding well, William Astor drafted a further question for Oliver Stanley on 8 November. No doubt his timing was far from coincidental, since Churchill would be making his, by now, almost annual Lord Mayor's speech at the Mansion House the following day. Astor asked 'whether Hong Kong or any other part of the Empire is excluded from the Prime Minister's declaration that it is not proposed to liquidate the British Empire'. By a twist of fate, however, Stanley was out of the Commons that day. It therefore fell to the deputy Prime Minister, Clement Attlee to interpret a lengthy pre-prepared Colonial Office answer, which stressed Britain's right to return to Hong Kong although not denying the opportunity for compromise; the formula was that the door was shut but not bolted. Attlee simply replied to Astor that 'no part of the British Empire or Commonwealth of Nations is excluded from the scope of the declaration referred to'. While expressing gratitude that Attlee had been unambiguous, Astor pressed on. Would British firms now be encouraged to prepare plans for re-establishing themselves in Hong Kong and with British export trade in the Far East? A man of few words, Attlee replied: 'This is obviously so.' From this brief parliamentary exchange, the government's determination to return to Hong Kong was set on record publicly for the first time. The green light had been given.[55]

The morning after Attlee's exchange with Astor, the London *Daily Express* headline blazed, 'Hong Kong remains in the British Empire.' Even Gerard Gent found Attlee's statement satisfactory, which was no mean feat, 'subject to a suitable distribution' to other government offices and departments. The Colonial Office's desire for a public declaration of policy had therefore been met, and helpfully, by the socialist internationalist deputy Prime Minister.[56]

Resuscitated: the Cabinet Far Eastern committee

At the same time as Clement Attlee was making his statement to the House of Commons, the joint Colonial and Foreign Office discussions were progressing. Under the hard-line Foreign Office official, Sir Maurice Peterson, a working party was set up to explore means of presenting British Far Eastern policy to the Americans, and this evolved into a formal Cabinet committee. The formation of this committee was enthusiastically encouraged by British officials in Washington who were still finding it 'chronically difficult' to present British policy in the US against the considerable post-war planning which the Americans had completed. The first meeting of the reconvened Far Eastern committee on 15 November, therefore, signified that the British were at last taking the Pacific war seriously. There was now in place a formal mechanism with which Far Eastern affairs could be discussed and communicated within Whitehall. Through this official Cabinet committee, the Foreign Office's stranglehold on policy was diluted as they had formally to acknowledge the concerns of other offices. This inevitably benefited the Colonial Office, offering them the perfect opportunity to raise their favourite issue: the future of Hong Kong.[57]

At the committee's first meeting in Whitehall, Gerard Gent lost no time in pressing home the importance of Clement Attlee's recent statement and outlining Colonial Office interests. As far as his office was concerned, there were only two problems; Hong Kong and Malaya.[58] The deputy Prime Minister, however, had 'considerably clarified' the Hong Kong situation.[59] This confident attitude was soon bolstered by the China Association who made a strong case for the continued British sovereignty of Hong Kong. Using the new supplementary Far Eastern economic subcommittee, the Colonial Office was presented with a forum in which to circulate economic arguments as well as political ones.[60]

Diplomatically, however, the British still expected strong opposition from the Americans in the Far East. The replacement of the Anglophobic American commander in China, General Joseph Stilwell, in November 1944 was not necessarily a precursor for improved Anglo-American relations. Indeed, the dismissal of Stilwell alarmed the Foreign Office who feared that the British would be tarnished with conspiring in his removal, and be sucked into the American whirlpool of recrimination and China-baiting.[61] Stilwell's replacement by General Wedemeyer also aroused mixed feelings. Although he had worked satisfactorily with Louis Mountbatten at SEAC as his deputy, the general was a midwesterner from Omaha, Nebraska, not an area traditionally known for its sympathy for the British Empire.[62] Mountbatten's political adviser, Esler Dening, had hardly allowed Wedemeyer to unpack before he was lapsing into deep melancholia concerning the new appointment. He told London that initially he thought that Anglo-American relations would improve substantially, but now he feared 'that the situation may well deteriorate further'; Wedemeyer had told him 'with conviction that there would not be a British Empire after the war'.[63] The same day (and it must have been a very bad day) Dening sent another message to the Foreign Office which struck a similarly downbeat note: 'To our critics, as well as to our well-wishers, we seem to be drifting aimlessly on the tide, and the doubt exists whether we have the strength or the ability to strike out in any given direction.' Anthony Eden, however, remained undaunted by Dening's pessimism; the Foreign Secretary was not convinced that all had gone sour with Wedemeyer yet, whatever the American's ignorance of the China situation. It was, after all, unlikely that Wedemeyer could prove more unpopular than his predecessor. He would soon learn the hard way, like Stilwell had, that China was the destroyer rather than the maker of reputations.[64] Moreover, both Cadogan and Eden felt that the British could do little more to support their Far Eastern interests than they were already doing; specifically, the setting up of a high-level Cabinet committee and an economic subcommittee for the region.

The collapse of China into virtual civil war, taking with it America's China policy, reinstated the power vacuum which was the basis of Hong Kong's existence as a British colony. The question was now being asked whether China would even survive as a political entity, rather than who would rule its vastness. As Neville Butler in the Foreign Office pointedly observed: 'A certain amount of the devil has been taken out of the Hong Kong controversy by the obvious uncertainty of the regime in China.'[65] Uncertainty in China increasingly alleviated the colony's exclusion from SEAC's command as Chiang Kai-shek was consumed by domestic troubles, curtailing his appetite for foreign adventures. There was now little possibility of the Chinese Nationalists recapturing Hong Kong. The efforts of the Colonial Office and SOE had also strengthened Britain's position in south China, guarding against the withdrawal of Japanese forces from the area or any other eventuality. It was not only Chinese weakness which was propelling London's Hong Kong policy forwards, but also the efforts of the British people.

7
Anglo-American Military Strategy in the Far East, 1942–44

The hard fact is that the Americans have got us by the short hairs . . . We can't do anything in this theatre, amphibious or otherwise, without material assistance from [America] . . . So if they don't approve they don't provide, and that brings the whole project automatically to an end. They will provide the stuff for north Burma operations . . . but they won't for anything else . . . Who pays the piper calls the tune.[1]

Louis Mountbatten's Chief of Staff at SEAC, 1944

If you listened to Washington gossip it would have been possible to believe that where the British offered rowing boats for the Pacific war, the Americans offered aircraft carriers. Unable to pack the military punch which their political aspirations yearned for, London was left to play a bad hand skilfully. The Foreign and Colonial Offices were acutely conscious of Britain's military weakness in the Far East, and were left placing their hopes in what the Chiefs of Staff could deliver militarily. It was not beyond possibility that the Chinese or Americans might recapture Hong Kong and refuse to hand it back, or at least stir up the Chinese population to resist British claims. British military problems, though, ran deeper than Hong Kong. Britain's political direction was analogised by Alexander Cadogan as 'a blind man searching for a black cat in a dark room'.[2] Luckily for the British, the feared Sino-American alliance began to crumble; at first imperceptibly, and then in 1944, in graphic detail as the military situation in China verged on collapse. This estrangement was instrumental in Britain's return to her Chinese colony.

The first signs of breakdown: the Sino-American relationship

1943 saw the marginalisation of the China theatre and brought the realisation among sections of American policymakers that Chiang Kai-shek was a 'reactionary, inefficient xenophobe whose aims were very different from those of Americans'.[3] This opinion had taken a long time to form and even then was not universally shared in Washington. Indeed, the Generalissimo spent hundreds of millions of dollars within America each year glossing over the corruption of the Soong dynasty while still begging for more.[4] Henry Luce's publications, *Time* and *Fortune*, also sold the deification of the Chinese and Chiang Kai-shek. Chou Enlai, deputy leader of the Chinese communists told an American intelligence officer that Washington's 'generosity excites contempt and gives them reason for pride in the effectiveness of their finesse'.

What lifted the lid on the reality of China and its corrupt leadership was the posting of General Stilwell to Chungking to command American forces in the China theatre, and later, nominally to command all forces in the theatre, both Chinese and American. Joseph Stilwell's nickname, 'Vinegar Joe', said a lot about his acerbic personality. His transfer to China also signified the importance which America attached to the Far Eastern theatre. When he was originally posted to Chiang Kai-shek's command in February 1942 he was the American Army's top China specialist and pencilled in to command the planned North African landings, Operation Gymnast, instead of Eisenhower. His initial assignment was seen as a significant military commitment. The Chinese army would be reformed and refitted before launching counterattacks against the Japanese while China would provide American bomber bases to hit Japan. Unfortunately for General Stilwell, however, he had been handed a poisoned chalice; a military *and* political role disguised as a purely combat position. In Chiang Kai-shek's China one could not exist without the other. His government was a coalition of factions and warlords; you simply could not survive unless you played politics.[5] Yet, never liable to let facts get in the way of their idealisation of China, the Americans threw money and favours at Chiang's feet without exacting specific commitments. And when those investments refused to come to fruition, Stilwell asked why. He did not question American involvement in China itself, in that way he was also captured by the China dream. But his attempt to reform the Chinese army into an effective fighting force brought the whole China theatre down on his head and with it Sino-American relations.

China's destiny?

As Americans began to realise that Chiang Kai-shek was not quite the democrat that they thought, Chiang failed to discourage them in this belief. The unguarded prose in Chiang's *China's Destiny* (widely accepted to accord with Chiang's own beliefs) paid little heed to democratic principles as Americans would understand them. The reader was led to believe that not only was Chiang responsible for writing all 100000 words in two months while running the war, but that all Chinese failures could be laid at the feet of the West. According to Sterling Seagrave the book 'oozed so much bigotry and dementia that those translating it into English began taking sick leave, rather than face foreigners who were reading it'.[6]

The American authorities wanted to suppress the book on the grounds that it would undermine Chiang's carefully crafted image as a liberal democrat.[7] But the evidence that Stilwell was reporting was becoming increasingly hard to ignore: militarily the Chinese had achieved little and it was a barely guarded secret that Chiang was more interested in fighting the communists than the Japanese. Teddy White, Henry Luce's China correspondent, finally managed to obtain an interview with Chiang in June 1941, where the Generalissimo explained that 'The Japanese are a disease of the skin, the communists are a disease of the heart.'[8] It was dawning on Roosevelt, furthermore, that Chiang was taking much more than he was giving. In April 1943 Chiang Kai-shek telexed the President with a fawning but thinly-veiled threat of blackmail:

As you know, I have to fight continually against demoralising doubts on the part of my officers, who conclude that America's attitude towards China is in essence no different from that held by other nations; that both in the all-important matters of joint-staff conferences and war supplies, China is treated not as an equal like Britain and Russia, but as a ward.

The president has consistently shown himself to be the one great friend of China, and I may say on our part we have been loyally responsive ... What a difference there is between our attitude towards the United States and that of Britain and Russia!

If in future the Anglo-American joint staff is not enlarged to include China ... then China would be just a pawn in the game. Gandhi told me when I visited India: 'They will never voluntarily treat us Indians as equals; why, they do not even admit your country to their staff talks.' If we are thus treated during the stress of war, what becomes of our position at the peace conference? You must insist that we have our own stand, and we have our own independent position to uphold.[9]

Despite Chiang's ulterior motive in securing yet more American aid, the message is illuminating on several levels of the Sino-American relationship. The Americans did not invite the Chinese to joint staff meetings for good reason – they were militarily peripheral and indiscreet – but, above all, because the Americans did not want them there. American public affection for China did not extend to allowing China to dictate Washington's policies. The paradox of American policy was that they only wanted a one-sided Sino-American relationship where the Chinese would follow the American lead and show everlasting gratitude. At the Casablanca conference Chinese affairs were discussed without the Chinese while their wishes at the Cairo conference were overruled without consultation.[10] Equally, Chiang's dependence on American sponsorship meant that the Nationalist government was diplomatically at the mercy of the Americans. The Generalissimo, however, believed that when push came to shove, Washington would not sever the long-established emotional investment given to his regime. In this, contrary to many other decisions, he would be proved correct.

At the end of the year, John Davies, Second Secretary of the American Embassy in Chungking, wrote to Harry Hopkins giving a damning indictment of America's China policy, and with it Chiang. Only weeks before, Ambassador Gauss had been warning of the Chinese desire for another huge political loan which was without a 'sound basis'.[11] What was required, Davies believed, was a realistic China policy. He argued that Chiang Kai-shek could secure his position by reforming his party and taking the lead in a genuine coalition government. However, 'the Generalissimo is not only personally incapable of this, he is a hostage of the corrupt forces he manipulates. In this uncertain situation we should avoid committing ourselves unalterably to Chiang.'[12] Unfortunately for America, these words went unheeded as Chiang had rightly surmised that Washington had invested too much in the Generalissimo to change horses, if one could be found.

Although American reporters and policymakers became increasingly sceptical of Chiang in 1943, Admiral Leahy, Roosevelt's Chief of Staff, reported that the changing atmosphere surrounding America's

China policy was also partly driven by domestic American politics. Leahy noted that Laughlin Currie

> stressed to me the necessity for a positive policy in our relations with our Far Eastern ally in order to avoid always being on the defensive in our relations with Chiang, and to mitigate attacks by political opposition in America which at that time used our China policy as a basis for criticism of the President.[13]

A more fundamental reason for growing scepticism towards China, however, was the increasing irrelevance of the China theatre to the winning of the war. The developing island hopping strategy formulated by Admiral Nimitz cut a swathe through the central Pacific, and eliminated dependency on Chinese bases. The strategy bypassed Japanese strongholds and utilised the superiority of American naval and air power, pushing ever onwards to the Japanese home islands. Critically, the strategy no longer required the wining and dining of Chiang Kai-shek.

London's 'realistic' China policy

Contrasting American and British policies towards China were clearly observable to others. The slippery and embezzling Chinese foreign secretary, T.V. Soong, brother-in-law to Chiang, told Stanley Hornbeck that 'discussion of policies and procedure with the British is very different from discussions of similar subjects with American officialdom.' 'Americans', he said, 'begin with principles and discuss possibilities and courses in the light thereof, with a certain emotional accompaniment. The British ... are matter-of-fact, "realistic", unemotional and they have constantly in mind the question of quid pro quo.'[14]

For all the pressures now exerting themselves on Sino-American relations, American policy remained consistent in its antipathy towards British colonialism. This was typified by McCracken Fisher of the Office of War Information (OWI). As the Chungking representative for OWI he was alarmed at the misguided views most Americans held concerning China. He was therefore pleased to see 'China debunking' articles from notables such as Pearl Buck. However, when Ashley Clarke asked what Britain could do for China short of an offensive in the Pacific, McCracken suggested that 'politically an offer to surrender our rights in Hong Kong to China would have a tremendous effect'.[15] But the question now emerging was whom London would actually give Hong Kong back to. The British watched with detachment as Chiang's regime began to totter and Mao's communists increased in strength.[16]

China's indirect diplomacy

Chungking's contrivance to channel post-war claims through Washington illustrated Chinese weakness. They were, however, particularly adept at persuading American opinion of the importance of supporting Chiang Kai-shek's version of the 'new China'. Teddy White remembered that 'one correspondent arrived in Chungking, was banqueted by the government the evening of his arrival, stayed drunk for his entire four-day visit, lurching from banquet to banquet, and let me, from my desk at the [Chinese Government] Information Committee, write all his dispatches', which were suitably enthusiastic about Nationalist China.[17] Other forms of propaganda consisted of playing on the American conscience about China's war-time commitment, the supposed similarity of American and Chinese anti-colonialism, the affinity of China for American benevolence, and the potential strength of an American-backed Nationalist China. The list was endless, and all these schemes were dedicated to propping up Chiang's corrupt regime and dragging America into internal Chinese politics. In this system of things, the State Department became a crucial component, amplifying and legitimising Chinese propaganda through its Sinophile staff. Both in Washington and at its Chungking Embassy, the State Department became a prime target for Chinese lobbying, including the return of Hong Kong. T.V. Soong had even broached the subject of the colony's return to China with Sumner Welles in March 1943. He did so, apparently, to discover the *British* attitude over the colony post-war, which was patently clear! It was more likely that Soong was hoping to elicit America's official support for their claim, but Welles was too astute to fall into the trap.[18]

The State Department and Hong Kong

At the same time that *China's Destiny* was published the American State Department received several unsolicited and anonymous reports from Chinese sources. These advocated the retrocession of the colony along the lines of the extraterritoriality treaties. One informant told the Washington China department that Sino-British negotiations were actively underway.[19] Another provided the Chungking Embassy with an in-depth plan for the future of the colony. The author maintained that the Chinese Government expected Hong Kong to be returned after the end of hostilities, when it would be kept as a free port. Such was the level of detail and thoroughness in this document, however, that it appears highly likely that this was an official Chinese document, and even perhaps, Chiang Kai-shek's hoped-for policy towards the colony. Its attempt to focus on the economic and industrial potential of Hong Kong implied that the Chinese were trying to commit America to supporting this policy with the incentive of economic concessions after the war. For example it stated:

> In Hong Kong all Powers who are willing to deal with China on a reciprocal basis could be invited to apply for locations for industry, approved by a Chinese commission set up for the purpose, on leases for 25 years (a sufficient time in which to write off buildings and improvements erected).

Interestingly, the report concluded with the suggestion that China's offer to keep Hong Kong as a free port, 'free from political intrigue, racketeering, squeeze and/or extortion . . . a "model" for New China', should be communicated to Britain 'through the USA or at the general Peace Conference'. There was even the hint that America might approach Britain directly which 'would meet an immediate and enthusiastic reception by all those who are interested in the Far East'.[20]

If this was indeed a ploy by the Chinese to push the Americans into the ring on their behalf, it deviated little from the established norm of Sino-American relations; America was clothing, arming, feeding, subsidising and dying on behalf of Nationalist China. And little of that aid ever reached its intended recipient. Lend-lease goods on reaching China from New York could be on sale in the black market in little under two hours. No wonder one British observer at the Washington Embassy believed that 'the Chinese want from [American] Lend-Lease the moon with chocolate sauce'.[21] It was also, no doubt, coincidental that T.V. Soong was ranked as 'reputedly the richest man in the world' by the *Encyclopaedia Britannica*.[22] As it was, American reaction to the Chinese document was subdued. It presented nothing new to American State Department officials who were already devout believers in the idea that Britain should retrocede Hong Kong.

Lord Halifax, though, received the impression from Stanley Hornbeck that no pressure would be brought to bear on Britain to return the colony. Instead, British sovereignty would be preserved if Hong Kong were to be placed at the disposal of the UN in any security pact that might be formed. However, this was not strictly the case: moral and political pressure *was* brought to bear by Washington on London as we have already seen. Although Hornbeck hoped that Britain would voluntarily return the colony to China, he also raised the subject in direct talks with the British when he visited London in November 1943.[23] At the talks, where it will be remembered Gerard Gent expressed apprehension over trusting the Foreign Office's resolution over Hong Kong, Hornbeck brought up his final point; the future of Hong Kong. 'The effect was electrifying', he observed regretting his decision. 'I had had no thought of injecting a discordant note. I felt at once that discretion in that context would be the better part of valour.' And if he remained under any illusions about British policy, these were swiftly dispelled. The next morning before he left for home the British ensured that he received an audience with Winston Churchill. According to Hornbeck, the Prime Minister launched into a tirade. He described:

> the acquisition by Great Britain of Hong Kong, and the develop-
> ment by Great Britain of a great port which he felt had benefited
> the whole world. He said that it was British territory and he saw no
> good reason why it should cease to be such. He went on to say
> that perhaps some arrangement could be made with the Chinese
> whereby the question of sovereignty could be adjusted but the
> political control and administrative responsibility remain with Great
> Britain. He referred to public utterances of his own to the effect that
> he was not Prime Minister for the purpose of being a party to the
> liquidation of the British Empire. He said that he had convictions
> on the subject and that he was perfectly willing to say so frankly
> to anybody.[24]

American attempts to force London to relinquish the colony were also being undermined by troubles within the State Department itself.

As America's China policy turned sour, American diplomats began to argue over who was to blame. There were tensions between Stanley Hornbeck and other State Department officials because he was withholding important papers from his Secretary of State, Cordell Hull, when he did not agree with them. Eventually these pressures exploded in 1944 and a palace revolt removed Hornbeck from his post as director of Far Eastern affairs. Recently, he has come in for severe criticism as the architect of America's doomed China policy that ended in Saigon in 1975. Accordingly, he was charged with being ignorant about the real China and, basing American policy on personalities and not fact, withholding cables that were critical of Chiang Kai-shek. One example of Hornbeck's inability to handle home truths about the Chinese Government was illustrated when John Service wrote a critical memorandum detailing the danger of backing a gangster like Chiang and the growing importance of internal Chinese politics. When Service returned to Washington in January 1943 Hornbeck received Service's report as 'ridiculous', 'preposterous' and 'scandalous'. Another scandal within the State Department was also about to break. The Federal Bureau of Investigation (FBI) had evidence that although secret China reports were not reaching the Secretary of State for Foreign Affairs, someone highly placed within the State Department was passing the information over to China Defence Supplies, T.V. Soong's Washington front for handling lend-lease. It appeared that the Chinese were better informed about American policymaking than the Washington administration was.[25] Nevertheless, despite the best attempts of some American historians to single out individuals, the difficulties of America's China policy should not be pinned on one man. The problems arose fundamentally from a misguided perception of American policy in general and of what it could do in China.

The Washington establishment's approach to its own ambassador to China, Gauss, was symbolic of their habit of seeing what they wanted to see in China. Gauss's valiant attempts to counter the American idealisation of the Chungking Government, for example over the Chinese loan of 1942, were profitless. Almost all his recommendations had been overruled in Washington. Laughlin Currie, one of Roosevelt's advisers, maintained that Gauss was 'considered undiplomatic' and only remained at his post on account of Wendell Wilkie's personal attacks on him.[26]

1944: the collapse of the China dream

London's attempt to reconcile her imperial ambitions in the Far East with Anglo-American friendship came to a head in 1944. As the Japanese were pushed from the offensive to the defensive, attention turned towards the Allied military strategy which would expel the Japanese from their conquered lands. The decision makers in London, especially Churchill, however, proved less than decisive in selecting a strategy that would best serve British interests. Instead, the attempt to balance political and military objectives led to a bitter and protracted struggle within Whitehall as to Britain's preferred military strategy. Should Britain, with her slender military resources, join with the Americans in a main thrust towards Japan, or should she use what little she had to reconquer her lost colonies in South East Asia?

Britain's dilemma was not helped by the actions of America. As 1944 wore on, it became increasingly apparent that Washington did not want to cooperate with Britain in any joint operations against Japan, or allow Britain to recapture her lost colonies. These were unpalatable truths for London. Instead, the British preferred to blame difficulties over military strategy on individual Americans, such as 'Vinegar Joe' or General Wedemeyer. A Foreign Office document understatedly remarked that it would be 'unwise to ignore the fact that while in one theatre General Stilwell is almost openly hostile to British interests, in the Pacific neither General MacArthur nor Admiral Nimitz have been disposed to give any publicity or credit to Empire forces taking part in operations'.[27]

The straw that broke America's China policy was the near-collapse of Chiang Kai-shek's regime in the face of Japan's Operation Ichigo. Despite billions of dollars of US aid and training, their efforts crumbled to dust as the Chinese army was pushed back hundreds of miles in disarray by Japanese troops. This was not the China which Roosevelt had sought to project as his fourth 'Global Policeman': America could no longer pretend that China was an emerging power, or that the China theatre was critical to forcing the defeat of Japan. The Chinese, 'acutely aware of their relative military exhaustion, of the fact that they can be no stronger politically than they are militarily' had consciously conserved military strength, leaving the fighting to the Americans.[28] But still the Chinese stretched the definition of an army. General Stilwell characterised Nationalist forces as being 'in desperate condition, underfed, unpaid, untrained, neglected, and rotten with corruption'.[29]

There were consequential effects on British policy. With every Chinese defeat, physical opposition to Britain's reoccupation of her Far Eastern colonies weakened. After Operation Ichigo, however, China would have trouble regaining her own territory, never mind recapturing British colonies. Washington's counter-balance to British imperialism had come to nothing. The British, on the other hand, utilising their command of SEAC and the leadership of General Slim, began to press ahead with the recapture of Burma and the other Far East colonies, turning the tide in their war against Japan.

America and Britain: strategies of self-interest

Unable to deny Britain a role in the Far East, America attempted to 'contain' British influence in her old colonies in South East Asia, which remained peripheral to the defeat of Japan itself. General Stilwell's State Department adviser, John Davies, wrote that:

In so far as we participate in SEAC operations, we become involved in the politically explosive colonial problem of the British, Dutch and possibly French. In so doing, we compromise ourselves not only with the colonial peoples of Asia, but also the free peoples of Asia, including the Chinese ... By concentrating our Asiatic effort on operations in and from China we keep to the minimum our involvement in colonial imperialism.[30]

The British could be equally explicit about their own interests if the situation moved them. When Churchill commented at one London policy meeting that Burma–India operations were being committed to construct and safeguard a supply line to China, Clement Attlee snapped, 'What do we care what the Americans want?'[31] The truth was that neither Washington nor London could avoid cooperating with the other: Britain needed American military supplies to regain her lost colonies, while America could not deny Britain's right to fight against Japan. The differing interests between the two Allies showed themselves in the separate military strategies that each developed in the Far East.

South East Asia Command and General Stilwell in China

British strategy focused on her only military command in the Far Eastern theatre, SEAC. This was born out of an agreement between Roosevelt and Churchill at the Quebec conference in 1943 to establish a joint military command in South East Asia to recapture Burma and open the overland supply line into China. In theory, Britain would use her base in India as a launch-pad for attacks against the Japanese through Burma and onwards. Since the Japanese had driven a wedge south through the Pacific, it was argued, not unreasonably, that the Allies could more effectively fight the geographically separated Pacific and South East Asian regions under two autonomous commands; SEAC in the south and MacArthur in the south-western Pacific, allowing each force to attack the Japanese flanks. Like everything else in the Far Eastern theatre, however, SEAC's role was not simply military.[32]

The structure of SEAC's command was exceedingly complex as a result of the need to balance American and British political aspirations. Because British troops would predominate in operations, and an American was in command of Operation Overlord on the same basis, it was agreed that Lord Louis Mountbatten would exercise overall command of SEAC.[33] The American General Stilwell, however, was named Deputy Supreme Commander while retaining his position as commander of Chinese and American armies in China. According to Christopher Thorne, 'even a more flexible man than "Vinegar Joe" would almost certainly have found the satisfactory fulfilment of all the roles involved beyond him'. Despite these unhappy omens, though, there was a great deal of hope that SEAC could revitalise Britain's war against Japan from India.[34] The brutal logic ran that American anti-colonial sentiment could be undercut by British deaths on the Far Eastern battlefield.

General Stilwell believed, along with President Roosevelt and many other American statesmen, that China was potentially the key to defeating Japan. It was held that by building Chiang Kai-shek's regime up and defeating the Japanese in set piece battles on the Asian mainland, the way would be cleared for strategic air attacks and the invasion of the Japanese home islands from China. The creation of SEAC, from the American point of view, would assist in this plan. America's aim in encouraging Britain to recapture Burma was primarily a strategy to help China and certainly did not signify approval for the British Empire. American military might was such, however, that Washington was able to maintain several parallel military strategies at the same time. Besides the China strategy, the Americans persisted in following two other strategies: General MacArthur's north-western drive towards the Philippines and Formosa, and Admiral Nimitz's island hopping charge across the central Pacific. The ability of Washington to shift emphasis between these three options depending upon their success would have a profound impact upon the Chinese theatre during 1944.

Britain searches for a Far Eastern strategy

It might have been expected, considering Britain's disabilities in the Far East, that she would have accepted the role cast for her in South East Asia, happy to be involved at all. Following, rather than leading, however, did not come naturally to Britain's governing elite. London's political ambitions were not necessarily circumscribed by her material limitations. Esler Dening, Foreign Office political adviser to Louis Mountbatten, was a vociferous critic of following American military strategy in the Far East. He maintained that:

> The present concept of Far Eastern strategy is an American one in which the British one is merely contributory and in which there is no place for an essentially British effort . . . For SEAC there appears to be no role at all except to cover General Stilwell's supply route,

and to employ British forces at the maximum disadvantage to themselves with the minimum effect upon the enemy... This concept runs contrary to Mr Eden's statement in the House of Commons on December 15th 1943 that we are principal in this war against Japan.[35]

Considering Britain's limited means and her diplomatic situation in the Far Eastern theatre, these aims were not wholly realistic. Even so, the Foreign Secretary persisted, believing that Britain had no choice. He wrote to the Prime Minister in early 1944 that:

I feel strongly that we must have a part of our own to play in the Far Eastern war. If we are merely dragged along at the tail of the Americans we shall get no credit whatsoever for our share in joint operations. I have a feeling that the Americans are not anxious that we should play any notable part in the Pacific war. *We want to make it plain to the world that we have played our part in regaining our Far Eastern Empire.* [Operation] Culverin would show this and would be an able contribution to assist, where an unenthusiastic Admiral King in the Pacific would not.[36] (emphasis added)

Operation Culverin was the Prime Minister's favoured strategy for securing British interests in the Far Eastern war. It involved bypassing the sodden jungles of Burma altogether in favour of an amphibious assault on Sumatra and Malaya; Malaya's natural mineral assets of oil and rubber being a major attraction for the Prime Minister. Churchill became increasingly obsessed with avoiding a slow slog through impenetrable jungle for little political gain. Throughout the next six months, therefore, he continually harped back to Culverin in an attempt fully to utilise SEAC and the Indian Army in order to restore the Empire. By September, Churchill was focusing on Singapore as the final goal of British strategy; 'the supreme British objective in the whole of the Indian and Far Eastern theatres ... the only prize that will restore British prestige in this region'.[37]

The Prime Minister's ambitions for SEAC, however, did not lead to a quick decision for British strategy. General Ismay wrote to a colleague that attempts to resolve British strategy in the Pacific 'will be one of the black spots in the record of British Higher Direction of War'.[38] Predictably, the Americans, who would have to provide the equipment and supplies, were strongly opposed to any talk of bypassing Burma. The British military were equally ambivalent, although for different reasons. Many policymakers in London argued that pursuing an operation like Culverin would not secure British interests in the Far East because South East Asia was peripheral to defeating Japan. If it was Britain's ambition to be at the centre of the Far Eastern war, they argued, Britain might combine with General MacArthur's thrust towards the Philippines and Taiwan, or focus its attack against Japan itself. The Chiefs of Staff wrote to Churchill rebutting his criticism that joint operations with the Americans would undermine Britain's position in her colonies.

> We conclude . . . that British participation in the quick main decisive thrust into Japan's inner zone will do more to restore British prestige in the whole of the Far East, and particularly in China, than a penetration of the outer zone from South East Asia. The launching of a large campaign from South East Asia must await the defeat of Germany and must, therefore, appear to the world as tardy and hesitating in comparison with the large strides being taken by the Americans in the Pacific. There is also the point that if we pursued this course, we should be open to the reproach that we had waited until the Americans had made it possible for us to walk in and recover our own possessions.[39]

It seemed as if there was a politically led choice between recovering Britain's colonies and playing an important role in defeating Japan, when in fact Britain wanted both. Faced with these contradictions, the Prime Minister equivocated over British strategy, acutely conscious that military strategy was not always his strongest point. Exhibiting his worst bloody-mindedness, he lectured the Chiefs of Staff on policy, accused them of ignoring political implications and denied that the Americans would have any use for the British in the Pacific until the Autumn of 1945. 'We are therefore free to consider the matter among ourselves and from the point of view of British interests only.'[40] The Prime Minister was always reluctant to admit that there were any costs to such a policy. As American anti-colonialism became more outspoken, though, it became an issue that Churchill could no longer evade.

The contradictions of Churchill, the contradictions of British foreign policy

1944 saw the Prime Minister more assured in his dealings with Washington. With the Americans successfully locked into a close relationship with Britain in Europe, Churchill was on stronger ground in pressing British interests in the secondary Far Eastern theatre. For all the faith that the Prime Minister placed in his personal understanding with President Roosevelt, Churchill realised that intrinsically they still held polar opposite views of the world. Churchill, therefore, remained sceptical of American pronouncements that Britain would not be forced to dissolve the Empire. He argued that:

> If the Japanese should withdraw from our Malayan possessions or make peace as a result of the main American thrust, the United States Government would after the victory feel greatly strengthened in its view that all possessions in the East Indian Archipelago should be placed under some international body upon which the United States would exercise a decisive control. They would feel with conviction: 'We have won our victory and liberated these places, and we must have the dominating say in their future and derive full profit from their produce, especially oil.'[41]

Roosevelt did not allay British suspicions. He had told Lord Halifax in January 1944 that he thought that Indo-China should not go back to France at the end of the war since 'France has milked it for a hundred years'. When Cordell Hull expressed a more conciliatory Anglo-American line the President reaffirmed his comments to the British Ambassador, believing that 'the people of Indo-China are entitled to something better than' French rule. This contradicted previous State Department reassurances, emphasising once more that it was FDR who made and set policy how and when it suited him.

There was an understandable fear in London that what happened to France would eventually happen to Britain. Indeed, Roosevelt was acutely aware of the wider implications of such an anti-colonial policy, seeing 'no reason to play in with the British Foreign Office in this matter. The only reason they seem to oppose it is that they fear the effect it would have on their own possessions and those of the Dutch.'[42]

Three into one: British strategic choices

Three strategic military options confronted or evolved for the British. First, as previously mentioned, was Churchill's favoured Culverin amphibious operation which promised to evade the 'rain sodden jungles' of Burma, recapturing Malaya and Singapore.[43] This, however, was circumscribed by military arguments and American opposition. D-Day, which was fast approaching, had priority on all landing craft and supplies over any Far Eastern operations, which meant that logistically Culverin was impossible.

The second option confronting the British was to utilise Australia as a base, and push in a north-western sweep at MacArthur's left flank towards Singapore. Once more, logistical difficulties intervened: Australia did not have the infrastructure or resources to fund such an operation, while politically British forces would have operated in the shadow of the egotistical MacArthur.

The third and final option received considerable support from the Chiefs of Staff. It envisaged the channelling of British resources into Admiral Nimitz's thrust across the Pacific, allowing Britain to be in at the kill with Japan. Militarily this had a lot in its favour, inflicting maximum damage on the Japanese, but it was restricted by Admiral King's hatred of the Royal Navy and the fact that British units would have to be entirely self-supporting. Even more problematic was the inability of the Royal Navy to form the large independent task force required to make the Americans take Britain's fleet seriously. America's preponderant power in the Pacific, though, made of these three strategic options something of a Hobson's choice.

The lack of clear direction (and understanding) attached to Britain's Far Eastern war meant that the choices that confronted the British left them at an impasse. No one had a firm understanding of where British interests lay or why the Americans did not want to cooperate with them in the Far East. Even Anthony Eden, the principal defender of an independent British foreign policy, could not force a swift decision. At a strategy meeting with the Chiefs of Staff in February he confided that 'The height of absurdity was reached when CCGS [Sir Alan Brooke] – who was in a bad temper throughout – insisted that Americans wanted our forces in the Pacific, as to which I had expressed doubts.'[44] Even Halifax failed to understand the pathological American dislike for British colonialism. He believed that with the failure of China to emerge as a strong and stable factor in Far Eastern affairs 'the [American] need for British co-operation may become more evident than it is at present'.[45] It did not. If the Americans could not secure the support of the Chinese in the Far East, they preferred their own company.

Caught up in a dispute with Claire Chennault[46] General Stilwell refused to accept three British Mosquito reconnaissance planes into the China theatre because they had British aircrews. Anthony Eden was incensed. He told Cadogan, 'If the [Chiefs of Staff] want my support at any time on this they can always have it . . . Don't give way.'[47] Admiral King, furthermore, refused point-blank New Zealand's offer of an air force in the Pacific because it offered Australia and New Zealand the excuse to claim Japanese islands! The sheer arrogance of this decision shocked even the usually philosophical Foreign Office. Ashley Clarke wondered on this basis whether any other country would have a say in the disposal of territories recaptured by American troops alone, including Hong Kong.[48] Despite America's high-handed actions, however, there was little Britain could do until it finalised its own Far Eastern strategy.

'A tragic waste'? Britain's military strategy is decided at last

The lack of any decision on our Far Eastern strategy is . . . most disturbing. Five months have elapsed since the conference at Cairo, but we have not yet progressed even as far enough to permit the Chiefs of Staff to exchange ideas with their American colleagues.

This was Ashley Clarke's stark warning to the Foreign Office in May. He also cautioned that 'it would be a mistake to over-estimate the effect which subsequent victories in Europe have had in redressing the adverse balance [on the British position in the Far East]'.[49] Diplomatic victories would count for little on their own, and had to be supported by military victories in the theatre of operations.

But from June to September the policy debate dragged on within Whitehall. It was very hard to claim that one strategy was politically superior to another when the paucity of British resources made any British decision peripheral to the main American military campaigns. The Prime Minister's inability to accept this fact encouraged his prevarication. What was required was a quick decision by the British and a commitment to it with all the resources and resolve they could muster. Failing to force Churchill into a decision, Eden was left complaining of a discussion that was 'meaningless when it was not explosive . . . W[inston] kept muttering that resources were available but provided no evidence and ended up accusing us all of trying to corner the Prime Minister'. A further discussion a week later was called 'two hours of wishful thinking' by Attlee on a note passed to Eden, 'and he was not far wrong'.[50] As the second in command, the Foreign Secretary must share some of the responsibility for prolonging Churchill's irresolution.

It was not until August that British policy at last became clear. SEAC would undertake an amphibious landing at Rangoon while the Royal Navy built up a subsidiary naval task force for the Pacific. At the second Quebec conference in September 1944 the British plan was presented to the Americans and finally agreed. Surprising the British, President Roosevelt unreservedly accepted the attachment of the Royal Navy task force to America's Pacific Fleet. 'The British delegation heaved a sigh of relief, and the story went the rounds that Admiral King went into a swoon and had to be carried out.'[51]

Roosevelt had decided that Britain's plan was an acceptable political compromise. With the Americans holding the purse strings the British were reluctantly forced to undertake the recapture of Burma. British scepticism, however, was vindicated by the rapid deterioration of the China theatre into an irrelevance. It was only through the exertions of General Slim, one of the most accomplished British commanders of the war, who was also on good terms with General Stilwell, that the Burma campaign was a success. Alan Levine argues that: 'The British war effort against Japan, largely at American insistence, was thus misdirected and a tragic waste. The forces committed in Burma would have been better used in Europe or fighting in the Pacific alongside the Americans in the decisive theatre.'[52] This assessment does, however, neglect the fact that the Americans did not want the British fighting side by side with them in the Pacific. After all, few people realise today that the British Pacific Fleet performed a valuable service against the Japanese at Okinawa.[53]

Operation Ichigo

Many British officials thought London's prevarication over strategy threatened to have disastrous consequences. If this was so, Japan's highly successful summer offensive into China helped destroy the American myth that the China theatre would be instrumental to the defeat of Japan: especially when it was the only place in the Far East where the Japanese were advancing and not retreating! Through his own foolishness, Chiang had radically altered military strategy in South East Asia in favour of the British. He was not only letting down the Chinese people but also the hopes of American anti-imperialism.

Starting in late April 1944, the Japanese China Army launched the two phase Operation Ichigo. It was planned to secure their coastal lines of communication and destroy American airfields that were being used to bomb coastal shipping and Japan itself. Its execution was a triumphant success, crushing all remaining Chinese resistance and raising the possibility of the capture of Chungking, the Nationalist capital. Everything the Americans had constructed in China, through great expenditure and patience, now came tumbling down; instead of the springboard they were hoping for to attack the Japanese home islands, China was reduced to an emergency theatre. Churchill greeted the disaster with a certain satisfaction in a confidential telex to his friend General Smuts, the South African Prime Minister:

[The] American illusion about China is being dispelled. The Soong family Oligarchy Regime is most insecure and very likely nearing an end. Chiang Kai-shek is in precarious position and of course there is grotesque Chinese military failure in spite of all Americans have done and their tremendous diversion effort over hump.[54]

With the collapse of the Chinese armies, America's China policy began to disintegrate. The Americans descended into internal bickering and recrimination over who was to blame: the State Department was racked by a palace revolt against Stanley Hornbeck's leadership, while in China itself Generals Stilwell and Chennault criticised each other for the looming debacle. As the Japanese pushed into central China in June, President Roosevelt was forced to telex Chiang Kai-shek that 'the extremely serious situation . . . leads me to the conclusion that drastic measures must be taken immediately if the situation is to be saved'.[55] The Generalissimo, however, had shown little interest in defeating the Japanese from the very beginning of the Sino-Japanese war, and he refused to change tack now. William Donovan, the head of American intelligence (OSS) told FDR that Chiang was 'paying no attention whatsoever to the domestic economic situation' and instead busied himself in local political matters and fighting the communists.[56] Chiang had no real conception of modern warfare, and believed that Chennault's American airpower could easily stem the Japanese advance. Ill-equipped and untrained Chinese peasant armies marched fatalistically to their deaths as the Japanese steamroller drove into the heart of China, destroying the American airfields.

Despite Chiang's follies, however, the Americans still refused to encourage political opposition to the Generalissimo and watched China sink deeper into the mire. Strategically, China's importance was vanishing. Faced with the successes of General MacArthur and Admiral Nimitz across the Pacific, the Americans found it easy to switch resources away from the China theatre. China was no longer useful to America's bombing campaign against Japan. When the Americans captured the Marianas in August, the need for B-29 bomber bases in

China vanished as alternative bases became available, offering a similar proximity for pounding Japan without the drawback of China politics.

The collapse of America's China policy

The removal of Chiang Kai-shek and his replacement by a more malleable leader offered the most obvious solution to America's China problems. T.V. Soong, now returned to high office after the late 1943 coup attempt, was the most prominent candidate. He told the Americans that he had 'the feeling that Chiang will eventually become discredited' and T.V. Soong's own political science group could take over.[57] Despite this, Washington turned a deaf ear to this coded plea for assistance. American policy continued to be fixated on Chiang Kai-shek despite the attempt of Stilwell and his political adviser, John Davies, to see the China situation in a broader perspective. Davies returned to Washington to put the case for a flexible American policy towards China. He argued that:

> We have made and are continuing to make the mistake of personalising our support of China. We think and speak of the Big Four in terms of four personalities – Roosevelt, Stalin, Churchill and Chiang. This is dangerous and misleading in the case of China. Our thinking is now so in error that if Chiang is abandoned or overthrown by dissident factions we shall imagine that China has disintegrated and ceased to be one of the Big Four ... If we assume a position of inflexible support of Chiang we may find ourselves discredited and our ends defeated through the repudiation and overthrow of the Chungking regime by a coalition commanding overwhelming public support.[58]

This effort, though, was in vain. Only in September did FDR start talking plainly with the Generalissimo. Chiang was dragging his feet over appointing Stilwell commander in chief of all forces in China, an unprecedented appointment but a logical one given the gravity of the situation. If Chiang persisted in refusing to follow American advice Roosevelt told him that he would have to 'be prepared to accept the consequences and assume personal responsibility'. Furthermore, 'the action I am asking you to take will fortify us in our decision and in the continued efforts the United States proposes to take to maintain and increase our aid to you'.[59] This direct threat to Chiang's foreign aid lifeline visibly shocked the Generalissimo. He was used to receiving toned down versions of such messages, but growing American distrust of his wife and his inner circle meant Stilwell (gleefully) handed him the message personally: 'The harpoon hit the little bugger right in the solar plexus, and went right through him. It was a clean hit, but beyond turning green and losing the power of speech he did not bat an eye. He just said to me, "I understand".'[60]

Having sponsored Chiang and presented him as the great unifier and saviour of China, President Roosevelt had become captive to the Nationalist regime. Replacing Chiang was no longer a viable option. There were few possible candidates to succeed him, largely because American support for Chiang had ensured the elimination of his rivals. T.V. Soong was as corrupt, if not more so, than his leader while Mao was tainted by being a communist. The failure of America's China strategy, therefore, resulted in the dismissal of its leading advocate, General Stilwell. On 19 October he received a cable from General Marshall recalling him from China. He was offered up as a sacrifice by President Roosevelt to appease Chiang Kai-shek who had insisted on his relief from command in exchange for concessions to the Americans.[61] 'Vinegar Joe's' dismissal left many Americans bewildered, and unleashed an avalanche of press criticism aimed at Chiang and Roosevelt. Sino-American relations would never recover the intimacy they once had, while American meddling in China had handed Britain control of military strategy in South East Asia.

China attempts to improve Sino-British relations

Throughout these tribulations, however, America's attitude towards the British in the Far East showed little sign of mellowing. On learning of Britain's finalised Far Eastern strategy, Stilwell wrote:

> I see the Limeys are going to rush to our rescue in the Pacific. Like hell. They are going to continue this fight with their mouths. Four or five old battleships will appear and about ten RAF planes will go to Australia but in twenty years the schoolbooks will be talking about 'shoulder to shoulder' and 'the Empire struck with all its might against the common enemy' and all that crap. The idea, of course, is to horn in at Hong Kong again, and our Booby [FDR] is sucked in.[62]

After Operation Ichigo such sentiments mattered less to the British. The Chinese, on the other hand, attempted to mend fences with London. The Chinese transformation, though, was a transparent and unconvincing one for the British. Instead, London came to see China's policy towards Hong Kong as a litmus test of their sincerity and on this last point the Chinese remained less than conciliatory. The first secretary of the British Embassy in Chungking, Berkeley Gage, met with the Chinese vice-minister for foreign affairs, K.C. Wu, in June. Wu explained that the Generalissimo wanted improved Sino-British relations 'and has given directions that interfering in neighbouring British territories is to cease'. While Gage accepted that this might be true, the circumstances were hardly auspicious. 'The military situation' according to Gage was 'worse than it has yet been, and the political situation also is far from encouraging'. Wu, furthermore, made it clear that Chiang had not relinquished his claim to Hong Kong. Chinese pleasantries aside, Gage noted that 'only a few days ago my attention had been drawn to posters put up in the town for "Opium Day" in which people were reminded of the Opium War against Britain a century ago, in spite of the fact that she was now an ally'. A.L. Scott at the Foreign Office saw Wu's conciliatory approach as a reaction to recent press criticism in Britain and America, and 'it is still we who are apparently to do all the giving'.[63]

The die had already been cast: it was too late for the Chinese to start playing footsie with the British because the Chungking Government had sold its soul to American aid long ago.

China, the Soviet Union and America

China's half-hearted attempts to build bridges with the British could also be seen as a response to the growing power of the Soviet Union in the Far East. During 1944 the Chinese Government was becoming increasingly worried about Soviet ambitions. At the end of March, Chiang Kai-shek was telexing Roosevelt concerning Soviet incursions into Sinkiang, in north-western China on the Outer Mongolian border, a region disputed by Chungking and Moscow.[64] Madame Chiang expressed these anxieties to Churchill's representative in Chungking, Carton de Wiart, while the Generalissimo was laid up in bed. 'She confessed for the first time how afraid they were of Russia, particularly after the bombing at Sinkiang in the north west. She said she hoped the British and Americans would take up business propositions there . . . Madame was very much more for the British than usual, and the American's shares are slumping.'[65]

The American response to the Sinkiang incident was surprising and demonstrated the contradictory nature of their China policy. Far from being drawn into the dispute, as might have been expected, Roosevelt urged on Chiang the necessity for 'the exercise of self-restraint and good-will' towards the Soviet Union. 'As a matter of practical realism, I suggest the present incidents be placed on ice until the end of this war.'[66] There was no question of jeopardising important relations with the Soviets at this increasingly crucial juncture of the war. American policy in the Far East rested on the construction of a balance of power: China would be built up to act as a bulwark against Soviet expansionism, and thus prevent direct Soviet and American conflict. The Chinese Nationalists' fall from grace, however, made it even more important to try to work with Stalin in the Far East. Cordell Hull advised Roosevelt that Ambassador Gauss understood that the Chinese were deliberately trying to foster 'increasing friction between the Anglo-American powers and Russia'.[67] For once, Gauss's opinions were accepted in Washington but for him it was too little too late. Gauss was driven to resign shortly after Stilwell's recall, embittered and frustrated at Washington's lack of support for a harder line on China. He shocked Stilwell's replacement by telling him: 'We should pull up the plug and let the whole Chinese Government go down the drain.'[68]

It was almost true to say that Chinese territorial integrity was secured by Chiang's success in playing off the surrounding foreign powers. The worst possible outcome for the Generalissimo was the formation of Anglo-American-Soviet unity in the Far East. Strangely, however, after all the atrocities perpetrated by the Japanese against the Chinese people, there was little rancour among the Chinese leadership against the Japanese invaders.[69]

Chiang's attempt to divert attention away from the failures of his regime threatened to backfire. William Donovan prophesied that the Generalissimo would refuse to confront pragmatically the huge problems facing him, with serious consequences for himself and America: 'Chiang's persisting in an active anti-Soviet policy, at a time when his policies (or lack of them) are accelerating economic collapse and increasing internal dissension, can only be characterised as reckless adventurism ... By doing so, Chiang may be digging his own grave.' Nonetheless, Donovan still believed America held all the answers for China: by using 'our tremendous and as yet unexploited influence with the Kuomintang to promote internal Chinese unity [there remains] the only possible and lasting foundation of progressive reform'.[70]

Roosevelt's strong line with Chiang over Outer Mongolia stands in stark contrast to his vacillating and weak stance with the Generalissimo over Stilwell's dismissal only months later. FDR did not, though, want to annoy Stalin. The fanaticism with which the Japanese were fighting made it more and more likely that America would need Soviet help in an invasion of Japan. The President's inclination to work with Stalin at the expense of Chinese interests found its natural conclusion at the Yalta conference.

Britain and the Far East: brightness at last

In November 1944, Sterndale Bennett, the new head of the Foreign Office Far Eastern section, looked back on the preceding year. He believed that:

> The story of our Far Eastern strategical discussions is, in my view, a sorry one. We spent nine months arguing which might have been devoted to more useful purposes. Whether the strategy ultimately decided was right or wrong is a matter of opinion which time will determine.[71]

Such pessimism was commonplace amongst British personnel, and a long way from the image which many Americans liked to apportion to the British as being 'very far-sighted, very tenacious and far "smarter" than [Americans] are'.[72] David MacDougall whose job it was to construct the Hong Kong Planning Unit was surprised to encounter so much doubt among British personnel when he toured the Far East. Many found it hard to believe that the Empire would be resurrected.[73] In Chungking, Ambassador Seymour adopted 'the rather melancholy view that undoubtedly China wanted and expected Hong Kong to pass into their possession after the war, and that it would be difficult not to accommodate her, at least to some extent'.[74]

It was true that American criticism showed little sign of diminishing. John Davies of the State Department continued to believe that Britain was carefully scheming her return to colonial South East Asia irrespective of the agreement to defeat Japan at all costs. Like many Americans he doubted Britain's commitment to finish the Pacific war. For him, 'South East Asia Command's plans for the future heavily discount the importance of China as an ally and the Chinese position on Japan's flank', while embarking on 'so circuitous and tardy an advance' that its contribution to Japan's defeat would be negligible.[75] The President also reiterated his insistence that Hong Kong would return to China. When Vice-President Wallace visited China in June he carried a personal message with him for Chiang Kai-shek from Roosevelt: 'Churchill is old. A new British Government will give Hong Kong to China and the next day China will make it a free port.'[76]

Events, nonetheless, did not validate such a gloomy prognosis for British interests in late 1944. The collapse of China meant that there would be no counter-balance to SEAC advances which America had hoped for. The possibility of American-backed Chinese forces recapturing Hong Kong, Indo-China or Malaya was increasingly fantastical. The architect of American policy, President Roosevelt, also showed signs of waning. Stettinius, the new under-secretary of state for foreign affairs, talking alone to Eden 'did not disguise his anxiety about the future of US policy. [The] President had been far from well lately. Harry [Hopkins] was rather ill and of course an irreplaceable loss.'[77] In these circumstances, Britain's prevarication over her Far Eastern strategy was not the tragedy which some British personnel believed.

8
The Cairo Conference

They [the Chinese] really like us and just between ourselves, they don't like the British. Now, we haven't the same aims as the British out there. For instance, Hong Kong. Now, I have a plan to make Hong Kong a free port: free to the commerce of all nations – of the whole world! But let's raise the Chinese flag there first, and then Chiang can the next day make a grand gesture and make it a free port. That's the way to handle that![1]

President Roosevelt, Cairo, 1943

No one was completely certain as to the aims of the Cairo conference, the one and only meeting of the Far Eastern Allied leaders. Held in late November 1943, it was meant to heal divisions between America, Britain and China. In fact, the talks exacerbated their misconceptions about each other. Winston Churchill and Anthony Eden were keen to align British and American policy for the invasion of France before meeting Stalin at Tehran immediately afterwards. Instead, the Americans seemed more interested in wooing the Chinese, and distancing themselves from the British. Chiang Kai-shek, in turn, attempted to bolster his international public image whilst his position within China began to deteriorate rapidly.

From Britain's point of view, it was a thoroughly demoralising experience, bringing home the unbalanced nature of the Anglo-American relationship. When Churchill recalled the conference as 'lengthy, complicated, and minor' he not only epitomised the general British attitude to what was regarded as a wasted conference but was also venting his frustration at Britain's lowly status amongst world powers.[2] Although Hong Kong was never brought up in open session at the conference, it was never far away from the surface as the Americans and Chinese talked of stripping Japan of its Far Eastern conquests. Cairo, with its riddle of the Sphinx, provided the perfect setting for such malcontents.

Meet President Chiang!

Neither Roosevelt nor Churchill had ever met Chiang Kai-shek before, which is surprising considering the former's great interest in China. While Churchill professed to being enamoured of Madame Chiang Kai-shek, and Eden was 'much impressed by Chiang', the reality of the conference was less amicable.³ Rooseveltian foreign policy was displayed with all its vagaries and idiosyncrasies. FDR brought with him neither State Department officials nor even his Secretary of State, Cordell Hull. Moreover, what America was trying to achieve in China remained ill-defined and confused. At the same time, Chiang Kai-shek's first conference appearance ironically marked the passing of his power. Whilst Chiang remained at Cairo, though, he was feted by Roosevelt as an important and intimate ally. It was all illusion of course; Chiang's position was so fragile within China that he was faced with a potential coup in his absence, while the Americans treated the Chinese as a subservient junior ally, to be manipulated for America's own political aims.

Cairo illustrated, if it were needed, just how far British policy in the Far East was constrained by Washington. At American insistence, the conference started with official photographs. Eden wrote that officials and generals 'stood about and sat for hours [at Roosevelt's villa], a desperate waste of time'.⁴ The British found themselves increasingly in the shade. General Ismay, Churchill's military representative, went to the conference expecting the Americans to finalise the plans for D-Day so that they could be presented to the Soviet leader at the following conference at Tehran. However:

> To our dismay we found that the Chinese delegation, under Gener-alissimo Chiang Kai-shek, was already on the spot. We understood that the primary object of meeting the American Chiefs of Staff at Cairo was to settle a number of outstanding questions connected with Overlord before meeting the Russians at Tehran . . . Until all this was settled it was impossible to say what resources, particularly landing-craft, would be necessary for Overlord and its subsidiaries, or to determine how much would be available for the residuary legatees, such as the Burma–Chinese theatre. We were now faced with the necessity of putting the cart before the horse.⁵

The Americans had previously been opposed to a joint Anglo-American meeting prior to the Big Three conference in Tehran for fear that Stalin would think they were ganging up on him. Of course, this is precisely what Churchill wanted. He had even reconnoitred the Pyramids so that Roosevelt could safely drive up to see them without having to suffer the indignity of being pushed in a wheelchair. When the President accepted Churchill as his guide, the Prime Minister was visibly aglow at the evident enjoyment FDR derived from the visit. Churchill's daughter described how the Prime Minister 'loved showing them to him. It really is wonderful how they both get on – they really like and understand each other.'[6] And yet the Americans were increasingly keen to distance themselves from the British for a number of reasons, giving advance warning of the dangers of placing too much trust in Anglo-American unity. From Washington's point of view, inviting Chiang Kai-shek to join the Allies at Cairo offered to moderate Stalin's suspicions of an Anglo-American conspiracy (a somewhat impossible task one feels) while also demonstrating America's preponderance in the Pacific theatre.

At the conference proper the British were frequently overlooked by the Americans in favour of the Chinese. Harry Hopkins and the President obviously conversed with the Chinese before the British were consulted, much to their chagrin. The Americans even suggested a 'United Chiefs of Staff' to include the Soviet Union and China to the astonishment of the British delegation. Unaccustomed to being on the outside of American relations, the British drifted into melancholia. Retrospectively, Anthony Eden realised that Britain's contribution to the Far Eastern theatre would be slight, while 'our American Allies were impressed, almost to the point of obsession, with the merits of General and Madame Chiang Kai-shek and their Government. I sensed that even the future of Hong Kong was in question with them.'[7] In his diary, he confided that things were not working for the British:

> W[inston] very kind and friendly tho' he accused me of looking sulky and being in bad temper. Wasn't conscious of it and think it was only lack of sleep which I told him. Also said that we didn't seem to be getting anywhere with our work. He agreed. FDR was a charming country gentlemen but business methods were almost non-existent, so W[inston] had to play the role of courtier and seize opportunities as and when they arose.[8]

Closeted away from the British, Roosevelt took it upon himself to promise things to Chiang Kai-shek which should not have been discussed in private. Churchill was livid to discover that Chiang had been promised a large operation across the Bay of Bengal before the coming monsoon. Louis Mountbatten, the head of SEAC, was further insulted at the way his openness with his American opposite number, General Stilwell, was thrown back in his face. Stilwell 'was constantly closeted with the United States and Chinese officials and maintained an attitude of extreme reserve and even secrecy'.[9]

The centrepiece of British war-time strategy was D-Day, irrespective of the need to take to the offensive in the Pacific. The reconquest of Europe was the most important operation for Churchill and the British staff, who rightly emphasised that its failure could put the war's end back a year, while letting the Soviet Union dominate Europe. Far Eastern operations depended on landing craft which were equally vital to land on the French beaches. There was a conflict of resources between the two hemispheres and it appeared to the British as if the Americans were putting the peripheral China theatre first out of pique by sponsoring an early amphibious operation across the Bay of Bengal.

Churchill's doctor was shocked by the vehemence of American criticism of the British, and especially their attacks on the Prime Minister: 'They are far more sceptical of him than they are of Stalin. Anyway, whoever is to blame, it is clear that we are going to Tehran without a common plan.'[10] Few members of the British party would have believed at this moment that the Americans were 100 per cent behind the Europe first strategy agreed in 1941. Admiral Leahy, Roosevelt's Chief of Staff, never had any doubts, however. He explained, using the example of Madame Chiang Kai-shek's celebrated visit to America in early 1943:

> So effective was [she] in presenting the case of China to many influential groups, including Congress, during her stay in Washington, that rumours sprang up that she might even persuade Roosevelt to change the grand strategy of the war and shift emphasis to the Pacific. Such rumours were baseless, of course, and the Joint Chiefs never considered them seriously.[11]

The Cairo communiqué

A further threat to British interests came from the seemingly innocuous wording of the Cairo communiqué. The original draft declaration, penned by the Americans and shown to the Chinese first, was greatly favourable to Chinese interests and ignored Britain completely. When the British were eventually shown the draft, Alexander Cadogan quickly realised that the Americans wanted to strip Japan of her empire and present it to China, although there was no mention of restoring Britain's possessions in the Far East. Harry Hopkins's draft also failed to state that the Allies were against territorial aggrandisement. It was this last ambiguous omission that the British seized upon and therefore charitably assumed that this meant that neither was the restoration of British colonies precluded. Churchill submitted a revised communiqué which toned down Chinese demands slightly and which ignored the issue of British colonies. Against the run of play this was accepted, but its modifications from the original were slight. For instance, it was still stated that China would recover Manchuria, something the British thought unwise without discussions with Stalin.[12]

It was not just Churchill who insisted on rewording the communiqué. Eden was equally perturbed by the slighting of British interests in the Far East. He told Hugh Dalton back in London that had he not stubbornly insisted on amending it, 'It was very doubtful whether, on a strict reading, either we or the Dutch would have got back anything of what the Japs have seized.'[13] In fact, there was an almost unanimous British consensus that Cairo was a setback for imperial interests. Leo Amery had his worst suspicions realised:

> As I had imagined, the communiqué about the Far East on the political side was the result of Chiang's capturing Roosevelt and getting from him an original draft, giving everything to China and saying nothing else about anybody else's rights, which it was impossible to do more than modify slightly afterwards.[14]

The anger of the British at their 'shabby treatment' at Cairo, though, should not have been unexpected. This had been the pattern for Far Eastern politics in general for a long while. London was paying the price of Churchill's excessive emphasis on a personalised Anglo-American relationship which failed to take into account the very real differences between the two Allies.

Cracks in Chiang Kai-shek's regime

If Cairo appeared to mark a transitionary stage in the nature of the Anglo-American relationship for the British, it may be surprising to learn that the Chinese also gained relatively little of lasting achievement. Far from Chiang Kai-shek 'capturing' Roosevelt as Leo Amery would have us believe, the Americans conducted negotiations with the Chinese very much on their own terms. It was the Americans who had everything to offer and the Chinese who held the begging bowl. The final Cairo communiqué was even at the American initiative. Tellingly, the Generalissimo, for all his loathing of Stilwell, invited him to accompany him to Cairo and present China's case for an invasion of Burma: for the promise of extra lend-lease *matériel* Chiang would use any ruse, even the insult of having an American Chief of Staff.[15] And while Chiang was away from Chungking moves were afoot from his own generals to try and save China because he would not.[16]

Lord Moran was summoned from the conference to attend to Madame Chiang who was laid up in bed with exhaustion brought on by stress. 'She was always tired, as the nettle-rash interfered with her sleep.' After the examination she asked anxiously; 'I shall soon get well, you think?' He replied, 'Madame, you will only get better when the strain of your life is relaxed.'[17] The truth was that the strain would not ease up. The Soong family were becoming divided and embittered. Chiang Kai-shek and Madame had effectively split up, even if legally it was dubious that the Generalissimo was really married to her in the first place: there was strong evidence that Chiang was a bigamist. He refused to put his false teeth in for her, keeping that a privilege for 'the other lady'. According to John Service, Chungking was now awash with rumours of marital discord. Normally,

Such gossip . . . would not be considered as within the scope of political reporting. This is hardly the case, however, in China where the person concerned is a dictator and where the relationship between him and his wife's family is so all-important . . . The Generalissimo at one time did not receive callers for four days because he had been bruised on the side of the head with a flower vase in a spat with the Madame.[18]

Chiang was also estranged from his brother-in-law and Madame's brother, T.V. Soong, the Foreign Secretary. Apparently, the other Soong family members were becoming increasingly jealous of T.V.'s growing independence and accumulated wealth from American lend-lease handouts. The schism was finally realised with his biting criticism of Chiang's mismanagement of the economy through his flunkey, the finance minister Dr Kung, just before Cairo. One version has it that in December, after the conference, the family attempted a reconciliation. However, this did not go well either. T.V.'s argument that effective control of the

Chinese economy had to be reinstated, with one dominant body run by himself, was not well received:

> Chiang countered that the setting up of such an agency would be unconstitutional. To which [T.V.] Soong retorted: 'You've always been able to change the Constitution whenever you wished, as for instance when you decided to be President.' This interview is supposed to have ended with Chiang throwing a teacup at Soong's head, and, of course, the abandonment of hope for any immediate reconciliation.[19]

Disenchantment with Chiang's rule reached a peak with the attempted coup in November while the Generalissimo was in Cairo. Events remain unclear, hidden by the darkness that envelopes so much of the Soong family history, although enough evidence has surfaced to outline the episode. Young, radical Nationalist generals removed from Chiang's usual power base, the Whampoa military academy, decided that the corrupt leadership must go if China was to be saved. The coup was planned for the anniversary of Chiang's kidnapping in the Sian incident (early December 1936).[20] Chiang would be presented on his return home from Egypt with a fait accompli. Some of the American commanders in China also had forewarning when the Chinese generals attempted to enlist American support. Brigadier General Thomas Timberman, in charge of training Chinese troops in eastern China was approached but gave an official no. The Office of Strategic Services, though, who had been suffering increasing interference from Tai Li, head of the Chinese Gestapo, were less unequivocal.

Unfortunately for the plotters, Tai Li rumbled the plot somehow. It could well have been from an American sympathetic to Chiang Kai-shek. In any event, 600 Chinese officers were arrested and 16 of the army's most promising generals were executed on Chiang's return. The repercussions, though, did not stop there. Shortly afterwards, Chiang sacked his corrupt and incompetent finance minister, Dr Kung (the *bête noire* of the British Foreign Office), and ordered him out of China, taking with him Madame Chiang Kai-shek and her sister, Madame Kung. It seems Tai Li found some evidence which implicated Chiang's own family with the plot, which uncoincidentally no doubt, served Tai Li's own interests by removing powerful rivals. The winner in all this was T.V. Soong who was soon restored to his old position with even more authority.[21] Although the secretive nature of the regime could conceal many of these explosions from the casual eye of Sinophile American observers, astute diplomats were in little doubt that China was once more sliding into the mire. President Roosevelt, however, was not especially interested in highlighting the defects of the Chinese regime. Since he had personally associated himself with supporting China and Chiang Kai-shek, any criticism of America's China policy was, in effect, a criticism of Roosevelt himself.

President Roosevelt's China policy

Roosevelt's conception of Washington's China policy was less than clear, which makes it hard for the historian to state what exactly the President did expect from American involvement in China. Although he was not completely ignorant of Chinese affairs, he had little impulse to push the real facts about Chiang Kai-shek's regime into the public spotlight. While he confided to his son, Elliott, that 'Chiang's troops aren't fighting at all – despite the reports that get printed in all the papers', the President continued to view Sino-American relations almost as a public relations exercise.[22] When General Stilwell asked him to define American policy at Cairo he rambled aimlessly on. Exasperated, Stilwell suggested that at least Washington was aiming to build China up as a power. Roosevelt replied, 'Yes, yes. Build her up. After the war there will be a great need of our help. They will want loans.' But according to the latest contemporary assessment of the Generalissimo's regime, it was unlikely that Chiang would survive. What then? 'Well, then we should look for some other man or group of men, to carry on.'[23] Unfortunately, Roosevelt had ensured that these people did not exist.

The photos of Chiang and FDR which were flashed around the world gave the impression of casual intimacy between the two, with one particular photograph projecting the image of a shared joke. In fact, Chiang Kai-shek spoke no English except the word 'Darling' which Madame had insisted on being called.[24] He had little or no knowledge of world affairs, although he was a mastermind in managing the internal warlord politics of China. To call Chiang a 'world leader' was therefore a travesty of the truth, and was something Churchill could not bear, even for the sake of Anglo-American relations. When the Generalissimo conversed with Roosevelt (or Churchill) he spoke through Madame Chiang who interpreted. Who was actually speaking was debatable. General Ismay recorded that Madame 'gave the impression of having decided opinions, and there is no knowing that she did not inject some of them in her translations of what her husband said'.[25]

Roosevelt was also visibly ignorant of Far Eastern affairs in general and seems to have had no idea that Hong Kong was in fact a free port under the British. His reliance on people like Patrick Hurley, a Republican firebrand, for information did him no favours either. Hurley's fatuous observations about complex situations are legendary, and one example will suffice: he sincerely believed after interviewing Chiang Kai-shek for a few hours that 'the Generalissimo and the Chinese people favour the principles of democracy and liberty'.[26] Whether FDR really thought that he 'could do with more men like Pat, whom I could depend [on]' is doubtful.[27] But it is categorical that he disliked the State Department and kept them divorced from his own personal diplomacy and decision making in general. Roosevelt appeared to believe that he could decide what was best for China and America single-handedly. The fact was, however, that Roosevelt did not have any very definite goals for America in China; all he appeared to have were platitudes, off-the-cuff policies and a convenient destination for sending political intriguers like Hurley and Vice-President Wallace. He did not even like Madame Chiang Kai-shek, thinking her a bloodsucking 'vamp'.[28] When she encamped at the White House during the first half of 1943, ostensibly for medical treatment but in reality for a publicity tour, she drove the White House and FDR mad. Morgenthau told his staff that, 'The President . . . is just crazy to get her out of the country.'[29] Unfortunately, the perception that Madame Chiang Kai-shek was so strongly associated with Roosevelt meant that he was essentially captive to her whim for fear of providing ammunition to his political opponents.

Roosevelt's secret meeting with Chiang

When the President met secretly with Chiang Kai-shek in Cairo, Roosevelt was attempting to paper over the contradictions of his own China policy. Ever one to spot a public relations opportunity, FDR made sure he was conspicuously seen with the Chinese leader in an attempt to distance America from the reactionary imperialism associated with Britain, France and the Dutch in the Far East.

It was to this end, therefore, that FDR held a meeting alone with Chiang at the President's villa. Unfortunately, the only official record surviving of the discussion is the incomplete Chinese version. This in itself does not really matter, however, because the meeting was more symbolic than substantial. The British were taken in, as they were meant to be, into believing that Chiang's time alone with Roosevelt signified the closeness of Sino-American relations and the importance of the Far Eastern war to America. The fact that we know so little about the discussions, moreover, makes it even more likely that Roosevelt deliberately wanted this to be the case. It was as if what he said to

Chiang was never meant to be recorded, because he knew it to be mere 'table talk'.

The recollections of Elliott Roosevelt, who talked to his father about the encounter with Chiang, (if they can be trusted) are the only significant record of the meeting. Over the issue of Hong Kong Chiang Kai-shek was very keen to solicit the support of America which Roosevelt tacitly agreed to in exchange for the reform of Chiang's government. Roosevelt told his son:

> We will support his contention that the British and other nations no longer enjoy special Empire rights to Hong Kong, Shanghai, and Canton. That's right . . . Actually, as far as he's concerned, the only earnest of our good faith that he expects is that when Japan is on her knees we make sure that no British warships come into Chinese ports. Only American warships. And I've given him my personal promise that that's what will happen.

Elliott demurred at this last point, suggesting that Churchill would never agree. Roosevelt was unmoved:

> There can't be much argument, inasmuch as it's ninety-nine per cent American matériel and American men bringing about the defeat of Japan. American foreign policy after the war must be along the lines of bringing about a realisation on the part of the British and the French and the Dutch that the way we have run the Philippines is the only way they can run their colonies.[30]

Roosevelt's arrogant and uninformed presumptuousness was further corroborated in private talks with General Stilwell, Harry Hopkins and John Davies. Apparently, the President had even offered Chiang French Indo-China 'point-blank', although the Generalissimo, with enough on his plate, understandably turned down the offer. The President also reaffirmed his commitment to force Britain to retrocede Hong Kong because the Chinese 'really like us'.[31] It was, perhaps, small wonder that a hardened military commander like Stilwell would be unimpressed by such woolly thinking. He confided to his diary, 'The man is a flighty fool. Christ, but he's terrible. We came out puking.'[32] Roosevelt's character, though, disinclined him from making firm promises or committing anything to written agreement. This made it far easier to renege on such commitments at a later date. There can be little doubt, therefore, that what the President agreed with Chiang Kai-shek owed more than a little to wishful thinking, including what was agreed over Hong Kong. Considering the untruths that Chiang fed the Americans, perhaps it was no more than he deserved in return.

Concluding at Tehran

There were no conclusions from the Cairo conference. That much is clear from Roosevelt and Churchill's meeting with Stalin at Tehran which followed it. The President's promise to Chiang Kai-shek that Burma would be invaded in 1944 was reversed without consultation as Roosevelt sought to ingratiate himself with the Soviet leader. Lord Moran wrote in his diary that Harry Hopkins had told him that FDR was determined to woo Stalin and reach agreement with him, whatever it cost, and he did. Once the Chinese had fulfilled their use at Cairo, the President had little compunction in dismissing them in favour of more important relations with Moscow.

Behind the front of Sino-American unity there was never any doubt about the subservient nature of Chinese interests to Washington's. While Roosevelt happily promised Chiang Kai-shek large-scale amphibious operations across the Bay of Bengal, he was equally ready to renege when faced with stiff British opposition. The Generalissimo had departed from Cairo content that he had secured the invasion of Burma in 1944. However, he was mortified to discover that the Americans had cancelled this plan on their return from Tehran for the final Cairo conference. Stalin, like the British, had insisted that Operation Overlord came first, giving Churchill the opportunity to reinforce the southern France 'Anvil' landings at the expense of SEAC's Burma operation.[33] If Roosevelt was prepared to overturn written agreements without Chiang's consent, even though they had been drawn up with him, there was little reason why the President would not do the same over Hong Kong.

When it became clear to Chiang that he was being sidelined and the China theatre with him, the Generalissimo demanded another huge $1 billion loan from Roosevelt which was, again, not politically necessary according to Gauss. He believed, as he had done for years, that 'our attitude towards China should be quietly and persistently firmed'.[34] Even a 'friend' of China like Morgenthau was becoming exasperated by this point. 'They [the Chinese] are just a bunch of crooks' he told his assistant Harry Dexter White in January 1944.[35] Although his remit on China only ran to financial affairs, the Secretary of the Treasury was appalled by the endemic corruption he saw in the Chinese hierarchy. Of the conditionless $500m 'loan' granted in March 1942 almost

$1m was traced back to Chiang's immediate family, the Kungs and Soongs. Despite all these regrets, however, Morgenthau was deeply implicated in America's China policy and had in fact approved the earlier 1942 loan.[36] In private, the Generalissimo made little pretence at his abdication of independence to American policy. Patrick Hurley reported back to the President that Chiang would 'follow your leadership on the diplomatic and political questions that will be considered in the impending conference'.[37] Placing one's trust in the hands of a political manipulator like Roosevelt, though, brought with it its fair share of disappointments. At Tehran when Stalin complained about Russia's lack of an ice-free port on the Pacific, Roosevelt obligingly offered him the Chinese port of Dairen under international treaty. The Chinese were not consulted, and neither were their views sought.[38] In the same manner, FDR would play fast and loose with Chinese sovereignty over the secret Yalta Far Eastern agreement.

Chiang Kai-shek was not the only person upset by the developing intimacy between Stalin and Roosevelt at Tehran. Alan Brooke, British Chief of Staff, spoke despondently. 'This conference is over when it has only just begun. Stalin has got the President in his pocket.'[39] While Roosevelt closeted himself with the Soviet leader the Prime Minister became increasingly agitated and depressed. When the President baited Churchill over Britain's colonies the Prime Minister's emotions finally spilt over. Specifically mentioning Hong Kong, he told Stalin and Roosevelt that 'nothing would be taken away from [Britain] without a war'.[40] Nevertheless, many Americans still insisted on proclaiming that Hong Kong would be returned to China. In this they were encouraged by the successful media presentation of Sino-American relations at Cairo, in particular the official group photographs which portrayed Chiang Kai-shek as an intimate of Roosevelt. The Chairman of the Senate Military Affairs Committee was even convinced that the Cairo declaration meant Britain would have to lose her Far Eastern colonies. The Chinese, however, remained noticeably silent over the issue of Hong Kong.

Sir Prideaux-Brune at the British Embassy in Chungking thought he knew why. His understanding was that the Nationalist government had issued instructions 'to soft-pedal or ignore the Hong Kong issue. As the Chinese – officially at any rate – are prepared to let it remain quiescent for the time being.'[41] He did not, though, ask why this might be so. Looking back and considering that Chiang's position was being openly challenged at home while Roosevelt's protestations of friendship were becoming increasingly empty, there were a good many reasons for the Chinese not to add to their troubles by rousing the British over Hong Kong. It was ironic that, despite their differences, both the Chinese and the British were suppressing their annoyance with President Roosevelt in the hope of securing closer relations with Washington. Even so, despite Britain's increasing resentment at American antics in the Far East the British remained optimistic that these differences could be resolved. Sir Eric Teichman, who according to Christopher Thorne was 'Britain's most experienced adviser on Chinese affairs', argued in a lengthy Foreign Office paper that Britain's current difficulties would prove transitory.[42] 'It does not follow', he elaborated, that 'because we have to yield pride and place politically at the present time in China to the US, that we should not in due course re-establish our great commercial interests and create in China one of the big post-war markets which will be so vitally needed for Britain's export trade.'[43] Such optimism was no doubt needed when surveying the economic ruin and human misery wrought over China by eight years of war.

9
Hard Choices: Yalta, the Death of a President and San Francisco, November 1944–June 1945

> The China question was on Roosevelt's mind constantly during the month preceding our departure for Yalta meetings because of the growing seriousness of opposition to the National Government of Chiang Kai-chek.[1]
>
> (Admiral Leahy)

With little time left to live, Roosevelt recognised that China would never live up to the role ascribed to it by American policymakers as the democratic anchor of Asia. Instead, Roosevelt looked to the Soviet Union to provide stability in the Far East. At Yalta, the proof was in the pudding; the President trampled over his promises to preserve the territorial integrity of China in order to gain Russian commitment for the Pacific war. Manchuria was to become a pre-eminent Soviet interest, while the warm water port of Port Arthur was leased. Despite the troubles which existed in Sino-British relations London was shocked by these negotiations. Anthony Eden made it explicit that Britain opposed any concessions to Stalin at the expense of China. Perhaps ashamed, President Roosevelt never had the courage to tell the Chinese of the deal he had struck in their name.

Death

With the sudden death of President Roosevelt on 12 April 1945 the impetus to American foreign policy collapsed. When FDR was buried he took with him not only his great charm, but also the architecture of America's Far Eastern policy. Few Presidents had kept as much information secret, or engaged in such widespread personal diplomacy, thereby sidelining the State Department. For all the attention that Roosevelt paid to their memoranda they might as well have spent their days playing golf. He had also groomed no successor and left few written instructions as to the future. With Truman's accession to power, the State Department may have regained much of its lost influence, but the system Roosevelt had left was almost damaged beyond repair: China was disintegrating, the Soviet Union was looming over all of central and eastern Europe, while relations with the British, for all their intimacy, were beset by mutual animosities. In many respects he bequeathed his Vice-President an unenviable task at a time when America (and the world) needed an experienced foreign statesman.

For the British, Roosevelt's death came as a mixed blessing. While the experience which he brought to the Anglo-American relationship was irreplaceable, at Yalta he had proven woolly and tiresome to Anthony Eden. Roosevelt appeared to neglect the real danger of Stalinism in favour of breaking up the British Empire, and giving Hong Kong back to China. For all its insignificant size, the colony still appeared to symbolise the battle between imperialism and progress for the President. Shortly after Roosevelt died, Lord Halifax heard a story of a visitor to the White House finding FDR lost in deep thought. 'When he went in, the President was sitting, staring into space and apparently completely absorbed in his own thoughts. He only spoke three times (not to the visitor, but to himself) – "If Churchill insists on Hong Kong, I will have to take it to the King".'[2] It is, though, a sensible question to ask how far Roosevelt could have gone in dissolving the Empire against British opposition. In many respects, Roosevelt was saved from having to face the failure of his own work. Regardless of British exertions to retain the colony, Hong Kong was still British territory under international law. Was he seriously suggesting that Britain be stripped of territory rightfully hers? Considering that the American sponsored United Nations was meant to uphold international law, the answer is probably no. Instead, the President hoped moral and military pressure would achieve his ends.[3]

The San Francisco conference (April–June 1945) which was held to inaugurate Roosevelt's cherished United Nations concept, reinforced the idea that American anti-colonialism was sentiment without substance. Although the colonial powers made some concessions over the idea of 'trusteeship', there was never any real chance that the British would willingly acquiesce in dismantling the Empire; that would come from visceral forces, in their own time. Indeed, British concern over Hong Kong transcended institutional barriers. A senior SOE officer characterised this attitude in hard-hitting terms, angered by continuing American pressure for the colony's retrocession:

Hong Kong is regarded as the touchstone for our future in the Far East. If we do not recover Hong Kong every Chinaman will consider that we are no longer a first-class power . . . The Americans, appear, nonetheless to have made up their minds to get Hong Kong away from us if they can . . . I realise that this is not an SOE affair [but] it seems to me to be our duty as an organisation to do everything we can to influence HMG on this crucial issue.[4]

It was fast becoming apparent in London that action physically to retake the colony was the only way to silence American criticism. But before that day arrived, the British were busy contemplating their business interests in the colony. This fact in itself manifested a certain confidence.

British commercial prospects

The fluid situation developing in mainland China reinforced the notion of a stable British trading base in Hong Kong. Ambassador Seymour observed that 'the experience of the last thirty years shows that trade with and in a disunited China is perfectly feasible'.[5] Possible or not, the Far Eastern committee chaired by G.H. Hall, the new parliamentary under-secretary of state at the Foreign Office, and its offshoot, the economic sub-committee, soon churned out copious papers on Far Eastern trade. Their conclusions were unsurprising: Britain lacked resources and post-war economic relations were uncertain.[6] In the economic committee, though, Hong Kong was portrayed as Britain's most vital interest in the Far East, to be re-established as quickly as possible, while the Colonial Office remained unhappy at the length of the New Territories lease. They argued that the fifty remaining years were 'manifestly much too short a period on which to base long-term reconstruction plans'.[7] Even if the Ministry of War Transport firmly supported this stance, which they did, the Foreign Office was never going to endorse such a controversial scheme; any extension of the lease would have been seen by most of the world as an extension of imperialism.[8]

Into the sea of uncertainty came news of Chinese trade liberalisation. Dr Sun Fo, president of the legislative Yuan, spoke to the Rotary Club of Chungking in November 1944, suggesting that the Chinese were going to make large concessions to international business after the war. China would not place restrictions on foreign ownership or management of Chinese firms post-war. This was one of the first semi-official Chinese utterances on foreign trade, and stood in opposition to the traditional Chinese discrimination against foreign traders.[9] (It is notable that Hong Kong's existence in the 1840s was partly attributed to the Chinese exclusion of colonial traders from Canton during the summer months.) Perhaps with the Chinese economy disintegrating this encouragement was academic but it was believed by many British China traders who embraced any information which promoted Hong Kong.

When Sir Prideaux-Brune, therefore, described British commercial prospects as being 'enveloped in a haze of uncertainties' he was not exaggerating. America's policy in China was partly to blame because they had helped destabilise the region through their muddled attempts to prop up Chiang Kai-shek. The Foreign Office believed that 'the vigour with which the Americans are acting in the China field suggests that they may not yet have formulated any very definite ideas of what it is all going to lead to'.[10] The breakdown of the Chinese regime, however, for all the British denials, favoured the retention of Hong Kong; a weak China could do little to stop the British sailing back into Hong Kong. But it would also be wrong to suggest that British policy would have been fundamentally different had China emerged as a strong developing power from World War II. A united China was not necessarily seen within Whitehall as incompatible with British imperial possessions in the Far East. Indeed, on many occasions the Foreign Office attempted to help the Chinese Government despite provocative slights from Chiang over Indian independence and Britain's military record. At the end of the war this policy had not changed; of their own accord the British donated a substantial batch of submarines and naval craft to the Chinese in April 1945.[11] For all this effort, though, the Americans remained loath to give the British any credit in the Far East.

Roosevelt and Yalta

All roads lead to Yalta; this has been a familiar cry from historians who have come to see this last meeting of Roosevelt, Churchill and Stalin as the Western Powers' culminating betrayal of Eastern Europe into Soviet enslavement. The Far Eastern agreement made at the conference is frequently (and understandably) overlooked, although this too can be labelled a betrayal of Chinese interests to the benefit of the Soviet Union. For President Roosevelt, however, it was a question of pragmatism. As Churchill's personal representative in Chungking had described, the Chinese situation was already close to catastrophe as the Japanese advanced towards the two key Nationalist cities of Kunming and Chungking. While General Hurley attempted to reconcile the irreconcilable with an agreement between the Nationalists and the communists, General Wedemeyer endeavoured to halt the Chinese rout.[12] American ideals were being replaced in a desperate struggle to keep the corrupt Nationalist regime afloat. In these circumstances Roosevelt told Hurley 'to emphasise the word "Russian" to' Chiang Kai-shek in order to force a Nationalist–communist agreement: FDR had decided that if Chiang could not stabilise the Far East, Stalin would.[13]

When the Big Three met in the Crimea in February 1945, the war in Europe was almost over and the Pacific war was in its last phase. Roosevelt went to the conference to charm Stalin, and also to obtain a Soviet commitment to enter the Far Eastern war after the defeat of Germany. This reasoning was based on the (false) assumption that a large-scale invasion of Japan itself would be required, inflicting thousands of casualties on American troops. Before the negotiations had even begun, Anthony Eden was despondent. The Foreign Secretary thought that the Soviet leader was the only one who could profit from the conference; 'the only one of the three who has a clear view of what he wants and . . . a tough negotiator. PM is all emotion in these matters, FDR vague and jealous of others.'[14] Eden's attempt, however, to coordinate the Anglo-American line entering one of the decisive conferences of the war met with little success.

En route to Yalta, the American and British delegations met at Malta but nothing constructive was achieved. For Eden it 'was impossible to get near to business' with the Americans, while Roosevelt gave 'the impression of failing powers'.[15] It was the same old story of the Cairo and Tehran conferences: Roosevelt had attempted to distance American policy from the British in the belief that he could broker a deal with Stalin; and the Soviet leader had walked all over him. Stalin now did so again at Yalta: in secret one-to-one talks with FDR it was agreed the price for Soviet entry into the Pacific war would be Soviet possession of South Sakhalin, the Kurile islands, Port Arthur and Dairen – the last two the legitimate possessions of China. The Soviet Union was also granted preeminent foreign interests in Mongolia and Manchuria.[16] Neither Chiang Kai-shek nor any Chinese representative was consulted over this agreement. Instead, it was going to be presented to them by the Americans as a fait accompli when the time was thought appropriate.

The secret deal cut at Yalta marked one more nail in Chiang Kai-shek's coffin. With the promise of 60 Russian divisions against Japan three months after the end of the war in Europe, the American need for Chinese bases and troops had disappeared. The Russians would now drive the Japanese into the sea, in all likelihood dragging the Nationalist regime with them.[17]

The Chinese were not the only ones kept in the dark about this agreement. Churchill and Eden were presented with it for approval on the last day of the conference, much to the Foreign Secretary's dismay. Despite an open argument developing between Churchill and Eden, the Prime Minister insisted on signing; failure to do, he maintained, would nullify British influence in the Far East.[18] Churchill's determination to endorse the agreement was in keeping with his previous policy of encouraging Soviet imperialism in the Far East in order to legitimise Britain's continued occupation of her colonies. In a personal minute to the Chiefs of Staff and Anthony Eden in late 1944, he explained how:

> It will be absolutely necessary to offer Russia substantial war objectives in the Far East, and I do not see what injury we should suffer if she had – in one form or another – all effective rights in Port Arthur. Any claim by Russia for indemnity at the expense of China, would be favourable to our resolve about Hong Kong.
>
> We should not show ourselves in any way hostile to the restoration of Russia's position in the Far East, nor commit ourselves in any way to any US wish to oppose it at this stage.[19]

It was the persistence of this attitude which so enraged Eden at Yalta. Far from being upset by this secret American–Soviet deal, therefore, the Prime Minister was, in all probability, very satisfied with its outcome. If Admiral Leahy's account can be trusted, Churchill's signature preserved British imperial interests in the Far East. Roosevelt had told his Chief of Staff prior to Yalta that he hoped to arrange for the return of Hong Kong to China at the conference. However, when the question of making Dairen a Soviet free port came up during FDR's secret negotiations with Stalin, Leahy 'leaned over to Roosevelt and said, "Mr President, you are going to lose out on Hong Kong if you agree to give the Russians half of Dairen." He shook his head in resignation and said, "Well, Bill, I can't help it".'[20]

The British Foreign Secretary used the example of the secret Far Eastern agreement as proof that although ill, the President was not mentally incapacitated, still having the energy to negotiate secretly with Stalin. Churchill's doctor, however, disagreed. He observed that Roosevelt:

Intervened very little in discussions, with his mouth open. If he has sometimes been short of facts about the subject under discussion his shrewdness has covered this up. Now, they say, the shrewdness has gone, and there is nothing left. I doubt, from what I have seen, whether he is fit for the job.[21]

FDR's personal adviser, Harry Hopkins, was physically no better, being only 'half in this world'.[22] All of this mattered because the State Department was, as usual, excluded from the important discussions. Whereas they believed that America should 'assume the leadership in assisting China to develop a strong, stable and unified government in order that she may become the principal stabilising factor in the Far East', Roosevelt had unilaterally decided that Stalin would do the job instead.[23] James Byrnes, Director of the Office of War Mobilisation and future Secretary of State, wrote that although the State Department had done extensive preparatory briefs for Yalta, it was the President's illness which prevented him from reading them. This, however, was a generous interpretation of the facts. Precedent suggested that Roosevelt would not have read them even had he been in better health. The President preferred to keep his own council. Stettinius, for example, remained in ignorance of the Far Eastern agreement although he had accompanied Roosevelt to Yalta as his Secretary of State!

The President's deliberate isolation from the Washington bureaucracy eventually caused America's China policy to implode. For a long period, however, these stresses were held in check using the adhesive of attacks on British imperialism. The State Department, apart from continuing to see China as an important fixture on the American foreign policy agenda, shared many of Roosevelt's suspicions of British imperialism. In their survey of the China theatre for Yalta, the State Department argued that 'the British are undoubtedly less optimistic – more cynical – than we are regarding the future of China', while certain British elements, acting 'out of imperial considerations, desire a weak and possibly disunited China'. The issue of Hong Kong was typically hoped to be resolved in China's favour. Amusingly, the document referred to 'the Big Three (or Four, if the Soviet Union is included)' after stating that 'our policy towards China is not based on sentiment' but upon 'enlightened national self-interest'![24] At this stage of the war it was not a question of optimism to maintain that China was a Great Power, but complete delusion.

The maverick General Hurley, ostensibly dispatched to China by Roosevelt to resolve Nationalist and communist differences, completed the destruction of America's China policy. After failing in his mission to prevent a renewal of civil war (and discrediting himself in the process), the general forced the dismissal of the State Department's John Davies and John Service, accusing them of communist sympathies.[25] These ruptures only helped to reinforce the view that America's China policy had run off the rails, falling back on the staple of anti-imperialism. Crucially, moreover, the architect of American policy, President Roosevelt, had single-handedly decided that China's usefulness had come to an end. Unfortunately, he had not bothered to tell anyone else. If the Chinese were not worthy of being informed of decisions which affected their sovereignty, the same could be said of the American people.

Unrepentant imperialists

American condemnation of the British Empire was retrospectively a futile act which offered little hope of success: it was a case of the pupil becoming the teacher, and the British did not like their traditional position being usurped. American 'values' were undermined at almost every turn by the hypocrisy that accompanied Washington's moralising. There was little mention of America's own 'colonies' acquired on her journey towards her 'Manifest Destiny'. It was as if the Philippines, Panama, Cuba and Puerto Rico did not exist, not to mention other American lands such as Hawaii, California and New Mexico which were annexed in questionable circumstances. In fact, American efforts re-inforced traditional British beliefs, which would change only through the pain of personal experience and political expediency. Lord Moran vividly captured the interminable conflict with the British when the Americans played the colonial card. He characterised Harry Hopkins at Yalta, like the President, as someone who 'seems to lose his balance when colonies are discussed; they might be back in the War of Independence, fighting their English oppressors at Yorktown'. Winston Churchill was similarly incapable of clear thought when he sniffed an American scheme to chip away at the Empire. During the conference, Stettinius brought up a report on trusteeship which in fact only applied to enemy territory. Without even attempting to ascertain this fact, the Prime Minister exploded to a visibly shaken Stettinius: 'He would not have the British Empire run by a lot of bunglers. He would refuse point-blank to countenance such folly. He spoke with heat . . . After the PM sat down he kept mumbling: "Never, never, never".' Moran held that these outbursts, were on balance, damaging to the British cause rather than constructive.

Yet, I wonder if I am fair to Winston. When the Prime Minister announced, 'I have not become the King's First Minister in order to preside over the liquidation of the British Empire,' it was not just bravado. He was affirming a faith for which he was prepared to give his life. The President knows this side of the PM, but he cannot leave the Empire alone. It seems to upset him, though he never turns a hair when a great chunk of Europe falls into the clutches of the Soviet Union.[26]

It was not only the Americans who risked inciting the ire of the Prime Minister over the colonial issue. As we have already seen, those closest to him in government, like Anthony Eden, were frequent victims of his spleen.[27] Often as not, however, these attacks were unjustified. It was, as Moran argued, a case of Churchill speaking without listening: 'If only he would listen occasionally!' he exclaimed after the Stettinius incident at Yalta.[28] There had always been a boorish tendency in the Prime Minister's personality, but this became increasingly exacerbated by physical fatigue brought about by years of war. Of course, it would have been more sensible to delegate and *trust* people to do their jobs but this was not his way. Again and again Churchill formed snap judgements on issues he only half-understood the background to, driven by his obsession to follow every aspect of the war.

Anthony Eden, in contrast to Churchill's ill-tempered letter on New Year's Eve 1944 which insinuated Eden's willingness to dissolve the Empire, replied with subdued anger. He pointed out that the trusteeship issue had already been discussed at Cabinet and agreed upon:

There is not the slightest question of liquidating the British empire. On the contrary, we are anxious to persuade the Americans not to go in for half-baked international regimes in any ex-enemy colonies they may take over, not to advocate them for others, but to accept colonial responsibilities on the same terms as ourselves.[29]

Clement Attlee was also increasingly disenchanted by the Prime Minister's lengthy Cabinet meetings, which often rambled on incoherently while Churchill dismissed the judgement of Cabinet committees in favour of his cronies, Brendan Bracken and Lord Beaverbrook. Courageously putting these opinions to paper, he brought the wrath of Churchill upon himself. After Churchill predictably fulminated against the socialist leader, he did, however, 'endeavour to profit by [Attlee's] counsels'.[30]

The Prime Minister's fears about his own government's stance towards the question of trusteeships (and the Empire) were therefore groundless. Both the pivotal offices of government responsible for the colonies were emphatically behind the Empire. His Foreign Secretary, although Churchill never acknowledged this, was even more sceptical of American foreign policy than he was himself. Exasperated by the need to refer everything to Washington for approval, Eden snapped at his private secretary, 'Can't we really have a foreign policy of our own?'[31]

If Eden was a safe pair of hands, Oliver Stanley's attitude at the Colonial Office was rock solid. On his January visit to Washington, Stanley met with the President who was in a typically flighty mood, expanding on his future plans for Indo-China and the Pacific islands as if he were recreating the world. He lectured Stanley that Churchill's 1942 Mansion House speech was ill-advised, and he hoped Hong Kong would be returned to China. Roosevelt's growing estrangement from Chiang Kai-shek obviously mattered little when the opportunity arose to put the British in the colonial dock. The President, though, was pushing his luck with the obdurate Stanley. When he told the Colonial Secretary:

'I do not want to be unkind or rude to the British, but in 1841, when you acquired Hong Kong, you did not acquire it by purchase.' Stanley's instant rejoinder was, 'Let me see, Mr President, that was about the time of the Mexican War.'

The President said that Chiang had confirmed in a letter his willingness to make a free port of Hong Kong. Stanley's only comment on the Hong Kong narrative was, 'It will be a long three days [of official visit], Mr President.'[32]

American double standards were nothing new to the British, but as the trusteeship issue came alive British attacks upon American policy became less guarded. Roosevelt himself also became a target. Richard Law, parliamentary under-secretary of state at the Foreign Office, had had a similar encounter to Oliver Stanley with the President the previous December. He advised that 'the President tends to be somewhat irresponsible in his table talk, and it would be unwise to base too much on any points of detail'.[33]

The hardening approach in the presentation of British colonial policy was also evident in London's preparations for the Ninth Institute of Pacific Relations conference, to be held at Hot Springs, Virginia in January 1945. At the 1942 Mount Tremblant conference in Quebec, the British had attached considerable importance to this unofficial gathering of academics, diplomats and politicians, despite attempting to cancel it. After the resounding Far Eastern defeats of early 1942 there was a feeling in Whitehall that Britain had to justify her colonies, if not the British Empire itself, to the assembled Allied delegations. With the forthcoming 1945 conference, however, the British had downgraded the conference's importance though a strong delegation was nevertheless fielded. Ashley Clarke's more hard-line replacement as head of the Far Eastern section of the Foreign Office, Sterndale Bennett, explained:

> These conferences of the IPR must arouse mixed feelings in our minds here. But there can be no doubt, I think, that as long as the Americans attach so much importance to them and send such a strong delegation . . . it is to our advantage to give every support and assistance to the British delegation, and to see it is also as strong as possible.[34]

At the conference itself the usual American criticisms of British imperialism were by now ritually aired, and once again met colourful resistance from the British socialist, Creech Jones. When the Americans droned on about colonies under the guise of 'dependent areas', Creech Jones struck a raw nerve, asking whether this included the 'fifteen million dependent peoples in the United States proper'; in other words, the American Negro! The British cross-party consensus was also displayed again when Creech Jones congratulated his usual foe Oliver Stanley on doing 'a reasonably good job'. He added that Labour and Conservative were 'now walking together' in colonial matters.[35] The importance of this meeting, however, should not be exaggerated; for the British it was only a talking shop which they reluctantly attended. The conference's real significance is, perhaps, indicated by the absence of British Foreign Office files in the archives: they were destroyed when the documents were 'weeded' for worthless material. Symbolically, the only remaining records are American.

Never ending: Anglo-American conflict in China

While it was true that Roosevelt increasingly overlooked Chiang Kai-shek's importance (for example, telexes became far less frequent between the two), it was certainly not the case that the British position in China became any easier. This was principally because American personnel within China remained exceedingly ill-disposed towards the British. At the end of November 1944, China's situation was on the edge. Carton de Wiart wrote to General Ismay from Chungking that 'the situation here is far worse than I have ever known it, and if the Japanese get Kweiyang, they can go for Kunming or Chungking, and I would not be surprised at anything happening then'. Even the new American commander remained extremely apprehensive in private at the gravity of the situation. When Japan's radio propagandist Tokyo Rose broadcast that 'General Wedemeyer will eat his thanksgiving dinner in India, if he eats any at all', she was being uncharacteristically truthful.[36]

Wedemeyer, however, like many other American service men in China, preferred to blame the British for the impending catastrophe. Superficially he improved Allied relations with his attempt to woo the media, although this was not difficult following General Stilwell. On the other hand, however, Wedemeyer promoted military plans which were partially designed to disadvantage the British position in the Far East. Despite his protestations to the contrary, he consistently sided with the Chinese against the British for political reasons masquerading as military necessity. The central tenet of this 'plan' was a joint Sino-American campaign, codenamed Carbonado, to seize the area of Canton and Hong Kong, on the pretext of opening up a supply route into China. This was to get underway in the summer of 1945. Carbonado, it should be added, could not have happened without American support and advisers. Before that operation became feasible, however, Wedemeyer attempted to coordinate all covert operations in the China theatre with obvious implications for Britain and Hong Kong.[37]

In October 1944, Oliver Stanley authorised Gerard Gent to discuss the possibility of forming an emergency civil affairs unit to infiltrate Hong Kong in the event of a Japanese withdrawal from the colony. This was an expansion on the earlier idea of utilising the British Army Aid Group had the Hong Kong Planning Unit not been ready in a crisis. There was a latent fear within the Colonial Office that Chinese irregular troops or bandits would seize the colony should the Japanese evacuate. In these circumstances, it was anticipated that the Chinese Government would attempt to control Chinese forces and reclaim the colony.[38] After receiving the approval of the Secretary of State for War, however, further consultations with Mountbatten and de Wiart were terminated by General Wedemeyer's insistence that all special operations in the China theatre be approved by himself.

Wedemeyer's reassertion of his authority over all the intelligence units was not without reasonable foundation. As far as he was concerned there were too many competing intelligence and commando units in his theatre (including 11 American ones), causing duplication and unnecessary bureaucracy. He even had to chastise one US Navy intelligence group for its independent attitude.[39] Nonetheless, Wedemeyer's new policy to clear all paramilitary operations through the Generalissimo meant British approaches to approve her emergency Hong Kong unit were now 'quite useless'. It was clear to the Colonial Office that neither Chiang nor Wedemeyer would ever sanction a British operation to retake their colony, and the Americans had now established the perfect bureaucratic alibi to disguise their anti-imperialism. Revealingly, General Hurley, still in China, had earlier telexed the President (after presumably consulting Wedemeyer) that the British Army Aid Group was unnecessary and served only imperial interests. Typically, he found it hard to resist an adventitious side-swipe at the colonial powers:

> All the British, Dutch, French diplomatic and other organisations in China are definitely opposing the American policy in China. The [British] Ambassador has said to General Wedemeyer and also to me that the American policy to unify China is detrimental, if not destructive, to the position of the White Man in Asia.[40]

Laying aside the implausibility of Sir Horace Seymour's remark to Wedemeyer, it was clear that the American high command in China wanted the British out of China, full stop. Wedemeyer's attempt to coordinate special operations should therefore be seen as the culmination of this resentment. There was also the question of the chicken and the egg: if there was British subterfuge and secrecy it was largely motivated by America's almost evangelical persecution of British imperial beliefs and policy. The Americans could hardly expect the British to be completely honest with them (even though they often were) if respect for each other's point of view was so clearly lacking on either side.

The American attempt to coerce British intelligence efforts sparked an internecine dispute between the BAAG and SOE, threatening Britain's only remaining toe-hold in Hong Kong. SOE pleaded with London to roll the BAAG into SOE, which was resisted by the BAAG causing endless (and futile) arguments within the British bureaucracy. SOE, furthermore, thought that they could circumvent Wedemeyer's order by proposing that the British retain jurisdiction for general intelligence duties around Kwangtung province, which of course included the area of Hong Kong. Such blatantly transparent manoeuvres tended to be a feature of SOE's planning and did not bode well for future operations.[41]

The stress of the period began to take its toll on tempers, particularly Colonel Ride's, the commander of the BAAG, who remained adamantly opposed to using his troops in south China to participate in the Colonial Office/SOE operation to retake the colony. Despite the fact that the BAAG consisted of many SOE personnel who had escaped Hong Kong on its capitulation in 1941, he was in no mood to compromise:

If the BAAG is used in the operation on Hong Kong for any other purposes outside its official role (escape and evasion of landing parties and airmen, rescuing of POWs, and security) we shall be damned in the eyes of both Chinese and Americans for a long time afterwards. The comment will be, 'There you are; we knew all along the perfidious British were up to their old games.'

Ride's outburst was regarded as hysterical at the Foreign Office and the Colonial Office, particularly in light of Chinese and American treatment of British interests in the theatre. The British were already damned in their Allies' eyes which undercut any further logic to appease them, especially when it concerned such an important issue as Hong Kong. A.L. Scott thought Ride's position 'remarkable'.[42] The report certainly put the cat among the pigeons; an impromptu interdepartmental meeting was convened on 5 July to discuss the next step. Gerard Gent, as usual, took the lead and did not restrain his opinions; Ride was wrong, and his first duty must be to the colony. 'He did not suppose the Foreign Office would wish to be faced with the embarrassing situation that would arise if Hong Kong were occupied by Chinese claiming to assert and retain authority in the colony.' Indeed they did not.[43]

When the British Embassy in Chungking was informed of the decision to use the BAAG in retaking Hong Kong, the story took a further twist. Churchill's personal representative to Chiang Kai-shek, Carton de Wiart, and the ambassador, firmly believed that the operation would be impractical due to expected opposition from the Americans, particularly General Wedemeyer.[44] The seriousness of the situation meant that the controversy and the danger it represented to Hong Kong permeated to the top of Whitehall. Oliver Stanley's private secretary, however, informed the Far Eastern department of the Colonial Office that there was no urgency to resolve affairs. SOE's head, Lord Selborne, backed by Stanley, was discussing the matter with Churchill, while David MacDougall, head of the Hong Kong Planning Unit, was visiting China for a month:

If it involves (as of course it does) the risk of a first-class row between General Wedemeyer and ourselves which could endanger the whole existence of our clandestine organisation in China (and no doubt in other American controlled areas), we should wait.[45]

American hypocrisy was on the agenda again: Selborne pointedly observed that although he was not 'desirous of intruding where we are not wanted . . . it is germane to remember that we invited OSS into the Balkans when it was a purely British theatre and shared our close integration'. Oliver Stanley was fully supportive of SOE's position believing that it was crucial to tackle the Americans head on at this juncture; failure to do so would see what little British influence had in China eradicated. If British covert operations were abandoned, the key mechanism for Britain's recapture of the colony would be lost. Stanley wrote to the Prime Minister arguing that, 'There are no British operational forces of the ordinary sort in either theatre and we have therefore to rely on paramilitary forces to show the flag in connection with the liberation of Borneo and Hong Kong.'[46] At the same time, Louis Mountbatten was arguing with Wedemeyer until he was blue in the face.

The American commander's proposals to coordinate all China operations extended to Indo-China where Louis Mountbatten thought he had a verbal agreement with Chiang Kai-shek that SEAC forces would predominate. Now, he was told this agreement no longer held (and since it was not written down, SEAC's claims were hard to prove). Churchill wrote to Roosevelt advising that Wedemeyer be overruled in favour of Mountbatten. Even though the President would not agree to this, the message sent by the British could not be ignored: they would defend their interests in the Far East at the highest level if need be.[47] And although Oliver Stanley's letter had arrived too late for a specific reference to Hong Kong in the Prime Minister's telex, the principle of mutual cooperation in Anglo-American relations raised by Churchill (in deed as well as word) held true for the colony. At a time when both the President and Churchill were increasingly preoccupied with deteriorating relations with the Soviets post-Yalta, the fact that Wedemeyer's actions could cause such consternation illustrated the continued importance of the Far East within British circles.

Ultimately, Britain's mobilisation against Wedemeyer's heavy-handed actions limited the damage to British capabilities in the China theatre. Although the general had his way, the British retained their hold on Kwangtung province using the BAAG and SOE. The price exacted, however, was extremely high. Sir Horace Seymour had to promise that he was 'completely committed to keeping General Wedemeyer informed of all British plans and activities in the military field'. In other words, no more secret plans to recapture Hong Kong from within China. Any emergency unit would now have to come from outside the China theatre, probably from India.[48] Carton de Wiart also took over the coordination of British covert operations in the theatre. While he was on relatively good terms with the Americans and Chinese in Chungking, believing Wedemeyer to be 'the right man for the job', de Wiart did not manifest the same determination to retain Hong Kong as many people within Whitehall did.[49]

General Wedemeyer's first months in command had realised a major set-back for independent British efforts to recapture Hong Kong. As Sir Horace Seymour explained, this was the American aim: both he and de Wiart had 'gained the impression that Wedemeyer [was] opposed to any action by the British in China directed to the reoccupation of Hong Kong'.[50] Instead, the British were now faced with the uphill task of securing Sino-American agreement for the attachment of an emergency civil affairs unit to advancing Chinese troops heading for Hong Kong.

David MacDougall's trip to China

When David MacDougall visited China in March 1945 in order to prepare the way for the Hong Kong Planning Unit's return to the colony, he encountered considerable doubts among British personnel that Britain would return there. These enquiries came 'from such widely differing sources as a Russian-born ex-employee of the Hong Kong Dairy Farm now working in Calcutta and a senior member of the Ambassador's staff in Chungking'. Major General Hayes, the British military representative in Chungking was also less than enthusiastic at MacDougall's visit. He was particularly keen to play down the Hong Kong issue so as not to complicate relations with Wedemeyer and the Americans even further. It was apparent that constant Sino-American intimidation of British personnel in China had drained some of their imperial spirit and pushed them into a defensive frame of mind. There were, however, more encouraging aspects to MacDougall's visit.

MacDougall learnt that the wooden-legged Admiral Chan Chuk, who had escaped from the colony with him in December 1941, was designated as the next mayor of Canton. While Chan was not particularly 'pro' anything, he had 'a soft spot for the British administration of Hong Kong'. If this appointment was confirmed, MacDougall saw it of the first importance: 'That should give us a good start. It is not difficult to imagine post-war conditions in which what Canton thinks is more important to Hong Kong than policies originating in Nanking (or wherever the capital of China is finally located).'[51] He observed, furthermore, that China's anticipation of the colony's retrocession was subsiding.

> If I interpreted correctly the nods and becks of those of my Chungking friends whom I managed to see in Chungking, the Chinese seem a good deal more reconciled to not getting possession of Hong Kong the day after tomorrow than they were in 1942: curiously enough, they show on the whole somewhat more faith in British tenacity . . . than our own Far Eastern communities.

MacDougall's presence amongst the embattled British personnel in the Far East, moreover, had its own salutary effect. After years of having to work in an American-dominated theatre, and no doubt make constant excuses for being British, people were gratified to discover that London had not forgotten them.[52]

Sir Horace Seymour, the British Ambassador in Chungking, was one of many people David MacDougall met in China who expressed scepticism at Britain's renewed imperial aspirations. Seymour's preference was to return Hong Kong. He warned that after the war the Chinese would 'do everything they can to get rid of the remaining foreign colonies on the coast [and] to make Hong Kong's position very difficult'.[53] This view, though, was increasingly out of step with the Foreign Office back in London. Yes, there would be problems reimposing British rule the way it was in 1941, but A.L. Scott disagreed 'with the thesis that the possession of the territory constitutes "imperialism"'. The Colonial Office, furthermore, 'attached considerable importance' to retaining Hong Kong as an anchor for British interests in the Far East.[54] An important consideration in the Foreign Office's hardening stance was the discrediting of any compromise solution. With China in confusion there was little realistic possibility of a halfway house where the Chinese would guarantee British interests in the colony. This, anyway, would not have removed Chinese grievances completely. The Hong Kong question had reached a point where a compromise could never satisfy both sides. T.H. Brewis of the Far Eastern department wrote, 'The fact is, I suppose, that Hong Kong is to remain as exactly as before, and that there is nothing which needs discussion with the Chinese . . . My impression is that this attitude has worked rather well so far.'[55]

General Hurley visited London in early April 1945 as Roosevelt's personal representative. It was sharp reminder of the Foreign Office's growing resistance towards American anti-colonialism. On hearing in late March that the general might not, after all, be coming, Anthony Eden noted, 'Thank God!'[56] Field Marshal Wilson at the British Embassy in Washington alerted General Ismay that Hurley's likely mission was trouble. Hurley had, apparently, already warned Wilson that both the State Department and the President were threatening Britain with a rough time over Hong Kong. As if this was not enough, Hurley raised the prospect of prohibiting Britain from using lend-lease *matériel* to regain her colonial Empire.[57] A.L. Scott was not impressed. He reacted to such threats in the same way that Oliver Stanley had when he visited America in January, casting aspersions upon the integrity of American policy. Scott argued that it was highly hypocritical for the Americans to maintain the 'pose of self-determination' when they had kicked the Mexicans out of south-west America, and forced the southern Confederacy to stay in the Union![58]

The Foreign Office brief for Eden and Churchill prior to meeting Hurley was equally robust. Since much of its contents was already implicitly agreed upon among Whitehall figures, the brief was, in many respects, predictable. It stated that the future of Hong Kong was a problem between Britain and China, which did not include the USA. What is more, 'having lost Hong Kong to the enemy, it [was] a point of national honour to recover it', just as General MacArthur claimed he would return to the Philippines. The British were also not convinced that they were acting from purely selfish reasons; the brief spoke of the 'heavy responsibility in respect of Hong Kong towards all nations interested in the stability and welfare of the Far East'.[59]

When Hurley did arrive, he did not disappoint. Sterndale Bennett described how Hurley 'passed so rapidly and so imperceptibly from subject to subject that there was not opportunity for taking him up on any one point'. Anthony Eden's meeting with the general no doubt took a similar course, although unfortunately he did not have time to make a record. As expected, though, we do know that Hurley raised the question of Hong Kong with Eden.[60] If the Foreign Secretary failed to communicate to the troublesome American general Britain's resolve over the colony, he was left in no doubt by Churchill. Hurley made the mistake of baiting the Prime Minister on this very subject. From Churchill's own words we know that

> General Hurley seemed to wish to confine the conversation to civil banalities. I took him up with violence about Hong Kong and said that never would we yield an inch of the territory that was under the British flag. As for the leased territory, in connection with the water

supply, that did not come up until 1998 or thereabouts. In the meanwhile we would set up distilling machinery which would give us all the water we wanted and more. The General-Ambassador accepted this without further demur. I do not think any harm could have been done by my talk with him. We shall see.[61]

If it was too much to hope that the Americans would accept Britain's attitude towards her 'colonies [as] one of responsibility and not privilege', which Sterndale Bennett thought it might be, American anti-imperialism was about to be dealt a tragic blow.[62] On the 12 April, one day after Hurley had seen the Prime Minister, President Roosevelt suffered a fatal brain haemorrhage. If his experience would be sorely missed by the British as peace approached, his obsessive arguments for the dissolution of the Empire would not.

The death of President Roosevelt and San Francisco

The death of Roosevelt should not have been unexpected but as Churchill's doctor wrote at Yalta, 'men shut their eyes when they do not want to see, and the Americans cannot bring themselves to believe that he is finished'.[63] The President's passing was deeply mourned by Churchill, who described him as 'the greatest champion of freedom who has ever brought help and comfort from the new world to the old'.[64] The cold fact remained, however, that Roosevelt's removal from office helped British foreign policy in many respects, including her attempt to reoccupy Hong Kong.

It was understandable why Churchill felt so grieved: as far as he was concerned the Anglo-American relationship was a personal (and special) relationship, jealously guarded between himself and Roosevelt. Roosevelt's death, therefore, broke up this comfortable twosome and restrained Churchill's wilder inclinations to trust in God and America. For the Americans themselves, the implications went far deeper.

Few people in American political history had concentrated so much power in their hands as Franklin Roosevelt. In many respects, he was the creator of the 'imperial presidency', but for all that he did not leave a coherent foreign policy behind. General Wedemeyer described how when he was assigned to the China theatre in November 1944 he was reminded of Stephen Leacock's remark: 'He mounted his horse and rode off in all directions.'[65] Perplexingly, even though he must have known he was dying, the President refused to leave a political will or testament, or anoint a successor. Harry Truman, Roosevelt's successor and deputy, was an experienced politician but had been kept in ignorance, like everyone else, of FDR's inner thoughts. He had no foreign policy experience and had to grapple with complex diplomatic problems from a cold start. It was, therefore, little surprise that the new President felt less strongly on colonial issues and Hong Kong's future. This was a man, moreover, who recognised the hypocritical aspects of American foreign policy. During a dinner for Oliver Stanley in January 1945, Truman asked what the American reaction would be if Puerto Rico were a British colony, and were treated the way the Americans treated it. The implication was that American anti-colonial criticism was reserved for other countries when America's treatment of her own dependent areas was not beyond reproach.[66]

Besides having to pick up the wreckage of Roosevelt's foreign policy idealism, Truman was faced with more pressing issues than Hong Kong's retrocession to China (on which he had never previously expressed a single opinion). Relations with the Soviet Union, in particular, were critical at this juncture, especially as Stalin was behaving more like his old thuggish self. Arguably, through his weakness with Stalin, Roosevelt had fanned the flames of Soviet expansionism himself. In such circumstances, the British found a new President who increasingly favoured a solid Anglo-American front with which to confront Stalin. Disputes which could weaken the Anglo-American alliance were therefore downplayed, including the issues of trusteeship and colonialism.

San Francisco

Despite President Truman's more conciliatory approach to Anglo-American relations, the effects did not immediately filter through to British policymakers. While Truman picked up the reins of American foreign policy, the State Department continued to pursue President Roosevelt's anti-imperialistic agenda. The British could thus be forgiven for thinking that Roosevelt's death had made little impact on American anti-colonialism.

At the San Francisco conference, which marked the inauguration of the United Nations Organisation, the American delegation led the way in establishing a trusteeship commission to visit colonies and report on them. The Commonwealth even showed signs of splitting, with the Australian delegation siding with the Americans.[67] The conference itself, however, was somewhat surreal; in many respects it resembled the British experience at the Institute of Pacific Relations conferences where the delegates had harangued British colonial policy until blue in the face, irrespective of practical considerations. Similarly, the proceedings at San Francisco, for all the importance the British attached to them, were largely irrelevant. Stalin would never have joined the United Nations or sent his Foreign Minister, Molotov, to the conference if there was any possibility of national sovereignty being undermined. The same principles applied to the British Empire. Even Winston Churchill had grudgingly come to this conclusion: he advised that the Americans be allowed to exempt any Japanese islands they required (for security purposes) from United Nations supervision, without exacting a quid pro quo.[68]

The Chinese, uncharacteristically, kept a low profile at the conference, even though they would receive one of the coveted five seats on the Security Council committee due to American sponsorship. Sir Horace Seymour noted that they resisted the temptation to stir up the Hong Kong issue, proclaiming with palpable sincerity that 'China has never taken advantage of the difficulties of others to absorb their territory'.[69] At a time when China's own weakness was more likely to be exploited by others, however, the Nationalists could stand accused of trading in empty gestures. Indeed, the city of San Francisco appeared a more absorbing distraction for the Chinese delegation than the tedium of diplomacy. One of their number passed out during mid-debate in the conference room, and had to be carried from the room. Reportedly, he had spent an entire afternoon with 'a most charming lady' in San Francisco![70]

The Colonial Office, however, were not now in a frame of mind in which they could readily decipher a real threat to the Empire from a harmless one. Churchill had frequently exhibited these characteristics as we have already seen, snapping at his ministers for seemingly innocuous proposals which touched upon the keyword, 'Empire'. Oliver Stanley now reacted similarly. After working himself up over British colonial concessions at San Francisco, the Colonial Secretary was in no mood for perceived divisions within the British ranks, least of all from the Foreign Office. Unfortunately for the latter, however, Hall-Patch of the Foreign Office's Far Eastern department made the mistake of emphasising the difficulties involved in Britain's return to Hong Kong at a Cabinet committee meeting.

During a Far Eastern economic meeting on 10 May, Hall-Patch (in the Chair) noted that unless the Chinese acquiesced with Britain's continued rule of the colony it would not be much use economically. 'He expressed doubts as to whether the future of Hong Kong as a British possession was clear enough to encourage British interests to assist in its rehabilitation.'[71] Oliver Stanley was furious. He wrote to Anthony Eden on 25 May:

> Every now and then I come across expressions of doubt in unexpected quarters as to our intention or capacity to resume the administration of Hong Kong, and one of the latest is the proceedings of one of the sub-committees of the Far Eastern committee (FE(E)(45) 5th meeting, paragraph 4). It is important that there should be no doubt about our resolution in the matter and none is justified least of all in official circles.

Sterndale Bennett at the Foreign Office thought Stanley's letter an overreaction. Few disagreed that the colony was British but he felt that 'no good purpose will be served by blinking [at] the difficulties which we are likely to meet in regard to Hong Kong'. On Eden's behalf, Richard Law was left to mollify the Colonial Office. He told Stanley that Churchill's minute of his conversation with General Hurley would be circulated within the Far Eastern department, but added that Hall-Patch was 'not throwing doubt' on British resolve, but 'merely referring to difficulties'.[72] It would appear that Foreign and Colonial Office mutual distrust remained an inescapable feature of the Whitehall landscape.

The British general election

The defeat of Germany on 7 May 1945 brought one half of the Second World War to an end, and with it came the demise of Churchill's coalition government. The Labour Party had insisted on a speedy general election (to be held in July) against the advice of Attlee and Churchill who wanted to keep the coalition together until the defeat of Japan. The fatigue, though, which had been stalking Churchill and Eden for the past few years resurfaced with a vengeance; Eden was taken ill with a duodenal ulcer and spent the entire month of June convalescing, missing the whole election campaign.[73] Churchill, too, needed a rest from government; he seemed 'too weary to think out a policy for the restoration of the country after the havoc of the war'. At his doctor's insistence he took a ten-day holiday in the south of France in early July, before the Potsdam conference.[74] It all seemed like the end of a long and arduous journey which no one had the fight left in them to carry on. Churchill's performance in the election campaign was lacklustre, while Eden's heart was not in it. He wrote just before the result in July at Potsdam: 'Depressed and cannot help an unworthy hope that we may lose, or rather have lost, this election. If it were not for the immediate

European situation I am sure it would be better thus, that is a big "if", I admit.'[75] Compounding his misery was the news that his son, Simon, was missing on active service in the Far East. For Eden the Burma war could not be a 'forgotten war'.

If it looked as if the government had reached its final destination, they could at least list a long line of achievements to match the defeats. Many of the pieces necessary for Britain's return to Hong Kong were already in place despite the increasingly pressing problem of Soviet imperialism. A foreign policy consensus, if not already existing, had been forged across political boundaries throughout the war years. This fact was exposed as the general election campaign unfolded; foreign affairs was reduced to a paragraph in Labour's election manifesto, the decisive issue being social reform. The legacy of the Churchill government, furthermore, was also relatively secure when compared to the American system of government. Whereas the death of Roosevelt had broken American foreign policy into splinters, the permanence of civil service staff and cross-party inclusiveness in London enabled continuity as well as change.

With their patron departed the Chinese were also given pause for thought. Li Shu Fan, who had visited the Colonial Office in early 1944 to discuss Hong Kong, was now acting as personal adviser to the Chinese Prime Minister, T.V. Soong in San Francisco. In discussions with a British representative, Li stated that the Chinese were increasingly concerned, not with Hong Kong, but with Soviet and American policies:

> There was no disposition to make an issue of the rendition of Hong Kong, in view of . . . misgivings engendered in official circles in Chungking as to the future attitude of Russia and the support accorded to the Communist Party of China. [Li] went further and stated that the attitude adopted by the United States in its sponsorship of a 'get together' policy between Chungking and the communist party in China had created grave concern in official quarters in Chungking.[76]

With the collapse of the Japanese war effort only months away, the British were about to discover whether this was one more Chinese deception. Either way, London knew like Stalin that ownership was nine-tenths possession.

10
Return of the Empire: the Defeat of Japan, July–September 1945

Perhaps the greatest problem . . . will be the destruction by three years of Japanese occupation of the British 'Legend'. Whatever else happens the deep feeling that British rule was inevitable has been shattered for ever. There is, however, another side to this picture; if the divine right of Britain to rule has been proved a myth, 'independence' at least under the dominance of any major Asiatic power, has proved a nightmare.[1]

SOE report, April 1945

The end of the war in the Pacific

Despite the exertions and scheming of the Allies to plot the course ahead, the situation remained as clear as the deep green sea which surrounded the colony. For all the momentum behind British foreign policy her return to Hong Kong was not inevitable, not least because there were factors over which London had no control. Most problematic was the continuing legacy of poor Anglo-American relations in the Far East. Besides Operation Carbonado, Anglo-American relations remained fraught in the China theatre generally, and it seemed obvious to British personnel that any reclamation of the colony would necessitate a British-led seizure. Sir Horace Seymour believed that 'If it could only be British forces which recapture Hong Kong, some at least of our troubles would be largely solved . . . But if we are merely given it back very reluctantly by our Allies, it will be a very long time before we hear the last of it.'[2]

Overshadowing Allied relations was the threat of a Japanese withdrawal from Hong Kong, up the China coast, leaving the colony wide open to Chinese irregular forces or loyal Nationalist armies. The British

Chiefs of Staff, who held a very low estimation of Chinese military prowess, expected this to be the only way the Chinese could recapture the colony. Political changes within the British Government, however, offered one last straw of hope for the Americans and Chinese. The theory was that a Labour government, with its more internationalist approach to diplomatic relations, would take a more conciliatory stance over Hong Kong. The acrimonious general election campaign of June and July seemed to point to major differences of opinion between the socialists and Conservatives. All of this was true of course, but Conservative–Labour schisms were principally concerned with domestic affairs. It was a misreading of the situation to link social radicalism with a progressive foreign policy. Churchill's defeat, on 26 July did not, therefore, mark a watershed in British diplomatic policy. In the end, it was Britain's foreign policy consensus which would triumph over the divisions of her two Allies, China and America.

Towards judgement day

The flicker of the war's end encouraged the Colonial and Foreign Offices to concentrate on the practicalities of returning British rule to the Far East. After an incredible five-month delay, Sir Horace Seymour received a reply to his telex which requested information on the future of Hong Kong. Apologising for the Ambassador's letter having been 'overlooked' by the Colonial Office, Sterndale Bennett informed him that 'nothing has been said on a ministerial level either privately or publicly to suggest that any change in the status of Hong Kong is contemplated'. For Seymour's information a China Association letter defending Britain's rights to the colony and the Colonial Office guidelines for the San Francisco conference were sent to Chungking.[3] The Foreign Office was now even prepared to blame Anglo-American difficulties on Britain's own lack of faith in the Empire! The liberal A.L. Scott was moved to write:

> I feel the root of the matter is that our people abroad are themselves half convinced that by retaining our Far Eastern territories under our control until they are fit for self-government, we are activated by purely selfish and reactionary motives. 'Refresher courses' may help to correct this.

Gladwyn Jebb thought this was 'very true'.[4] The colonial lethargy which had epitomised Britain's defence of the colony in 1941 had been replaced by a hard-bitten, do-it-yourself philosophy which attempted to wipe out the shameful defeats of earlier years. There was little illusion about the importance of recapturing the colony using British troops.[5] The problems of cooperating with her Allies in the China theatre provided, if it were needed, a continuing reminder of the dangers of trusting British policy to others.

The ever present David MacDougall was one of many people who encountered complications. Attempting to recruit British Chinese personnel for the Hong Kong Planning Unit, he faced the obstacle that many of the people on his 'hit list' remained working in China. To extricate them would require a Chinese Government visa, which would be hard to obtain if the Chinese knew why they were returning to England.[6] The situation was little better for British forces in China itself. Sir Horace Seymour reported that the Americans were still extremely suspicious of the BAAG and the British military situation in China 'is now so difficult and precarious' that any special operations plan to recapture Hong Kong would have to be cleared with the Americans and Chinese at the highest level.[7]

The final wartime conference of the Big Three, codenamed Terminal, which met at Potsdam in the middle of July, marked a further ebbing of Britain's world power. The commitment to restore her sovereignty over Hong Kong was, however, successfully passed from Churchill's administration to Attlee's.

Potsdam

When Churchill arrived in Berlin on 15 July after his convalescence, he brought in tow his shadow from the Labour Party, Clement Attlee. Anthony Eden also joined the delegation after recovering from his duodenal ulcer. The reason for Attlee's presence was that Churchill's government was in limbo. Polling day had been on 5 July, but to enable the services to vote, the result was staggered until 26 July, towards the end of the Potsdam conference. Such a situation was not ideal. Indeed, in one melancholic moment Churchill thought that 'nothing will be decided at the conference at Potsdam. I shall be only half the man until the result of the poll. I shall keep in the background of the conference.'[8] It was true that Potsdam was not a decisive conference simply because many decisions had been taken long before; its function from the British and American point of view was largely to stem the deterioration of relations with Stalin. On the other hand, Churchill had the opportunity to assess the new American President and his Secretary of State, James Byrnes. With 'terrible deeds ... being done' in Eastern

Europe, however, Allied relations with the Soviet Union could not but overshadow the conference.[9]

All the same, the Far Eastern war was discussed at Potsdam and the issue of Hong Kong was an item the Foreign and Colonial Office hoped to raise with President Truman. The Far Eastern department of the Foreign Office suggested that Britain's defence of the colony should rest on three points: Britain had built the colony from nothing; with the abolition of extraterritoriality, British traders needed a secure trading base; and 'Having lost Hong Kong to the enemy, it is a point of national honour for us to recover it, and restore it to its national state of order and prosperity.'[10]

Chinese officials were conspicuous by their absence at Terminal, symbolising the status to which China had descended in inter-Allied diplomacy. T.V. Soong had held exceedingly gloomy talks with the British Ambassador to Moscow, Clark Kerr, in late July. Soong explained how President Truman had only informed the Chinese of the secret Yalta agreement in June, which came as a nasty shock to Chiang Kai-shek. 'He was sore about the terms of the Yalta agreement on the Far East and about China's not having been consulted.' Now the Russians were insisting on even more favourable agreement with the Chinese. Having few cards left to play, the Chinese had to give.[11] Internal events in China also made for reliably pessimistic reading. At the time of Potsdam there had been a recent gold scandal in the finance ministry which stripped the Chinese of any remaining financial credibility. More worrying, perhaps, was America's willingness openly to dictate China's foreign policy.

As if the Yalta agreement were not enough, the Americans had forced the Chinese to drive on the right-hand side of the road. This concealed significant economic implications for US exports into what had been a traditionally (British) left-hand sided country. SOE reported that while most senior Chinese government figures were appreciative of American aid, others were coming to the conclusion that even this was not enough; they hoped that America would openly intervene on behalf of the increasingly desperate Nationalist side. It was a common Nationalist belief 'that Washington would not . . . stand by and see the KMT Government overwhelmed by the [communist] Yenan, or any other regime'.[12] While this view may have been representative of most Americans within China itself, opinion in Washington was undergoing a sea change. The decisive voices in the American capital had wearied of China's begging hand, and there was certainly no stomach for large-scale intervention on the Chinese mainland.

While the Great Powers met at Potsdam, the British were frantically trying to balance any diplomatic agreement over Hong Kong with the threat of physical force.

'Great urgency': the Colonial Office and the reoccupation of Hong Kong

With the news from the Joint Chiefs of Staff of the upcoming Sino-American offensive towards Hong Kong, the Colonial Office attempted to reinstate their emergency commando unit. Even though the War Office believed that it remained highly unlikely that Chinese forces would recapture the Hong Kong–Canton area in the near future, the possibility remained. It was at this juncture, therefore, that the Colonial Office embarked on a two-track policy. In the event of a sudden Japanese capitulation or withdrawal from Hong Kong, a secret emergency commando unit would be prepared and waiting. On the other hand, Operation Carbonado necessitated an approach to Chiang Kai-shek to gain the attachment of British civil affairs personnel to advancing Chinese armies. These plans provided the final framework for British policy to recapture Hong Kong. Before such an approach could occur, however, Oliver Stanley felt that American approval at the highest possible level should be secured, preferably at Potsdam.[13]

Stanley's thinking indicated that from the British point of view, it was the American hand that rocked the Chinese cradle. Moreover, the British had learnt from the Wedemeyer debacle over intelligence coordination in the China theatre. If there was any hope of securing American approval for this sensitive project a direct approach to Washington was held out as the best available option. With an American general who was antipathetic to British claims to Hong Kong, and who also commanded the Chinese armies and advised Chiang Kai-shek, it was clear that Wedemeyer would have to be overruled by the President or his Secretary of State.[14] The issue had reached such a critical state for Oliver Stanley that he wrote one of his final letters as Colonial Secretary to Anthony Eden on the future of Hong Kong. It was the culmination of years of uncertainty, inter-office rivalry and personal involvement. On the 25 July, Stanley wrote to Eden, beginning 'My dear Anthony,'

> I should very much have liked to have a talk with you tomorrow about the matter connected with Hong Kong. It is of great urgency as it may be that the only way for it to be dealt with is that it should

be raised in personal conversation with the Americans, either between you and Byrnes or between the PM and the President. But unfortunately I cannot get back from Bristol until the Friday morning and I hear that you are planning, if all goes well, to leave then for Potsdam. I do hope you can spare a few minutes tomorrow to let George Gater explain the position to you. Orme Sargent is, I think, already aware of it and it has been discussed with your office. Of course you could not give a decision at such short notice, but you might be able to advise me as to the best course to pursue.[15]

Time was against Stanley and the Colonial Office, however. The next day Eden, Stanley and all the other Conservative ministers were swept out of office by a Labour landslide as the general election result was announced. The Colonial Office's position, furthermore, was handicapped by Stanley's absence from Potsdam in the first place. Traditionally, the Colonial Secretary had never gone to any inter-Allied conference (and did not expect to go), but once again it illustrated the Colonial Office's inherent inferiority within the Whitehall structure; it was forever having to rely on the Foreign Office to put its point of view across even if the time had come when both offices agreed over the colony.

Pushed to one side: Hong Kong at Potsdam

For all the concern of the Colonial and Foreign Offices to raise the Hong Kong question at Potsdam, circumstances were not conducive. When the conference officially started on 17 July, European matters dominated proceedings and it quickly became apparent that Churchill's increasing age was beginning to show. Eden noted how

W[inston] was very bad. He had read no brief and was confused and woolly and verbose especially about new council of foreign ministers. We had an anti-Chinese tirade from him. Americans not a little exasperated . . . In fact Alec and I and Bob have never seen W[inston] worse. I tried alone with him and again urged him not to give up our few cards without return. But W[inston] is again under Stalin's spell. He kept repeating 'I like that man' and 'I am full of admiration of Stalin'.[16]

The Foreign Secretary was himself troubled by personal tragedy, even if he did not let it show. On the 20 July he heard that his son, Simon, had been killed in a plane crash in Burma. His diary entry simply recorded that 'life seems so desperately empty'.[17]

The interruption of the conference timetable also created problems for the British delegation. The opportunity to discuss Hong Kong was circumscribed by the timing of Terminal. With the bulk of the work sealed, the conference adjourned on 25 July for a few days to allow Eden, Churchill and Attlee to return home to receive the election result the following day. Few of the Allied delegates expected a socialist victory. Even the Soviet Foreign Secretary (and Stalin's little echo), Molotov, gave his best wishes for Eden's return much to his amusement: 'I must be a very bad Foreign Secretary and give way too often if they want me back!'[18] Churchill's doctor was so confident of a Conservative victory, despite an uneven campaign, that he had left his luggage behind at Potsdam.[19] The verdict of the British people, however, was a resounding endorsement of the Labour Party programme for domestic reform, electing Clement Attlee as the new Prime Minister. Winston Churchill and Anthony Eden would not return to Potsdam for the final part of the conference.

Oliver Stanley's letter to Eden asking him to raise the Hong Kong issue with Truman or Byrnes, therefore, remained an impossibility. With the bulk of the conference questions settled and discussed before the break in the conference, the prime opportunity to broach the subject had been lost. Irrespective of this, however, and more important, was the continuity of British foreign policy despite the change of Prime Ministers.

Changing ship but not course: Clement Attlee as Prime Minister

The announcement of Churchill's dismissal allowed people around the world to speculate that British policy would become more accommodating over colonial issues. The London correspondent of the Chinese paper, *Ta Kung Pao*, now anticipated 'a happy solution of such questions as Hong Kong'.[20] This, though, was a superficial reading of British politics, often from people who had much to gain from such a change. British foreign policy was more than the sum of one man, being deeply ingrained across party lines. Clement Attlee wrote to Churchill in the closing hours of the resumed Potsdam conference:

> We have, of course, been building on the foundation laid by you, and there has been no change of policy . . . My having been present [at Potsdam] from the start was a great advantage, but Bevin picked

up all the points extremely quickly and showed his quality as an experienced negotiator.[21]

Attlee had flown with his Foreign Secretary, Ernest Bevin, for the final stage of Terminal on 28 July. And when the new Prime Minister stated that there had been 'no change of policy', he was, of course, sincere. The new Foreign Secretary had not only been favoured by Eden as his successor, but had actively sought out Eden's advice before he left for Germany to ensure the continuity of Britain's negotiating stance. There had even been the possibility of Anthony Eden accompanying the Labour Party delegation back to Potsdam![22] Churchill, similarly, remained confident that Attlee and Bevin would not upset the British diplomatic applecart, even if the Americans reacted unfavourably towards a socialist Britain. He characterised them as 'strong men', unwilling to 'allow chaos if they can help it'.[23]

The Foreign Office undoubtedly favoured Bevin as their next Foreign Secretary for reasons which Sir Alexander Cadogan soon made apparent. He thought that Bevin 'was the heavyweight of the Cabinet, so if he can be put on the right line, that may be all right'.[24] In other words, if handled the right way, the Foreign Office bureaucrats had the potential to manage their own foreign policy, rather than letting Bevin do it. There was nothing new in this, but it demonstrated once again the capacity of Whitehall to set its own agendas and ensure the continuity of policy from one incumbent to the next. The King, hitherto unmentioned in the narrative, also intervened at this point to dissuade Attlee from appointing the unpopular Hugh Dalton as Foreign Secretary. Dalton made no bones about his dislike for the way the Foreign Office was run, suggesting that there would have been blood on the carpet in King Charles Street had he been appointed. King George VI, however, wrote to Churchill that he had been 'astonished' when Attlee had told him of his inclination to put Dalton at the Foreign Office. He told the new Prime Minister that 'Foreign Affairs could be the most important subject for a very long time and I told him to think again and put Bevin there'.[25]

Despite a successful change of government, it was not completely seamless. The Colonial Office's attempt to raise the issue of Hong Kong at Potsdam with the Americans was one obvious casualty. Although Bob Dixon, Eden's and now Bevin's private secretary, had been sent a brief on Hong Kong for Attlee at Terminal, the issue was not discussed at the conference.[26] Paskin at the Colonial Office found out from the Foreign Office that the matter 'was put to the PM at Terminal, and that he intended to raise it with President Truman. There was, however, no opportunity' to do so. Instead, Bevin had approved the Foreign Office's suggestion that the Americans be approached through the usual diplomatic channels.[27]

While the War Office continued to believe that the Japanese in the Hong Kong vicinity would fight to the last as they did in Okinawa, the Colonial Office remained fearful that the Japanese could still withdraw. British weakness in the Far Eastern war was, in many ways, responsible for bequeathing this drawn out and convoluted predicament. If the Chinese lacked the ability openly to seize the colony from the Japanese, the same could be said of British efforts. Indeed, London was having difficulty mustering a token invasion force never mind a battle group to overwhelm an opposed Japanese defence. The future of Hong Kong was therefore being held in limbo by the inadequacies of the Allied powers in the Far East, and the uncertainties of Japanese strategy.[28]

At an important interdepartmental meeting on 29 July in Whitehall, it was recognised that if the Japanese should evacuate the colony, the most probable outcome was that Chinese communist guerrillas would attempt to enter it. The communist domination of the area surrounding Hong Kong has frequently been overlooked as a factor limiting Chiang Kai-shek's intentions to recapture Hong Kong. With the Chinese civil war re-emerging, there was little chance of communist troops surrendering Hong Kong to their hated enemies, the Nationalist government. For once, the Colonial Office recognised the fractured nature of the Chinese body politic and planned accordingly since Chiang Kai-shek 'would not recognise Chinese communist troops or their ability to take Hong Kong'. Restrained by Sir Horace Seymour's agreement to keep General Wedemeyer informed of any British operations within the China theatre, the Colonial Office looked outside China for an emergency commando unit. On the 3 August Paskin and his colleague, Miss Ruston, saw Brigadier J.M. Calvert of the Special Air Service (SAS) in connection with forming a Hong Kong volunteer company in India. The meeting certainly enthused the Colonial Office, who no doubt thought themselves lucky to obtain the assistance of such highly-trained commandos short of alternative missions now the war in Europe was over. Miss Ruston elaborated, 'this proposal seems to be exactly what we are looking for in connection with our plans' for Hong Kong.[29] If in the meantime, however, a civil affairs agreement with the Americans and Chinese could obtain an attachment of British administrators to Operation Carbonado, 'so much the better'.[30]

Bearing the unbearable: the Japanese surrender

British planning for the recapture of Hong Kong, based on Operation Carbonado was rendered superfluous by the sudden Japanese surrender on 14 August. The unexpected capitulation of Japan was the best news the British could have received; Sino-American operations were left in disarray, leaving the colony wide open for the British fleet.

The Japanese had, over a long period of time, come to realise that their task was fruitless: the Americans had begun systematically to destroy one Japanese city after another using waves of B-29 bombers, decimating remaining fuel reserves. There was not even enough to eat; Japan was isolated from the outside world by the American naval blockade and was slowly starving to death. Her only hope was based on a compromise peace, and the Allies had rejected this out of hand in the Potsdam Declaration, while the supposedly neutral Soviet Union had rebuffed Japanese peace feelers. To the British and Americans it had seemed a question of how long Japanese resistance could continue and what price in blood they would make Allied troops pay. The fanatical Japanese defence of Iwo Jima and Okinawa indicated that the cost would be high. It was this fear, the dread of having to invade Japan itself with enormous casualties, that had encouraged the Americans to seek Stalin's commitment to the Far Eastern war. The combination of Allied forces aligned against them, coupled with the devastation wrought on Japan itself through carpet bombing and the atomic bomb brought Japan to its knees. There remained, however, a strong military faction within the Japanese Government which preferred a fight to the end. The deadlock was broken in the early hours of 10 August by the intervention of the Emperor when he sanctioned the acceptance of the Potsdam Declaration. Japan offered to surrender unconditionally, subject to a guarantee retaining the Imperial House, on that same day.

Although the American State Department was opposed to any conditions imposed by the Japanese, Admiral Leahy and President Truman accepted the Japanese offer to surrender as it stood in conjunction with Britain, Russia and China on 11 August.[31] The Emperor, crushing the military faction's continued opposition to peace, again accepted the Allied peace terms after a lengthy Imperial conference on 14 August. The following day Hirohito broadcast to the Japanese people for the first time, urging them to 'bear the unbearable' in accepting a peace settlement. The Second World War was over, a month short of six whole years. The problems of the peace were just beginning.[32]

The surrender of Hong Kong

The suddenness of the Japanese capitulation on 14 August brought to the surface with a vengeance the fears and recriminations which had plagued Hong Kong during wartime. Although British plans to attach civil affairs planners to Chinese Nationalist forces were defunct as Operation Carbonado was cancelled, London moved swiftly to reassert its sovereignty over the colony. On 11 August the joint Anglo-American Combined Chiefs of Staff were informed that Britain considered 'it of paramount political importance that we should, at the earliest possible moment, send a British Commonwealth force to accept the surrender of the Japanese at Hong Kong'.[33] In response, the American Chiefs of Staff agreed to release the British Pacific Fleet back into British jurisdiction, considering that the future of Hong Kong should be arranged between the Chinese and British. The evidence for America's real sympathies, however, remained in the small print. The American Chiefs of Staff, attempting to distance themselves from London's reoccupation of Hong Kong, pointed out that the release of the British Pacific Fleet should 'not . . . be construed as assistance to or arrangement for their intended purposes'.[34] The British, however, were not interested in the qualifications of American policy, only in the task at hand. The Colonial Office in collaboration with the Admiralty and War Office readied a task force (codenamed Shield) from the British Pacific Fleet to steam forthwith to Hong Kong. Rear Admiral Cecil Harcourt was nominated for this mission, gathering a fleet of some 24 vessels at Subic Bay in the Philippines, including two aircraft carriers, HMS *Indomitable* and HMS *Venerable*. Also assigned to the force were 3000 personnel from an RAF construction unit. Preparations, however, took time and it was not until the 27 August that Admiral Harcourt actually set sail for Hong Kong.[35]

The Hong Kong Planning Unit was also 'militarised' to command British forces and flown out to India from London and Australia in preparation for entry into the colony.[36] Despite their isolation from diplomatic events, the Colonial Office and Foreign Office did not overlook the importance of British POWs in the colony itself. The Foreign Office told the British Embassy in Chungking that it was 'a matter of the greatest importance' that the interned Franklin Gimson, Colonial Secretary of Hong Kong pre-war, be given a message authorising him to administer the colony until Admiral Harcourt arrived.[37] The sense of urgency within Whitehall was contagious. Trepidation at Chinese designs on Hong Kong would only be exorcised when the Union Jack was firmly planted in the colony once again.

The British expectation that the Chinese would attempt to manipulate the surrender of the colony to their own advantage was the sum of all fears. After the problems that the Chinese had caused the British during the war, little trust in Chiang Kai-shek's 'honour' remained. Indeed, in June 1942 Chinese troops had advanced into northern Burma, pulled down boundary markers and announced that the British had left and they were taking over the country. When the Japanese eventually advanced into this isolated region in late 1943, the Chinese simply retreated and made no attempt to engage the enemy. The suspicion was indelibly left on British minds that China had advanced into Burma simply to acquire British territory.[38] The same course of events, it was speculated, threatened to occur with Hong Kong.

Chinese threats, however, would remain only that. When Japan surrendered, the official British history noted that the 39 Chinese divisions Wedemeyer required to take Hong Kong were still in training:

> Only sixteen divisions . . . had had American training and were fully equipped; of the remaining twenty-three, none were fully equipped . . . No officers or NCO's had yet passed through the training school opened by Wedemeyer in the summer of 1945, and the administrative arrangements for supplying the thirty-nine divisions were far from complete.

The Chinese army in general, moreover, despite the tireless efforts of Generals Stilwell and Wedemeyer, was still an empty shell:

> Most of the other 250 to 290 Chinese Nationalist divisions were under strength, untrained, under-nourished and ill-equipped. Apart from the sixteen divisions from Burma and Yunnan, the fighting value of Chiang Kai-shek's armies at the end of the war with Japan were thus negligible.

The reality of Chiang Kai-shek's military weakness was now completely revealed. Even General Wedemeyer's optimism wavered when he was faced with the curtailment of lend-lease supplies at the end of the war. He urgently telexed Washington that America could not turn her back on Chiang at this critical stage of the war. The general admitted that American-trained Chinese forces were still woefully unprepared to maintain order across China; he wanted large amounts of US aid and the commitment of American troops to key Chinese ports. It was the usual request to be expected from Chiang Kai-shek: more aid, more money, more troops; everything but his own commitment to their useful application. The replies Wedemeyer received from Washington were telling: while America would help Chiang's attempts to reoccupy the country, he was instructed on 10 August that the United States would not support Chiang in any civil war. Furthermore, on 22 August Wedemeyer was ordered to suspend all training of Chinese troops, including the elaborate training organisations built up by the Americans in China. Washington was effectively pulling the plug on the Nationalist regime.[39]

Chiang Kai-shek and the surrender of the colony

With the end of the Pacific war, the Generalissimo lost his main argument for sustained American support. Even the State Department, the pre-eminent lobbyer of Chinese interests in Washington, turned its back on China, distracted with the occupation of Japan. Dunn of the State Department, told General Lincoln in a telephone conversation that as far as he was concerned America was 'not a party to' the problem of Hong Kong any longer, regardless of the British 'charging about the place raising the flag'.[40] With so much bad news flowing in the Nationalists' direction it was clear to British diplomats in Chungking that all the ingredients for an unholy row with Chiang were brewing. Wallinger at the embassy remained deeply concerned that Britain should tread gently on the surrender of Hong Kong, making sure that nothing underhand was done which could inflame American and Chinese opinion at this sensitive time. He informed London that the 'American staff here have been frank with us and it would be good policy to reciprocate'.[41] Nonetheless, on that same day, the embassy received a British ultimatum for Chiang Kai-shek which informed him that the London authorities were going to reoccupy and restore their administration to Hong Kong. This was the beginning of two weeks of protracted and emotional wrangling over the surrender of the colony.

In response to the British ultimatum, the Chinese acting Minister of Foreign Affairs told Sir Horace Seymour that the Chinese Government was deeply unhappy with such a unilateral move. He explained that while the Chinese had no territorial ambitions towards Hong Kong, they regarded the British announcement as 'rather high-handed'. The Chinese argued that it was they who should accept the surrender as the colony was in the China theatre, and therefore technically under the jurisdiction of the Generalissimo. Once again Ambassador Seymour was placed in a delicate situation, and attempted to explain Chiang's actions by reference to loss of 'face', a term frequently synonymous with allowing the Chinese to get whatever they wanted.

Ernest Bevin, the Foreign Secretary, however, rejected out of hand any attempt to conciliate the Chinese, with full Cabinet approval. He held that Hong Kong was British territory and had nothing to do with the Chinese. If Chungking was so concerned with the question of face, then they could have a representative present at the surrender, but nothing else.[42] While Bevin was patently subscribing to the established Foreign Office view on the colony, the more independently-minded Clement Attlee was kept in line by the new Colonial Secretary, George Hall, who reminded him of his own personal commitment in parliament to resume British authority.[43] Alan Brooke, the British Chief of Staff, also resisted the idea of taking the surrender on behalf of the Chinese because it 'would weaken our position in any subsequent negotiations [over Hong Kong] which might take place'.[44] The strong British reaction to the surrender issue was precipitated by the perception that the Chinese (with American support) remained untrustworthy.

It was into this atmosphere that Colonel Ride in China telexed London detailing American plans for a 'Humanitarian Reconnaissance Mission' to Hong Kong. He had been informed by the Americans that they intended to fly two planes into Hong Kong prior to the official surrender, ostensibly to help POWs interned in the colony.[45] Considering that the majority of prisoners in the Hong Kong camp were British, however, Ride ascribed sinister motives to the American plan, especially after they declined his offer to obtain a RAF Halifax plane from India. He warned London that 'we have reason to believe that Americans may fly in Chinese officials to accept formal surrender'. To forestall them, Ride advocated implementing the Colonial Office–SOE emergency operation to seize the colony using the BAAG, codenamed Operation Tidings. With this news, pandemonium broke out in London.[46]

Ride's previous respect for decorum with Chinese and American forces during July quickly dissipated as he became increasingly convinced that neither would help Britain reoccupy Hong Kong. Instead, Ride now swung to the opposite extreme and wanted to disregard Allied opinion altogether. He openly advocated that the British pursue the (potentially explosive) option of fighting their way into the colony before the Chinese and Americans arrived. The Foreign Office, however, shrank from such a provocative action. With a British task force on the way they were not prepared to countenance such a dangerous gamble. From their point of view Britain's disagreement with Chiang was diplomatic and not military because the Nationalists lacked the resources to capture the colony. As a precaution, however, Ride had already been ordered on 13 August to accompany any Chinese or American force that went into Hong Kong before the fleet arrived.[47] Faced with the BAAG's increasing tendency to act like a loose cannon, Colonel Ride was ordered by Carton de Wiart not to enter Hong Kong 'with a show of force' under any circumstances.[48] De Wiart's liaison officer reiterated this warning, threatening the BAAG that if they did not join the American mission into Hong Kong, other British servicemen would be found who would go.[49] At the last Ride backed down and agreed to participate in the American mission, securing a commitment that prior approval from the Japanese in the colony would be obtained for any landings there. The decision in London, however, to pursue a strong diplomatic line without escalating the military side infuriated SOE troops in China.

An SOE agent at the important Chinese supply base of Kunming characterised Wedemeyer's 'humanitarian mission' to the colony as 'presumably [inspired] to make headlines in the American papers, as there seems no other purpose to their crazy scheme'. Moreover,

This still leaves [a] British full colonel under [the] direction of [an] American captain on British soil. [The] effect on POWs will be disastrous as they have been pinning all hopes on [the] BAAG for years and will not take kindly to wearing American uniforms. Meanwhile we vomit. Repeat, vomit with disgust and pray for further details.[50]

The incident seemed an appropriate finale to all the backbiting and jealousies which had riven the Far Eastern theatre. But it should be remembered that while there were disagreements between British forces in China, partly exacerbated by their distance from London, Whitehall's united front towards Hong Kong was far removed from the schisms of previous years. The Cabinet had unanimously agreed that only Britain would take the surrender and that Chiang Kai-shek would be excluded. His only concession would be a Chinese observer at the signing ceremony. London had also promptly dispatched a significant task force for the colony as a sign of her commitment to retake Hong Kong. H.V. Kitson, a councillor at the Chungking Embassy, now transferred to the Foreign Office, believed that the arrival of these British forces in the colony would be pivotal, and present the Chinese leader with a 'fait accompli'. It would put Britain 'in a stronger position to resist Chiang

Kai-shek's desire to send a representative to accept the surrender'.[51] Unfortunately, however, Admiral Harcourt's task force was delayed in Subic Bay by logistical problems, pushing back the estimated date for their arrival in Hong Kong. While this lag gave Chiang time to elaborate on his argument as to why the surrender should be made to him, the British fretted and assertively counter-argued, destroying the last remnants of trust in Sino-British relations.

The growing estrangement between China and Britain was increasingly hard to disguise to the outside world. As stories began to circulate of a race to recover Hong Kong, the Dominions Office was forced to issue a message playing down the issue. On 18 August, the gravity of the situation left the British Prime Minister no choice but to write to President Truman and ask for his cooperation. The Supreme Allied Commander of the Pacific Theatre was an American, General MacArthur, and his interpretation of surrender directives remained critical. 'Order no. 1', the Japanese surrender order, was far from clear. If Chiang was not prepared to listen to the British, then perhaps he would listen to his erstwhile ally, America. Clement Attlee told Truman, that 'we cannot accept any interpretation of General Order no. 1 as meaning that Hong Kong, which is British territory, is included in the expression "within China"'. Therefore, he asked that MacArthur be told to order the Japanese in Hong Kong to surrender only to the British in case there was any confusion over the matter.[52] Anxious not to delay the surrender any further and well aware of British feelings, President Truman replied on 19 August agreeing to Attlee's position; the colony was to be removed from the China theatre for surrender purposes. MacArthur would arrange the surrender of Hong Kong to the British, 'providing full military co-ordination is effected beforehand by the British with the Generalissimo'.[53] This last caveat caused the British endless problems because MacArthur and other American commanders were unsympathetic to British claims, and would not therefore pressurise Chiang Kai-shek. British assurances to General Wedemeyer that they would cooperate with Chiang were greeted with scepticism in Washington. The American Chiefs of Staff argued that before Wedemeyer could 'give the all-clear to MacArthur he must have it first hand from the Generalissimo that the latter is satisfied' with arrangements.[54]

American policy increasingly found itself captive to its own unrealistic and contradictory aims. While they were acutely aware of their own failure to continue propping up the Nationalist regime, the Americans had also sanctioned the release of British naval vessels which had made up the British Hong Kong task force. There was a certain amount of guilt motivating American actions for having let Chiang down. In an effort to exonerate themselves in American and Chinese eyes, Washington attempted to extract guarantees of British assistance to Chiang when the Americans would offer none. They advocated that the Generalissimo be given full access to Hong Kong's facilities to secure his reoccupation of southern China, including the port itself. Such a policy offered to save Chinese face (and American), without the employment of any American troops.[55] Whichever way one looked at it, though, the British were back to square one as regarded effecting the official surrender of the colony. With America's tacit acquiescence the Generalissimo was even less willing to compromise his perceived authority to settle the question. An impasse had been reached, with the villain clearly defined from London's point of view. A.L. Scott, back at the Foreign Office, felt 'sure we have the Americans to thank for Chiang Kai-shek's obstinacy'.[56]

Retrospectively, however, the British held a relatively strong hand on the Hong Kong issue compared to the war years, irrespective of the local situation in the colony. Importantly, American diplomatic interference was contained. Although Ambassador Hurley tried to lobby President Truman on Chiang's behalf, the President pursued a much more circumspect policy than Roosevelt had. With the British acting so vigorously, Truman could only attempt to broker a compromise without the threat of arms. He wrote: 'Much as I deplored this friction between two of our Allies, there seemed little else that could be done by us.'[57] The prevarication behind American policy was recognised by British diplomats in America as 'a growing willingness to acquiesce in our return to Hong Kong'. In its weekly political summary, the Washington Embassy reported that the death of FDR had tempered American anti-colonialism, believing that 'the present administration feels less strongly about changing the status of Hong Kong and other Imperial possessions than President Roosevelt is alleged to have done'. Moreover, 'America's acquisitive mood towards the Pacific in any case undercuts much of their earlier criticism'.[58] While the Americans sympathised with the Chinese, Washington was forced to recognise the established rights of the matter which underpinned American foreign policy. The American Joint Chiefs of Staff had also agreed to treat the issue pragmatically, as a military concern only. In a June 1945 paper, they stated that 'Hong Kong is legally a British Crown Colony' which the 'United States should avoid involving itself in'.[59]

Soviet actions in Manchuria, furthermore, provided a useful justification for Britain's retention of the colony. On the day of Japan's decision to end the Pacific war, Kitson at the Foreign Office bluntly stated that 'the future Russian position in Manchuria will . . . initially affect our policy in regard to Hong Kong'.[60] When General Wedemeyer suggested to the British that their high-handedness over the colony set 'a bad example to the Russians',[61] the Foreign Office reacted indifferently. For all the heartache over the surrender, however, London need not have worried itself unduly. Overlooked and underrated, the bedraggled and starved POWs in the colony took it upon themselves, under the leadership of Franklin Gimson, to seize the colony and resurrect British rule. Through their own courage, the survivors of three and a half years of Japanese deprivation and hardship had solved the immediate Hong Kong question.

The man of the hour: Franklin Gimson

Franklin Gimson had an unfortunate sense of timing. In 1941 he arrived in Hong Kong from Ceylon just in time to be captured by the Japanese and spent the next few years as a Japanese POW. Unperturbed by his incarceration, however, Gimson insisted on continuing the job he had been sent to the colony to do in the first place: administering British interests. In this respect he was faced with several difficulties, some of his own making. Initially he had been separated from the other prisoners, and the other internees had done what all Englishmen do in adversity; they had formed a committee. When he was released back into the main British civilian prisoner camp at Stanley in mid-1942, he therefore had to reassert his authority among disillusioned internees. In pursuit of this goal he was also hampered by an overbearing manner which many found hard to stomach; understandably, perhaps, when such arrogance and confidence had been Britain's undoing in the defence of the colony. Nevertheless, always willing to follow someone who gave the impression that they knew where they were going, the other prisoners soon allowed Gimson control of the prisoners' committee.

Once established as the leading POW representative in the camp, Gimson committed one act which made him very unpopular in the camp but would have lasting repercussions for British authority in Hong Kong: he denied a demand for civilian repatriation inside the camp. As far as he was concerned, 'A colony was to me British territory as much as Britain itself. Rightly or wrongly, I agreed that internees as British subjects resident in British territory would not be entitled to repatriation.' This action meant that when the Japanese surrendered, senior British administrators would be in situ to take control of the colony. Meanwhile, Gimson's committee planned for a British takeover in the event of a Japanese evacuation. As it happened, however, the nature of the surrender was not foreseen by the prisoners and they did not have to fill a power vacuum left by their captors. Instead, with Hirohito's surrender order the Japanese soldiers remained in Hong Kong and were reluctant to let their prisoners become their new masters.[62]

Ignorant of the diplomatic firestorm developing over the small colony, and of London's instructions for him to resume control (which were being delivered by hand),[63] Gimson's sense of imperial mission remained indomitable. He took it upon himself to confront the Japanese with the changed situation and asked for the control of Hong Kong to be handed over to the British. The Japanese, however, were initially uncooperative. They

> stated that the future of Hong Kong was not decided. There was no certainty it would continue to be British. I replied that the view was merely an expression of opinion which I was not concerned [sic]. I intended to carry out those duties to which I had been appointed by HM's Government. I required accommodation for myself and for my officers, and also the use of the wireless station.

Faced with such logic, the Japanese agreed. Ignoring American leaflets which told the prisoners to remain in the camp, a nucleus under Gimson left for the centre of Hong Kong to resuscitate British rule. The journey there was a memorable one for the prisoners who had suffered years of starvation and humiliation.

> This journey more than any other incident of this momentous period filled our hearts with more emotion than we had previously experienced and made us appreciate to the full the truly providential survival after enduring the privations of the Japanese regime. Our route took us through the fishing village of Aberdeen and my most vivid memory of it is the sight of the faces of the Chinese there, who at the noise of the approach of the bus, cast their eyes down to avoid possibly meeting the glances of its Japanese occupants. The faces were slowly raised and beaming smiles appeared in answer to ours as our identity was recognised.

Their part in the retention of Hong Kong, however, was not yet over. While many internees left to reconstruct the shattered remnants of their businesses, Gimson broadcast to London and the colony, informing them of Britain's resumed administration. He also had to contend with returning Japanese morale as the British awaited Admiral Harcourt's arrival. In this respect, Colonel Ride's insistence that the American mission from China should first receive Japanese authorisation appears well founded. Initially, the Japanese refused any landing of Allied planes on the grounds that Kai Tak airport was 'under water'. After Gimson pointed out that there had been no rain for three weeks, the Japanese withdrew this argument. Eventually, he had to threaten the Japanese in order to allow the planes to land and the situation remained tense.[64] Ride, who accompanied the Americans into the colony, reported how the younger Japanese officers were 'arrogant and menacing', forcing the Allies to return post-haste to Kunming.[65] Until Admiral Harcourt arrived, no further attempts were made to enter the colony by the Americans. Franklin Gimson had presented Chiang Kai-shek with the Foreign Office's much hoped for fait accompli.

'Never have I seen him so moved as he was today': Chiang is forced to compromise

With events in the colony concealed from the outside world, the British authorities continued in their attempt to force Chiang Kai-shek to accede to the surrender of Hong Kong on their terms. On 20 August, Ernest Bevin made his first major foreign policy speech in the House of Commons to the general approval of the British press. In his broad analysis of the diplomatic problems facing Britain he restated that there would be no change in the status of Hong Kong. The consensus driving British policy was reinforced by Anthony Eden's parliamentary reply for the Conservative Party which 'endorsed what Mr Bevin said about Hong Kong. The position he had taken up was just and fair and was one which everybody in the country would wish to uphold.'[66] Winston Churchill's near obsessive interest in the colony, moreover, remained. In a parliamentary question he asked Clement Attlee whether or not he was committed to retaining Britain's position in the colony. The new Prime Minister replied,

Yes, Sir. As stated by the Foreign Secretary on Monday, arrangements are being made for the Japanese surrender of Hong Kong to be accepted by the British Force Commander. Plans for re-establishing British administration in the colony are fully prepared.

Churchill, expressing his contentment at this answer, continued, reminding Attlee of Churchill's numerous wartime commitments to the integrity of British colonies in the Far East. The Prime Minister answered that he had a very 'full recollection of those statements and I will bear them in mind'.[67] The unanimity underlying British policy, however, remained irrelevant to Chiang Kai-shek. He acted as if Britain's attitude over the surrender of the colony was anything but fair and was based on opportunism rather than ideological commitment. Believing that he had nothing to lose from continuing obstinacy, the Generalissimo held out for British concessions.

The symbolic importance of the colony was clear to Chiang but he attempted to dampen speculation that China was casting a covetous eye in its direction. He told his Nationalist Party on 24 August that he would not send Chinese troops into Hong Kong because it would 'cause misunderstanding' between Allies. He continued:

> I now declare to the nation and the world at large that the status of Hong Kong which is based on treaties, will not be changed without going through negotiations with Britain. China will only resort to diplomatic means to restore concessions and leased territories including Kowloon from other powers.[68]

Considering the state of the Chinese army, these were empty words as Chiang well knew. The main difficulty for Chiang, though, was that he appeared to show no comprehension of British policymaking. The British interpreted Chiang Kai-shek's speech to mean that he was attempting to obtain Hong Kong through manipulation of the surrender negotiations. With the Americans he always stalled for time, and usually secured a favourable compromise for himself. (That he frequently squandered these advantages was neither here nor there.) Now dealing with the British, Chiang transferred these tactics without modification. What he seemed incapable of understanding was that the British felt very strongly about the Hong Kong issue as a matter of principle, something he was not used to seeing in the Americans. The American Ambassador to London talked to Sterndale Bennett of the Foreign Office and reported to Washington, 'that for prestige reasons, if for no other, there could be no question of [the] British not returning and resuming sovereignty'.[69]

With newspaper reports from Chungking stating that the Chinese military were actually negotiating the surrender of Hong Kong, including a provision for its occupation by Chinese forces, Chiang's protestations were unlikely to be believed.[70] Indeed, the more he protested the innocence of Chinese claims, the more the British worried. The Foreign Office telexed Seymour in Chungking: 'We feel that Chiang Kai-shek's present attitude is unreasonable and out of keeping with his recent statesmanlike pronouncement about Hong Kong in his statement of August 24'.[71]

The continuing uncertainty over the surrender highlighted the dynamics of British policy and the strains within the Whitehall bureaucracy. As negotiations dragged on, certain sections on the British side came to see their differences with Chiang as semantic and thus unimportant. Sir Horace Seymour, true to past experiences, attempted to temper the hard-line approach coming from the Colonial and Foreign Offices. Under the guidance of Sterndale Bennett and Gerard Gent, British policy held firmly to the belief that under no circumstances could London accept the surrender of Hong Kong under delegation from Chiang Kai-shek. Instead, the surrender would remain wholly British with a Chinese and an American witness if they so wished.

It was apparent that Seymour was uncomfortable in having to justify a policy with which he did not wholeheartedly agree, especially since he had to communicate the bad news directly to the Chinese authorities. He argued that London should compromise and accept the surrender from Chiang for what the ambassador saw as only a question of saving Chiang's face: 'I cannot believe that the Chinese will accept a solution under which their representative is to sign any surrender document merely as a witness, and so far as I can judge here, they would have American support in resisting this proposal.'[72] General Ismay, the Prime Minister's representative to the Chiefs of Staff, also suggested that such a compromise, 'although not entirely satisfactory, was from the military point of view, acceptable', enabling Britain 'to tidy up once and for all a situation which had become extremely involved'.[73] No doubt influenced by his experienced colleague Sir Horace Seymour, Carton de Wiart, now Attlee's personal representative to Chiang Kai-shek, also expressed disquiet with British diplomacy. He attempted a further compromise, suggesting two surrenders: a territorial one for Britain, and a military one for Chiang as commander of the China theatre. This, however, was quickly struck down by London as unrealistic.[74] During the entire surrender period, Whitehall dominated policy decisions and refused to allow itself to be distracted by British diplomats on the ground. They resisted the temptation for the dog to be wagged by its tail.

The British diplomats in Chungking were finding it increasingly difficult to empathise with British policy because they did not consider that Chiang Kai-shek posed any threat to the sovereignty of Hong Kong. They saw the argument as one of procedure, and not importance.

During an interview with the Generalissimo, Carton de Wiart noted that Chiang was 'most insistent that I study the text of his speech made on 24th August', and he never once pretended that Hong Kong was part of China. Moreover, de Wiart argued that: 'Had we been able to contribute to the capture of Hong Kong I feel we might have had some reason to object, but unfortunately we have done nothing and had the war lasted a few weeks longer the colony would undoubtedly have been liberated by Chinese forces.' This, of course, was nonsense as we have already seen. It should be remembered that de Wiart also had another agenda. As a bitter anti-communist, he believed that Britain's intransigent attitude would humiliate the Nationalists so much that it would score a major propaganda victory for the communists.[75] Regardless, the Foreign Office, with strong Colonial Office support, remained unmoved.[76]

When Carton de Wiart saw Chiang again on 27 August, there was no disguising the seriousness of the situation. It must have been clear to the Chinese leader that events were moving against him. In an emotional meeting, the Generalissimo deplored British actions which he said threatened to undermine Sino-British relations. De Wiart described how during the many meetings he had had with Chiang, 'he has always been entirely frank and ingenuous but never have I seen him so moved as he was today'. Seymour corroborated this opinion, arguing that the controversy would hamper the re-establishment of British interests in China itself.[77]

The solution to the dilemma, when it came at last, was a unilateral decision by the British to sign the surrender equally on behalf of Chiang Kai-shek as commander in chief of the China theatre. London instructed Harcourt to sign for Britain and Chiang. Given little alternative, Chiang Kai-shek agreed to nominate an American and a Chinese witness to attend the ceremony. Previously, the Chinese Vice-Minister for Foreign Affairs, had confided to Seymour that Chiang would not compromise, and so if Britain would not either, then she ought to leave the matter be and go ahead with the surrender arrangements as planned.[78] Unable to allow the negotiations to collapse without one more try, however, the Prime Minister and Foreign Secretary argued that Britain must be prepared for one last concession to save Chiang's face. After considerable discussion late into the night at the Foreign Office, Gerard Gent persuaded Attlee and Bevin to split the surrender, with Harcourt signing for the British, and a British military representative in China signing for Chiang.[79] When this was telexed to the Chinese leader, however, he once again refused. Fed up with the impasse, the British decided to sign on behalf of Chiang Kai-shek, approval or no approval. At the barrel of a gun, the Generalissimo agreed.[80] The date was 31 August, two weeks after the initial Japanese capitulation.

Admiral Harcourt arrives in Hong Kong

While London and Chungking locked horns over the terms of Hong Kong's surrender, Admiral Harcourt's task force had arrived off the colony on 29 August. Harcourt sent a message to the Japanese informing them that a British aircraft would land at Kai Tak at a specific time and fly a Japanese envoy back to HMS *Indomitable* to arrange for Britain's entry into the harbour. True to form, however, events did not go smoothly. Once again it was the intervention of Franklin Gimson which came at the crucial moment. Gimson's colleagues had spotted the British fleet on the horizon and so Gimson asked the Japanese if any messages had been received from the boats. The Japanese replied that they had but they were unable to negotiate since they had no orders to that effect. It was at this point that Gimson insisted that the Japanese should reply affirmatively to the British radio message, allowing the British plane to land. The Japanese eventually agreed and a plane was landed and departed back to the fleet with a Japanese envoy and British naval Commander D.H.S. Craven. After having received detailed information from the Japanese envoy as to the location of the (American) magnetic minefields in the harbour, he was flown back to Kai Tak with instructions for the entry of the British fleet the next day. Unfortunately, this scheme also went awry. As the weather closed in, the plane got lost and crashed in the New Territories, being captured by Chinese communist guerrillas who wanted to slit the Japanese officer's throat. After talking the guerrillas out of this course of action, the British pilot with his Japanese prisoner had to wait until the next day to be rescued.

Unable to delay, Harcourt sent Craven back to Kai Tak the following day with instructions for the Japanese on his entry into Hong Kong later that day. After moving all the Japanese into the dockyard area, the British dispatched naval ratings and Marine landing parties into the centre of the colony around midday. Although the situation remained tense, most of the Japanese remained calm.[81] As Harcourt's new flagship, *Swiftsure*, entered the harbour, Gimson

could not suppress fears that some Japanese fanatics might react to the landing of British forces. In fact, amidst the intense explosion of Chinese firecrackers, I thought I detected an ominous crackle which seemed to describe machine gun fire. However, the noise was merely that of precautionary bursts fired into cavities at the naval base which might have harboured Japanese intent on a final display of opposition before acknowledging defeat.[82]

The only drama, however, came when Hellfire planes from *Indomitable* spotted Japanese suicide speedboats leaving Picnic Bay on Lamma island in the direction of the British fleet. With the bombing of the leading vessels, the remaining hundred-odd boats scattered and were beached or returned to harbour.[83]

Once established on the mainland, Harcourt quickly restored order to the war damaged and looted colony although many Chinese civilians took the opportunity to exact revenge on Japanese war criminals. Japanese using public transport were repeatedly attacked, some with hammers, while the Japanese executioner, caught in disguise, 'came to an untimely end'.[84] His name was Takiyawa and he was a notorious sadist. His fate was, perhaps, appropriate: 'After the Japanese surrender he was seized, half-drowned, then lynched by a Chinese mob before being hanged, still alive, from the Star Ferry terminal and left to rot.'[85] Harcourt also had the delicate task of managing Gimson's administration. Although tired and ill, Gimson wanted to continue the administration, subject to reinforcements from the Hong Kong Planning Unit. Perhaps he saw it as his golden opportunity to become governor of the colony. Whatever the truth of the matter, London was insistent that the POWs should be relieved for a well-deserved rest. With the arrival of David MacDougall and his staff on 7 September, a British military administration was set up with the unenviable task of tackling the postwar problems of the colony.[86] There remained one last episode to complete Britain's return to Hong Kong: the local surrender of the colony.

Securing the surrender of the colony on their terms, the British decided they could act with a degree of magnanimity towards the Chinese over the date for the signing of the surrender document. Sterndale Bennett suggested that 'on general grounds and for the particular reasons connected with our commercial interests in China itself', it was desirable to sign the Japanese surrender of Hong Kong after the surrender in China, which was planned to take place at Nanking. Even so, the Foreign Office remained suspicious in victory of Chinese aims. Sterndale Bennett thought that:

> It is possible that Chiang Kai-shek's attitude over the surrender in Hong Kong is not merely a question of immediate prestige, but is

designed to give the Generalissimo a basis for maintaining after the surrender in Hong Kong, that he must continue to direct and supervise the implementation of that surrender. It is conceivable that the surrender document at Nanking may contain provisions relating to Hong Kong.[87]

On this basis, the British military commander in China, General Hayes, who was attending the Nanking surrender, was warned to check for any surreptitious claim to Hong Kong inserted by the Chinese before he signed! Similar fears also lay behind Britain's defiant refusal to sign a written agreement with the Chinese for the transhipment of their troops through the colony. While London was happy to help with the transport of Chinese soldiers to northern China to fight the communists, Britain would stipulate the conditions as she saw fit.[88]

Agreeing to delay the Hong Kong surrender until after the Nanking ceremony, however, proved once again a frustrating experience for the British. The Chinese surrender was continually postponed by what Harcourt characterised as 'Chinese incompetence'. Fed up with this state of affairs, he pressed London to sign at will but was asked not to sign without approval. After keeping his American and Chinese representatives as guests for a whole week, Admiral Harcourt at long last signed the surrender of Hong Kong on 16 September: 'In the evening there was a searchlight and fireworks display by the Fleet which was excellent and greatly delighted the local population.'[89] Hong Kong was again a British colony.

Conclusion

> The Colonial Empire is our fifth, and will be our last. This is the last chance that the British will ever have of doing something for which, with all their blunders and even crimes, they have shown a peculiar genius.[1]
>
> Sir George Moss, 1944

Winston Churchill was once overheard to have said that 'there is only one thing worse than fighting with Allies, and that is fighting without them'.[2] This sentiment could easily be applied to Britain's attempt to recover her colony of Hong Kong during the Second World War. At times it seemed as if Japan's occupation of Hong Kong was incidental to Britain recapturing it at all. Opposition to London's continued sovereignty over Hong Kong from her Allies, China and America, was vociferous and constant. While China had a strong claim to the colony, however, she lacked the strength to extinguish Britain's legal rights to return. Instead, what little influence Chiang Kai-shek's government had over London was derived from her dependency on American sponsorship.

The British understood that China was unlikely to act independently of America. Anthony Eden told Lord Halifax in August 1944, that 'China would be so dependent on the other Great Powers that she would not be likely to pursue any very independent policy . . . in matters affecting international peace and security.'[3] The Sino-American alliance never lived up to the expectations of either the Chinese or Americans. Washington's dreams and Chiang Kai-shek's grabbing hand ensured that it was a temporary marriage of misconceptions. Its strength lay in its propaganda value not in its reality.

In the end, however, British interests in Hong Kong were best defended by Chiang Kai-shek's own incompetence rather than the relentless imperial dogmatism of Winston Churchill. Always preferring to do more of the 'issimoing' than the 'generalling', Chiang Kai-shek failed to deliver the China that Washington expected. With American despondency in the China theatre came the momentum to shift the centre of gravity of the Far Eastern war into the Pacific. As American support ebbed away, China's opportunity to reconquer the colony disappeared; it was patently obvious that Chiang could not recapture Nanking, never mind Hong Kong, without US troops. Chiang's reckless behaviour, however, was not uncharacteristic of the corrupt Nationalist dictatorship which would do little to help itself. While T.V. Soong was having Kansas steaks flown into Chungking, Chinese soldiers were dying in their bedrolls from neglect, only a mile away.[4]

America's shift from a regional to a global strategy towards the end of the war also greatly undermined Washington's pressure on Britain to retrocede Hong Kong. By 1944 American efforts to exclude Britain from the Far East and elevate China to a regional power had faltered while Soviet power grew inexorably. It was in such circumstances that President Roosevelt attempted to conciliate Stalin's appetite for Soviet expansion, even at the expense of facilitating Britain's return to Hong Kong. As he told Admiral Leahy when he accepted Russian control of the Chinese port, Dairen: 'Well, Bill, I can't help it.'[5] Porter and Stockwell have described the tempering of America's anti-colonial ambitions as a reaction to the complexities of world problems:

It is true that US anti-imperialism grew more muted as the war proceeded but British resistance and Colonial Office polemic were less influential in curbing the enthusiasm of Americans for Afro-Asian independence than the Americans' own exercise of world power and their anticipation of the profits of free-trade imperialism after the war.[6]

Roosevelt's attempt to demolish the British Empire was at best confused, and at worst, breathtakingly hypocritical. At Tehran he had talked of a post-war world without the French and British empires. Stalin's empire was consciously excluded by the President, and thus unthreatened by any scheme which America and Russia could agree.[7] Nor should we forget America's own colonial empire which in 1941 stretched from the Caribbean, through Latin America and across the Pacific. Republican President William McKinley told a Boston audience in 1899 that control of the Philippines, Cuba and Puerto Rico was a 'great trust' that America carried 'under the providence of God and in the name of human progress and civilisation'. The parallels with British imperial sentiment were striking, but something that few Americans would admit to during the Second World War. Seemingly unable to look at themselves in the mirror, Americans often found it easier to reprove the British for what they denied in themselves.[8]

Britain's defence of her colony, however, rested on much more than the divisions and contradictions of her Allies. Without the determination of British personnel to rebuild her lost Empire, there would never have been a question mark hanging over Hong Kong during the war. Driven by a consensus which saw Empire inextricably linked to Britain's position as a Great Power, British policymakers remained unrepentant imperialists. Criticism of Britain's position in the Far East by America and China was counter-productive and only served to reinforce Britain's belief in Empire. Led by Winston Churchill, the London government set its face against any peace settlement which would prejudice their Far Eastern interests.

It is misleading, though, to maintain that Churchill was instrumental in forcing Britain's return to Hong Kong; this is the interpretation that he himself would like us to accept and something the legacy of his written records makes hard to escape. Churchill said of one of his books: 'This is not history, this is my case.'[9] Even a revisionist interpretation of the Churchill myth by Clive Ponting puts the Prime Minister centre stage in resisting colonial change. Ponting claims that: 'In order to strengthen opposition to change he insisted on appointing men of similar views to his own as Colonial Secretary – for example Lord Lloyd in 1940 and Oliver Stanley, who held the post from November 1942 until the end of the war.'[10] This is to overestimate the importance of Winston Churchill to British foreign policy. Oliver Stanley's appointment was more of a carefully crafted political appeasement than a deliberate attempt to prevent imperial reform. The truth was that the vast majority of British servicemen, civil servants and politicians believed in the sanctity of the Empire, and opposed the abandonment of British territory overseas. Foreign policy could not be set by one man, and had personnel in SOE, the Colonial Office or the Foreign Office not believed in Britain's right to return to Hong Kong, Churchill's sentiments would have been shown to be empty. These were the people who turned British thought into action. Even a man like Clement Attlee, behind the posturing of international socialism, firmly believed in the British Empire; it was only over its purpose that he dissented.

It could also be argued that Churchill's vituperative outpourings actually retarded London's attempt to defend British interests. Roosevelt's tendency to see the world in idealistic (and simplistic) terms was exacerbated by Churchill's reactionary stance and disguised the Prime Minister's own ambivalence towards Anglo-American cooperation. In a black moment, Anthony Eden's private secretary wrote: 'If allowed to, [Churchill] will win the war and lose us the peace as certain as certain.'[11] That Churchill could not interfere with British colonial policy any more than he did, due to other policy commitments, was perhaps a blessing in disguise.

The fact that Hong Kong's future became such a burning issue during wartime can partly be blamed on the Prime Minister's emotional handling of the situation. It need not have been: a calmer and more measured approach to this tiny island colony would not have endangered British sovereignty, as the more subdued determination of the Foreign Office and Colonial Office showed. G.V. Kitson at the Foreign Office thought 'that as regards such politically explosive issues as Hong Kong, the Burma frontier and Tibet, it is much better to let sleeping dogs lie. "Qu'on excuse, n'accuse"!' [If we excuse them, they won't blame us.][12] A sensible person does not pick arguments that endanger what is most important to him. Fighting over Hong Kong hurt Anglo-American cooperation while doing little to secure the integrity of the British Empire, the two cornerstones of British policy. Churchill should have admitted that the Americans could not have dismantled the Empire without British acquiescence. To have done so, however, would have been to deflate his own importance within the British Government and popular imagination; something he was never keen to do. Lady Churchill told Churchill's doctor:

> Winston has always seen things in blinkers... He sees nothing outside that beam. You probably don't realise... that he knows nothing of the life of ordinary people. He's never been in a bus, and only once on the Underground. [She smiled.] That was during the General Strike, when I deposited him at South Kensington. He went round and round, not knowing where to get out, and had to be rescued eventually. Winston is selfish; he doesn't mean to be, he's just built that way. He's an egoist, I suppose, like Napoleon. You see, he has always had the ability and force to live his life exactly as he wanted to.[13]

This dangerous self-centredness could be seen in the Prime Minister's attempt to monopolise the London end of the Anglo-American relations with President Roosevelt. It is ironic, therefore, that to depreciate

Churchill's significance we have to focus upon it in the first place. Nonetheless, this needs to be done because he himself has left voluminous records of his own actions for historians to follow. It is worth considering whether Oliver Stanley would have been so widely ignored had he left a ready prepared archive of his own. Instead, we are forced to rely upon others' interpretations of the Colonial Secretary and his own scant annotations scribbled on official papers. We should, perhaps, be wary of over-emphasising the individual over the general, particularly in such complex circumstances as diplomacy.

Britain's return to Hong Kong finds its true significance in the context of the imperial mentality which permeated British society. Imbued by a narrow educational curriculum which focused on Britain's past military endeavours, there was little doubt in most people's minds that Britain would return to Hong Kong. Sir Ralph Furse, an old Etonian and Oxbridge graduate, was representative of the single-mindedness of Britain's governing elite. In charge of Colonial Office recruitment between 1910 and 1948, he was a leading proponent of Britain's imperial destiny and followed the teaching of an old Jesuit: 'It is wonderful how much good a man can do for the world if he does not want to take credit for it.'[14] Without the many hundreds of similar 'quiet crusaders' who were used to thinking imperially, there would have been no Hong Kong question during the Second World War. Lord Rosebery stated in 1899 that 'Imperialism, sane imperialism, as distinguished from what I may call wild-cat imperialism, is nothing but this – a larger patriotism.'[15]

Epilogue

If consistency often eludes practitioners of diplomacy, the reversal of Washington's Hong Kong strategy in the aftermath of the Pacific war was ironic to say the least. In 1957, National Security Council (NSC) paper 5717 stated that 'It is in the interest of the United States that the British maintain their position in Hong Kong.'[1] In fact, America's switch to support Britain's hold on the colony was highly embarrassing after the strident anti-colonialism of the war years. The onset of the cold war forced Washington to reassess her attitude towards colonialism. As the CIA noted in 1948, 'the loss of their dependencies weakens the colonial powers, which are the chief prospective US allies' while depriving America 'of an assured access to bases and raw materials'. It was 'a serious dilemma' for a country which had set itself up as a champion of anti-colonialism. With the outbreak of the Korean War in 1950, Britain had convinced America that Hong Kong was no longer a colonial issue but one of national defence.[2]

Prior to the Korean War, America's attitude remained highly ambivalent towards the colony as Washington was mesmerised by the implosion of its China policy. Hong Kong could not escape the ructions on the Chinese mainland. Suppressed while the Japanese burned their way through the country, the revolutionary battle between the Nationalists and communists quickly resurfaced once the invaders had surrendered. Unfortunately for the Nationalists, and some might say for China, they were led by Chiang Kai-shek's clique, who had more than proved their incompetence during the Pacific war. Their armies had rarely engaged the Japanese and little would change against Mao's communists. With the Nationalist armies melting away, a despondent T.V. Soong pinned his hopes on a third world war breaking out.[3] As the Americans argued over who was to blame for the Nationalists' defeat, the People's

217

Republic of China was declared in October 1949. The troublesome Hong Kong question had just become even more complicated: now Hong Kong was claimed by two rival governments, the Nationalist remnants on Taiwan and the communists in Peking!

The anachronism that was Hong Kong, however, remained. The colony was a pitiful sight in 1945. It had the dubious honour of being called the most looted city in the world. It had been looted immediately after the British defeat, looted constantly during the occupation, and looted again after the Japanese surrender. Few of the city's clubs were recognisable; the golf course had allotments dug all over it, the Jockey Club was literally a shell of its former self. Even the floorboards had been stolen! No one had escaped the ravages of war. And yet, George Hopper, American consul general, was soon telling Lieutenant General Wedemeyer on his China mission that the British had quickly and miraculously restored the life of the colony, so much so that the population had doubled from 1 million to 2 million by August 1947. British success was even encouraging some Chinese to leave China. It was also interesting to juxtapose the colony with its mother country: the vibrant entrepreneurialism which was let loose across the colony once more stood in stark contrast to regulations back in socialist Britain.

All the same, after the war the colony declined in importance. With the mother country's economy in ruins and decolonisation accelerating, Hong Kong was low down on London's list of priorities. In reality, the colony had returned to its pre-war status. Sir Alexander Grantham, Governor of Hong Kong from 1947 to 1958, knew perfectly well that 'the electorate of Britain didn't care a brass farthing about Hong Kong'.[4] The Hong Kong Chinese were hardly more concerned. They remained apathetic towards British rule in any positive sense and only wished to be free to pursue the creation of wealth as they always had. A newspaper noted that, 'In the cinemas "God save the King" is a sign that the doors are open.' Most of the refugee population fleeing mainland China 'regarded the island as little more than a reasonable hotel'.[5]

With Mao's triumphant communists reaching the China–Hong Kong border, the colony was gripped by the fear that it was about to be invaded for the second time in a decade. Once again Hong Kong pitted the Foreign Office against the Colonial Office. The Colonial Office, bolstered by the hard-line governor of the colony, Sir Alexander Grantham, pressed for an unequivocal statement that Britain would hold on to Hong Kong at all costs.[6] This was familiar ground for the Colonial Office's Paskin who lamented that, 'The attempt on the part of the C[olonial]O[ffice] to get some positive decision on policy as regards the retention of Hong Kong . . . has been going on interminably, at any rate since 1943.'[7] And with Creech Jones as Colonial Secretary this was not about to change. Like his predecessor Oliver Stanley, Creech Jones knew that a Colonial Secretary 'cannot break the adamant view of the Foreign Secretary'.[8] Behind the seemingly endless Colonial Office–Foreign Office conflict, however, stood a determination to resist any renewed Chinese claim to Hong Kong.

The Foreign Office's public reticence over the colony was driven by its usual pragmatism. It was appreciated that without American support 'our only hope of hanging on to Hong Kong is to keep quiet about it'.[9] Even so, under the pressures of the cold war, the British chose to send 30000 military reinforcements, including armour and air cover, to strengthen the colony's defence. This time they were not Canadian. Before American policy recovered its interventionist nerve in Asia with the Korean War, it was the British who were left to develop and implement the 'domino theory'. It was believed that 'If we surrender Hong Kong to the communists, there will be nothing to prevent the flood from pouring into South East Asia. It is necessary to call a halt somewhere, and we consider that Hong Kong will therefore become the symbol of the resistance of the rest of Asia to the communist advance.'[10] This idea presupposed that Hong Kong actually led somewhere and defended something.[11] Ultimately, however, the government could not afford its bluff being called by the Chinese. In preparation for such a humiliation, British rhetoric was toned down and contingencies prepared for a retreat.[12]

But for some reason, Mao chose not to move. As the cold war engulfed the Far East, Hong Kong remained a crossroads for east and west. Hong Kong was useful to everyone, including the Americans who used the colony to collect intelligence on the Chinese mainland. There were parallels with West Berlin. Hong Kong projected a shop window of Western prosperity and freedom in contrast to the austere totalitarian blandness of communism. Mao's reasoning for leaving the colony alone, though, was harder to interpret and more consequential. It is possible that he believed an invasion of Hong Kong would have involved the communists in a war with Britain and America for which he was not ready. The financial importance of the colony to China was clear, with half her foreign income being channelled through Hong Kong. Some Chinese officials even admitted that Hong Kong had been China's 'lifeline' during the Korean War, providing petroleum, chemicals and other strategic products denied them by the UN embargo. Mao even obtained his Hollywood movies and medical drugs through the port.[13]

These reasons alone probably do not provide the whole answer. It is likely that Taiwan held the key. Hong Kong, like Chiang Kai-shek's last refuge, was more useful to Mao 'outside the house', rather than in it. He told his personal doctor that he preferred to keep Taiwan in his grip as a baton to 'keep Khruschev and Eisenhower dancing'.[14] In other words, it was a foreign policy tap which he could turn on or off at will. Considering the anguish which the communist threat posed to Hong Kong for the British and the Americans, it worked. Mao informed Stalin during his December 1949 trip to Moscow that he wanted to bring about order and stability in China before talking to 'foreign imperialists'.[15] Whatever the merits of these arguments, an informal *modus vivendi* had been reached within China that Britain would retain control.

By 1960 the colony had become the eyes and ears of America's cold war containment strategy in the Far East. From Hong Kong, the Americans ran their spy networks into China and retained an intelligence-gathering position on the Chinese mainland. The United States Consulate General in Hong Kong was 'the most important American source of hard economic, political and military information on Communist China'.[16] America's new found support for Hong Kong, though, was received with equivocation by Hong Kong's Governor, Sir Alexander Grantham. The swollen consulate staff, obviously including many CIA operatives, were 'extremely ham-handed' in their operations and had to be told to stop 'being so stupid'![17] The potential extraction of the 2500 Americans living in the colony in 1957 was, therefore, a critical influence on Washington's policy. With associated foreign nationals 'of interest to the United States' this rose to 3300.

Like British strategists before them, Washington realised that Hong Kong was indefensible against a determined attack. It was calculated that a successful defence of the colony could only be undertaken in depth, which meant securing a defensive perimeter on mainland China. Technology had not made the defence of Hong Kong any easier or more practicable. As such, 'US intervention would probably not be operationally feasible in case of direct communist attack on Hong Kong.'[18] The consequences of armed intervention in defence of Hong Kong was likely escalation with no stopping point. An earlier assessment had made this chilling observation: 'It would be unwise for the United States to contribute forces for the defence of Hong Kong or Macao unless we are willing to risk major military involvement in China and possibly global war.'[19]

America's China policy had been destroyed by Mao's victory. All that was left to do was apportion the blame. In an attempt to pre-empt any criticism, the State Department published its 1949 China White Paper which vilified the Generalissimo. A report by the Joint Munitions Allocation Committee to the JCS confirmed this was 99 per cent correct. 'However, the United States failed to warn the Chinese Nationalists what the United States would do if they would not accept her advice. Anticipating the United States' endless aid, Chiang and his clique let the corruption go on.'[20] For all that, the 'loss of China' or more pointedly, the rejection of American friendship was never readily accepted in American policymaking circles.

It is interesting to note that while China at the beginning of the twenty-first century is an acknowledged world power it lacks many of the traditional trappings. Gerald Segal suggests that China today is not a world apart from Chiang Kai-shek's time, retaining many of the period's characteristics, being skilled in the manipulation of foreign powers but militarily weak, economically backward, and politically corrupt:

> At best, China is a second-rank middle power that has mastered the art of diplomatic theatre... In 1997 China['s]... per capita GDP ranking was 81st, just ahead of Georgia and behind Papua New Guinea [while remaining] a second-rate military power [with no international allies of significance]... Once prominent on the map of aid suppliers, [it] has become the largest recipient of foreign aid.[21]

Whatever the attributes of China, past and present, in 1949 the British were no closer to scuttling and running from the colony than they had been in wartime. The new plain-speaking British Foreign Secretary, Ernest Bevin, told Dean Acheson, Secretary of State, that while Britain would be prepared to discuss the future of Hong Kong 'with a friendly and stable Government of a unified China', those conditions did not currently exist. The word 'democratic' had been deleted from Bevin's draft.[22] These conditions would not exist for another fifty years. In 1997, a unified and stable Chinese government received the colony of Hong Kong back into Chinese rule. If the communists had decided to walk unarmed and en masse into the colony prior to this date, it is unlikely that the British could have responded. But these remain other voices, other rooms.

Notes

Introduction

1 *Daily Telegraph*, 20 February 1997, obituary.
2 Winston Churchill, speech at Harvard, 6 September 1943, in *Onwards to Victory* (London, 1944).
3 Raymond Seitz, *Over Here* (London, 1998), p. 341.
4 John Harvey (ed.), *The War Diaries of Oliver Harvey 1941–1945* (London, 1978), p. 194, 1 December 1942.
5 For example see Louis, *Imperialism at Bay* and Christopher Thorne's *Allies of a Kind, the United States, Britain and the War against Japan* (London, 1978).

1 Return and departure

1 John King Fairbank, *The United States and China* (Cambridge, MA, 1971), p. 138.
2 Ibid., pp. 137–49.
3 Norman Miners, *Hong Kong under Imperial Rule, 1912–1941* (Oxford, 1987), p. 43.
4 Mr T. Reid, Labour Party Advisory Committee on Imperial Questions, Memo no.244, 'Official appointments in dependencies' 1942, Labour Party Archive at the National Museum of Labour History, Manchester.
5 Major General Woodburn Kirby, *The War against Japan vol. I: Official History* (HMSO, 1957), p. 19.
6 Prem 3/90/5A, COS memo to Churchill on HMS *Duke of York*, 21 December 1941.
7 'The valour and the horror: Canada and the fall of Hong Kong', CBC TV programme, 1991.
8 CO 968/13/2, COS (41) 28, Churchill in Annex 1 to Maj. Gen. Ismay, 7 January 1941.
9 Kirby, p. 108.
10 Prem 3/157/1, Eden to Churchill, 8 February 1941.
11 CO 968/13/2, Maj. Grasett to Air Ministry, 6 January 1941.
12 Galen Perras, ' "Our position in the Far East would be stronger without this unsatisfactory commitment": Britain and the reinforcement of Hong Kong, 1941', *Canadian Journal of History*, 30 (August 1995), p. 246.
13 Winston Churchill, *The Second World War, vol. III* (London, 1950), p. 157. Churchill to Maj. Gen. Ismay, 7 January 1941.
14 CO 968/13/2, COS (41) 28, 10 January 1941. Telex to C in C FE.
15 Perras.
16 CO 968/13/2, COS to PM, 8 September 1941.
17 For an expansion of this idea see Correlli Barnett, *Lost Victory* (London, 1995), e.g. pp. 14–15.

18 CO 967/69, 1941, personal correspondence of Sir Mark Young, Governor Hong Kong. Letters 14 October and 2 December 1941.
19 Kirby, p. 112.
20 CO 968/13/2, Hong Kong Defence policy 1941.
21 G. Wright-Nooth with Mark Adkins, *Prisoner of the Turnip Heads* (Cassell Edition, London, 1999), p. 40.
22 'The valour and the horror'.
23 FO 371/63392/f564, General Maltby's Hong Kong reassessment, 1947.
24 'The valour and the horror'. The programme emphasises the bitterness felt by Canadians towards Mackenzie King and the British, and the general military ineptitude that resulted.
25 MacDougall papers, Rhodes House, Oxford. MSS Ind.Ocn. 73. Item 1, notebook on the fall of Hong Kong.
26 Wright-Nooth, pp. 48–9.
27 PREM 3/157/2, 21 December 1941.
28 Kirby, p. 145.
29 FO 371/31671/f4000, 1942 situation in Hong Kong. This file contains a wealth of material relating to Japanese atrocities perpetrated against the defenders and inhabitants of the colony. The FO pushed for publicity to be given to these crimes, although the Colonial Secretary and India Office were afraid for the 'sensibilities of Canadian and Indian troops'. See also F6407.
30 James Bertram, *The Shadow of a War* (London, 1947), p. 120. Bertram was a Marxist.
31 Ibid. p. 150.
32 Kirby, p. 469.
33 PREM 3/90/5A, 12 March 1942, C in C India to War Office.

2   The meaning of Empire

1 Quoted in L.C.B. Seaman, *Victorian England* (London, 1973), p. 331.
2 *Speeches of Churchill, vol. VII*, pp. 6918–24. 'The future of the Empire', House of Commons, 21 April 1944.
3 See Lawrence James, *The British Empire* (London, 1994).
4 Frank Welsh, *A History of Hong Kong* (London, 1994), pp. 124–5.
5 FO 371/31777/f6440, Sir Maurice Peterson minute, 1 September 1942.
6 Sir Reginald Stubbs, 16 September 1922 to CO while on leave in London. Quoted in Welsh, *Hong Kong*, p. 386.
7 FO 371/35679/f23, memorandum by Mr Ewer of the *Daily Herald* submitted to the Foreign Office, December 1942.
8 Christopher M. Bell, 'Our most exposed outpost', *Journal of Military History*, 60 (January 1996).
9 Ibid., p. 65.
10 Welsh, p. 30.
11 Ibid. For example see pp. 133–4.
12 The politics and history of the opium trade in Hong Kong are beyond the limits of this book. However, it is instructive to note that in 1918 revenue from opium sales reached the not untypical figure of 46.5 per cent of all Hong Kong Government revenue. Ibid., p. 364.

13 CAB 96/FE(E)(45)10, 3 February 1945, War Cabinet Far Eastern committee, BOT paper on 'Certain aspects of commercial policy in China'.

14 CO 133/111, Blue Book 1940.

15 FO 371/46232/f1331, Cavendish-Bentinck minute, 13 March 1945.

16 CAB 134/280, Cabinet Far Eastern committee, 'British foreign policy in the Far East', 31 December 1945. The paper went on to state: 'The UK trade with the area under consideration [Far East] was not quantitatively of the first importance. It accounted for about 4.5% of UK imports and 5.25% of UK exports (1937–39 average).'

17 FO 371/46251/f2382, Eden on FO brief prepared for visit of General Hurley, 4 April 1945.

18 FO 371/35680/ f412/G, Brenan and Ashley Clarke, January 1943.

19 Seaman, p. 339. Adam Smith's *The Wealth of Nations* systematically demolished the economic case for empire in 1776.

20 WP(44) 643, CAB 66/57, Stanley memo to Cabinet, ref. CDWA, on 15 November 1944. Quoted in Louis, p. 103.

21 J. Gardiner and N. Wenborn (eds), *The History Today Companion to British History* (London, 1995), p. 100.

22 Quoted in Seaman, p. 301.

23 Correlli Barnett, *The Audit of War* (London, 1986), p. 221.

24 Franklin Gimson diary, Rhodes House Library, Oxford, MSS Ind.Ocn. 222, 13 September 1943.

25 Later on in life Clement Attlee reminisced nostalgically about his time at Oxford University, wishing to recapture 'the magic of those days and of that city'. See Trevor Burridge, *Clement Attlee, a Political Biography* (London, 1985), p. 16.

26 See Correlli Barnett's trilogy; *The Collapse of British Power; The Audit of War,* and *Lost Victory.*

27 Gladwyn Jebb, *The Memoirs of Lord Gladwyn* (London, 1972), p. 106.

28 Barnett, *Audit,* p. 221. Quotation from Sir Ralph Furse in Robert Heussler, *Yesterday's Rulers* (NY, 1963), pp. 82–3.

29 CAB 66/57, WP(44) 643, Stanley memo to Cabinet on colonial development loans, 15 November 1944.

30 ADM 116/4271, memo by Deputy Chief of Naval Staff, 3 January 1940. Quoted in Bell.

31 Harvey diary, p. 191, 23 November 1942.

32 A.N. Porter and A.J. Stockwell, *British Imperial Policy and Decolonization, 1938–64* (London, 1987), pp. 8–11.

33 FO 371/31715/f5553, China post-war settlement, minute by Ashley Clarke, 7 August 1942. Sir Maurice Peterson agreed but argued American 'intervention will not necessarily be a grounds for altering our attitudes' on Hong Kong.

34 Charles Cruishank, *SOE in the Far East* (Oxford, 1983), p. 154.

35 Jebb, pp. 101–7.

36 FO 954/24/f123, Eden to Churchill on the role of SOE, 5 April 1942.

37 FO 371/41657/f5341, Churchill's Mansion House speech, 10 November 1942.

38 Martin Gilbert, *Road to Victory, Winston S. Churchill, 1941–1945, vol. VII* (London, 1986), p. 780. PM personal minute, 25 May 1944.

39 Anthony Eden, *The Reckoning* (London, 1965), p. 513.
40 PREM 3/157/4, Eden, 20 October 1942.
41 Hugh Dalton, *Memoirs, 1931–1945: the Fateful Years* (London, 1957), p. 630, 2 September 1943.
42 Dilks, D. (ed.), *The Diaries of Sir Alexander Cadogan* (London, 1982), p. 697, 22 January 1945.
43 Harvey diary, p. 191, 23 November 1942. Eden's supporters found much to criticise in Stanley. Not only was he a loyal Chamberlainite but he was also a poor public speaker, overly diffident and was tainted by the disastrous Norwegian campaign in 1940. See entry in forthcoming *New Dictionary of National Biography* (Oxford University Press).
44 Ben Pimlott (ed.), *The Second World War Diary of Hugh Dalton, 1940–45* (London, 1986), pp. 189–92, 28 April 1941.
45 Churchill papers, Churchill College, Cambridge. Char 20/11/62–64, Oliver Stanley to Churchill, 13 May 1940.
46 John Colville, *The Fringes of Power: the Downing Street Diaries, 1939–55* (London, 1985), p. 444, 26 September 1941.
47 PREM 4/43A/5, Oliver Stanley speech: 'No outside control of colonies', 5 March 1943.
48 After the war, Gent was appointed Governor of the Malayan Union and was tragically killed in a plane crash following his recall to London in 1948. See A.J. Stockwell (ed.), *Documents on the end of Empire: Malaya, II*, (London, 1994), p. 34.
49 CAB 129/1, CP (45)144, Attlee memo on defence, 1 September 1945. In an essay written in 1937, he had also postulated 'rejecting altogether the concepts of imperialism, and by establishing through the League of Nations international control of raw materials'. See George Bennett (ed.), *The Concept of Empire, Burke to Attlee 1774–1947* (London, 1953), p. 407.
50 Kenneth Harris, *Attlee* (London, 1982), pp. 205–7.
51 Ibid., p. 216.
52 FO 954/22/62–96, Attlee's copy of post-war Far East settlement, October 1942.
53 Porter and Stockwell, p. 48.

3   The Anglo-American relationship at war

1 FO 371/41657/f2172, Moss memo to Sir Alexander Blackburn FO, May 1944.
2 Elliott Roosevelt, *As He Saw It* (NY, 1946), p. 71.
3 CO 967/18, report by Richard Law on Washington DC talks, September, 1942.
4 Wedemeyer, A.C., *Wedemeyer Reports!* (NY, 1958), pp. 252–3.
5 Harvey, p. 197, 7 December 1942.
6 David Reynolds, *The Creation of the Anglo-American Alliance, 1937–41* (London, 1981), p. 58.
7 FO 954/22/f168, Eden in Washington DC to Churchill, 29 March 1943. He met Hull, Winant, Welles, Hopkins and FDR.
8 CO 825/35/55104, minute by Lord Cranborne, 14 July 1942.
9 Quoted in Thorne, p. 394.

10 FO 371/31777/f2947, Richard Law, April 1942.
11 HS 1/349, Madame Chiang Kai-shek article in *New York Times* magazine, 19 April 1942.
12 HS 1/349, John Keswick report on failure of British commando unit in Chungking, 13 April 1942.
13 Sterling Seagrave, *The Soong Dynasty* (NY, 1985), p. 10.
14 Ibid., p. 285.
15 FO 371/31704/f3187, reaction to Madame Chiang Kai-shek article. Apparently Chiang Kai-shek himself did not approve of his wife's article.
16 FO 954/6/f580–2, Eden to Madame Chiang Kai-shek, 1 June 1942.
17 FO 371/31616/f2918, Seymour telex no. 500, 13 April 1942.
18 The influence of British missionaries in China and their effect on British foreign policy is largely unexplored. The London Missionary Society (LMS), with its links to non-conformism and the Liberal Party, were, however, known to be active in China.
19 FO 371/31616/f2918, Seymour telex no. 500, 13 April 1942.
20 FO 371/31616/f3588, May 1942.
21 FO 371/31617/f4276, June 1942.
22 AP 20/19/572, Churchill to Eden, 22 July 1943. Refers to publication of Gallup opinion poll in *News Chronicle*. (Avon papers)
23 Gilbert, *Churchill VI*, pp. 1162–3.
24 Thorne, p. 161 and Rhodes James, *Churchill Speeches, vol. VI*, p. 6481, 9 September 1941.
25 FO 371/31777/f2947, Eden, 2 May 1942. (All quotes in this paragraph.)
26 FO 371/31627/f5964, Leo Amery to Eden, 13 August 1942.
27 *Speeches of Churchill, vol. VII*, pp. 6918–24. 'The future of the Empire', House of Commons, 21 April 1944.
28 FO 371/54073, Churchill minute to COS, 23 October 1944.
29 Avon papers, Birmingham University. AP 20/12/768, Churchill to Eden, 31 December 1944.
30 Harvey diary, pp. 160–2, 22–5 September 1942 for dislike of Stanley amongst Eden's supporters.
31 Leo Amery diary, p. 942, 21 September 1943. Also, Harvey diary, p. 297, 21 September 1943.
32 Irwin Gellman, *Secret Affairs, Franklin Roosevelt, Cordell Hull, and Sumner Welles* (Baltimore, 1995), pp. ix–2.
33 Ibid., p. 315. Hull conversation with Morgenthau, 9 July 1943.
34 Ibid., p. xi.
35 Reynolds, p. 25.
36 Leahy, W.D., *I Was There* (London, 1950), p. 187.
37 Reynolds, pp. 26–7.
38 FO 371/41750/f1418, Sir George Sansom in Washington DC to FO, March 1944. Hornbeck was appointed Ambassador to Holland in late 1944.
39 Wedemeyer, p. 180.

4 An Empire brought into question

1 FO 371/4072/f8170, G.P. Young minute, 9 December 1942.
2 FO 371/31662/f7822.

3   FO 371/31777/f2063, dinner discussion in NYC, 19 January 1942.
4   National Archive and Records Administration, College Park, USA. RG59, Box 5098, letter dated 12 September 1944 inquiring whether Hong Kong was returning to China.
5   Eden diary, 27 February 1942.
6   Lord Moran, *Winston Churchill, the Struggle for Survival, 1940–65* (London, 1966), p. 27.
7   MacDougall papers, Steve Tsang interview with MacDougall, 26 February 1987.
8   Winston Churchill, *The Hinge of Fate* (London, 1964), p. 61 and Robert Rhodes James (ed.), *Winston S. Churchill, his Complete Speeches, vol. VI, 1935–42* (London, 1974), p. 6464, 27 January 1942.
9   CO 825/35/4, minute by Gent, 30 June 1942.
10 FO 371/31777/f5965, Gladwyn Jebb minute, 7 September 1942.
11 Eden diary, 30 May 1942.
12 FO 371/31633/f3962, A.L. Scott responding to a parliamentary question on Chinese troops in Malaya, 27 May 1942. 'No offer of Chinese troops for the defence of Malaya was ever made. In May 1939, however, General Chiang Kai-shek offered 200000 troops to assist in the defence of Hong Kong, an offer which was not accepted and was subsequently withdrawn.'
13 MacDougall papers, notebook on the fall of Hong Kong. Undated.
14 PREM 4/28/5, parliamentary mission to China report issued February 1943, undertaken November 1942.
15 FO 371/31633/f2775, A.L. Scott minute on future of Hong Kong, 8 April 1942.
16 FO 371/31715/f5087, Ashley Clarke minute, 19 July 1942.
17 CO 825/35/4, Gent minute, June 1942.
18 FO 371/31801/f4369, Miss McGeachy minute, 13 June 1942.
19 FO 371/31801/f3814, Sir Maurice Peterson on IPR conference, 13 May 1942.
20 FO 371/31801/f4369, Sir John Brenan, 13 June 1942.
21 CO 825/42/53104, Stanley, minute, 23 August 1943. He was referring to the French defence of their colonies and the general future of the Far East.
22 *The Value of a Pound: Prices and Incomes in Britain, 1900–1993* (London, 1995).
23 FO 954/6/f585, Eden to Seymour, 9 July 1942.
24 FO 371/31619/f3043, Treasury meeting, April 1942.
25 *Foreign Relations of the United States* series (FRUS), 1942 China, p. 421. Sir Frederick Phillips to Morgenthau, Washington DC, 3 January.
26 FO 954/6/f497, Niemeyer to Eden, 8 January 1942.
27 FRUS, 1942 China, pp. 419–20. A.M. Fox to Morgenthau, Washington DC, 3 January.
28 Ibid., p. 425. Gauss to Cordell Hull, 8 January.
29 CAB 65/25, 2 February 1942.
30 FRUS, 1942 China, p. 438. Meeting in Washington DC, 26 January.
31 Ibid., p. 423. Meeting in Washington DC, 8 January.
32 Ibid., p. 438. Meeting in Washington DC, 13 January.
33 Ibid., p. 446. Meeting in Washington DC, 26 January.
34 Ibid., pp. 486–8. Memo by Hornbeck, 19 March. He belatedly came to see that Chiang was treating the loan as a 'poker game', manoeuvring the US

Government into a 'without strings' only position. Which would 'score for them a first-class diplomatic victory the consequences of which in the long run will be good neither for this country or China'.

35   FO 954/6/f572, Eden interview with Koo, 20 April 1942.
36   FRUS, China 1942, pp. 509–15. Luthringer memo on amelioration of China's financial difficulties, 24 April.
37   FO 371/31619/f5341, Hall Patch in Chunking to Treasury, 25 July 1942.
38   FRUS, 1942 China, p. 454. Hull to FDR, 31 January.
39   Ibid., p. 519. Luthringer to Hamilton, 21 May.
40   Ibid., pp. 521–3. 22, 23 and 25 May.
41   FO 371/31619/f3468, Eden minute on Chinese blackmail, 10 May 1942.
42   FO 371/31619/f4252, Wood and Eden discussion, 8 June 1942.
43   FO 371/31715/f5553, Peterson minute, 7 August 1942 and FO telex to Chungking, 9 August 1942.
44   FO 371/31715/f5087, Eden on Far Eastern post-war settlement, 21 July 1942.
45   FO 371/31715/f5553, Peterson minute, 7 August 1942 and FO telex to Chungking, 9 August 1942.
46   FO 371/31704/f4297, Ashley Clarke minute, 16 June 1942.
47   FO 371/31704/f4297, Eden minute, 17 June 1942.
48   CO 825/35/55104, Cranborne minute, 14 July 1942.
49   CO 825/35/55104, Cranborne minute, 14 July 1942.
50   FO 371/31773/f5506, 'Britain's post-war prospects in the Far East', G.F. Hudson, 5 August 1942.
51   FO 371/31773/f5506, Sir John Brenan minute, 8 August 1942.
52   In 1920 Hong Kong engineers demanded increased wages and, with the employers failing to agree, withdrew their labour to Canton, quickly bringing the colony to a standstill. The same occurred in 1921–22, when the exploited Chinese seamen gathered more widespread support (almost all the colony's workforce of 120 000) and marched off to Canton. The colonial government's repressive measures only met with further agitation, forcing the government to concede a famous victory to the seamen. Matters went a stage further in the 1925–26 blockade of Hong Kong when anti-foreign feeling swept the colony. It was caused by the deaths of Chinese civilians in the Shanghai international settlement and Canton at the hands of foreign troops (mostly British, one might add), and the agitation of a left-wing regime in Canton. Once more Hong Kong's workforce departed for Canton, the strikers demanding a huge $20 million payment. The Hong Kong Government, left in a perilous situation, considered what to do. At the time, Sir John Brenan was British consul in Canton. He adamantly opposed the idea of coercion which was being put forward by the new Hong Kong Governor, Sir Cecil Clementi, with the support of the Colonial Office (Welsh, pp. 369–76). A further coincidence was the fact that Leo Amery was the Colonial Secretary supporting Clementi in his use of force. Amery later wrote of his concern that 'the growth of an aggressive anti-European nationalism in China . . . led to much controversy between the Foreign Office, out of appeasement, and those of us who were more concerned to defend the interests built up by British enterprise in a prosperous colony like Hong Kong' (Leo Amery, *Life, vol. II* (London, 1953), p. 305). It would appear that Foreign–Colonial Office conflict over the colony was nothing new.

In October 1926 the boycott ended without a penny being paid to the strikers. Ironically, the reason was the intervention of Chiang Kai-shek who had succeeded Sun Yat-sen as leader of the Kuomintang. In an attempt to reassert central authority throughout China, a pro-Chiang coup took place in Canton during March 1926. Chiang moved quickly to end the boycott because it was distracting from his military campaign against dissident warlords (Welsh, pp. 376–7). This assistance is, unsurprisingly however, rarely acknowledged in British history at a time when the colony's future was in great jeopardy. Retrospectively, the convergence of Chiang Kai-shek, Brenan and Amery almost twenty years later over the same issue remains one of the quirks of history. In preparation for a northern expedition to re-establish central authority in Shanghai and Nanking, he needed to secure his position in Canton.

53 FO 371/31773/f5506, Sir Maurice Peterson minute, 17 August 1942.
54 FO 954/6/f592, Seymour talks to Chiang Kai-shek about India, 12 August 1942.
55 FO 371/31633/f5964, Amery letter to Eden, 13 August 1942.
56 FO 371/31777/f5965, official minutes of Foreign Office–Colonial Office meeting by Gent, 20 August 1942.
57 FO 371/31777/f5965, official minutes of Foreign Office–Colonial Office meeting by Gent, 20 August 1942.
58 FO 371/31777/f5965, Ashley Clarke minute, 27 August 1942.
59 FO 371/31777/f5965, Eden, 24 August 1942.
60 FO 371/31777/f5965, Sir Maurice Peterson minute, 28 August 1942.
61 FO 371/31777/f6440, Sir Maurice Peterson minute, 1 September 1942.
62 FO 371/31777/f6440, Ashley Clarke minute, 31 August 1942.
63 FO 954/22/post-war plans and reconstruction, October 1942.
64 HS 1/176, SOE, November 1942 paper, 'Present political and military aspects of the regime in China'.
65 FO 954/22/post-war plans and reconstruction. Attlee's copy of the revised Eden–Cranborne Far Eastern paper presented to Cabinet. Dated 9 September 1942.
66 Quoted in Welsh, p. 424.
67 FO 371/31777/f6425, interdepartmental meeting, 10 September 1942.
68 Cranborne, however, conscious of the need for consensus with the Labour Party, did not wish a split at Cabinet level. Paul Emrys-Evans (Dominions Parliamentary under-secretary) and Richard Law of the Foreign Office, on behalf of Cranborne, helped persuade Attlee to see the merits of the Colonial Office position. (Louis, p. 196)
69 FO 371/31777/f6425, F.G. Coultas minute, 21 September.
70 FO 371/31777/f6441, amended Foreign Office–Colonial Office paper, 9 September 1942.
71 CO 967/18, report by Richard Law on Washington talks, September 1942.
72 FO 954/29/f513–5, conversation between British journalist David Ewer and William Bullitt, former ambassador to Paris and Moscow, 11 August 1942.
73 CO 967/18, report by Richard Law on Washington talks, September 1942.

5　China claims Hong Kong

1　FO 371/31662/f7822, Cadogan minute on impending breakdown of extra-territoriality negotiations, 21 November 1942.

2　FO 371/31662/f7822, Ashley Clarke minute, 20 November 1942.

3　CAB 23/88, Cabinet conclusion 24 (37), March 1931.

4　FO 371/31633, Eden minute, 2 March 1942.

5　Joseph W. Ballentine, director of the Office of Far Eastern Affairs in the State Department, quoted in Kit-ching, 'The US and the question of Hong Kong 1941–45', *Journal of the Hong Kong Branch of the Royal Asiatic Society*, 19 (1979).

6　FO 371/31620/f5489, Eden minute, undated August 1942.

7　FRUS, 1942 China, pp. 277–8. Letter Hull to Halifax in Washington DC, 6 May.

8　FRUS, 1942 China, pp. 269–71. Memo by Walter Adams of FE section, Washington DC, 19 March. He reflected that American help to China 'may spill over the level of appropriateness and good taste to the detriment both of the interest of China and of the US'.

9　Quoted in Thorne, p. 489 and p. 533.

10　FO 954/Political/f520, Churchill to Eden on Four Power Plan, 18 October 1942.

11　FO 954/Political/f520, Eden reply to Churchill, 19 October 1942. PM/42/228.

12　FRUS, 1942 China, p. 287. Cordell Hull to Gauss, 5 September.

13　FO 371/f8539/54/10, British and American policy towards China, 28 December 1942.

14　FO 371/ 31627/f6518, 17 September 1942.

15　*The Times*, 14 October 1942.

16　FRUS, 1942, p. 289. Ambassador Gauss to Cordell Hull, September 8.

17　FO 371/31664/f8036, Ashley Clarke minute, December 1942.

18　Sir John Brenan, though, later pointed out when the China Association was still adamantly pushing for equality of trade, that Britain also had similar problems to the American states: London was negotiating on behalf of India, Burma and her other colonies which possessed more open trade policies than the motherland. FO 371/31664/f8109, Brenan minute, 10 December 1942.

19　FO 371/31662/f7845, meeting of the China Association and the Federation of British Industry with Eden, 19 November 1942.

20　FO 371/31664/f8081, Brenan minute, 3 December 1942. Also Cadogan letter to Winant, 7 December.

21　FO 371/31662/f7822, Ashley Clarke minute, 20 November 1942.

22　Hansard, 14 October 1942. Mr Sorenson parliamentary question to Richard Law under-secretary state of FO. Ibid., 20 October 1942.

23　PREM 3/157/4, Seymour to FO, 16 October 1942. Ibid., Eden reply, 20 October.

24　FO 371/31662/f7742, Seymour to FO, 14 November 1942.

25　Wendell Wilkie was the Republican Party's Presidential candidate in 1940.

26　FO 371/31664/f8287, *Time* article, 'Bitter tea', 9 November 1942.

27　FO 371/31663/f7822, Ashley Clarke minute, 20 November 1942, quoting governor of Hong Kong, 20 June 1931.

28 FO 371/31663/f7822, Ashley Clarke minute, 20 November 1942.
29 FO 371/31663/f7822, Eden minute, 22 November 1942.
30 FO 371/31663/f7950, Chinese pushing for American agreement, 25 November 1942.
31 FO 371/31663/f7822, Ashley Clarke to Monson, CO, 25 November 1942.
32 FO 371/31662/f7973, Halifax telex to Eden, 26 November 1942. Ibid., Eden reply, 4 December.
33 FO 371/31664/f8188, Seymour telex, 7 December 1942. Ibid., Eden 11 December.
34 FO 371/35679/f123, Seymour and Teichman talk with T.V. Soong and K.C. Wu, 14 December 1942.
35 FO 371/31664/f8287, Seymour telex, 15 December 1942. Ibid., Ashley Clarke, Cadogan and Eden, 17 December. Eden added an aside that it was 'Interesting this time we did not give everything at the start.'
36 CAB 65/28, WM173(42), extraterritoriality, 28 December 1942.
37 Cadogan diary, pp. 500–1, 28 December 1942.
38 FRUS, China 1942, pp. 414–5. Eden to US Chargé in London, 29 December.
39 FO 371/35679/f23, David Ewer memorandum, 29 December 1942. Also Sir Maurice Peterson minute, 31 December.
40 FO 371/35679/f23, Cordell Hull press conference, 30 December 1942. Ibid., f1, Halifax to Eden, 31 December.
41 Thorne, p. 179.
42 FO 371/35679/f1, Foulds minute, 1 January 1943. Ibid., Ashley Clarke, 2 January, and Cadogan, 3 January.
43 Eden diary, 31 December 1942.
44 FO 371/3569/f1, Ashley Clarke to Hornbeck, 13 January 1943.
45 William L. Tung, *Wellington Koo and China's Wartime Diplomacy* (NY, 1978), p. 53.
46 Shian Li, 'The extraterritoriality negotiations of 1943 and the New Territories', *Modern Asian Studies*, 30, 3 (1996).
47 FO 371/35680/f285, Seymour to FO, 12 January 1943.
48 FO 371/35679/f1, Ashley Clarke to Hornbeck, 13 January 1943.
49 Tung, *Wellington Koo*, p. 93. Apparent comments of Soong to Koo after the signing ceremony.
50 FO 371/35739/f2529, May 1943. The Western edition, delayed by Chiang, had many of the 'fascistic' anti-Western references removed.
51 'Nations and their past', *The Economist*, 21 December 1996.
52 FO 371/41657/f5341, Churchill's Mansion House speech, 10 November 1944.
53 Eden diary, 11 November 1942: 'Talk with Winston on telephone. His speech has gone very well.'
54 FO 371/35824/f2913, the future of Hong Kong 1943. China Association document, circa December 1942, forwarded by CO.
55 Quoted in Thorne, p. 65.
56 Arthur Creech Jones papers, Rhodes House, Oxford University, 17/12, ff. 40–2. 'Report of the Weekend Conference', New Fabian Research Bureau, 19–20 March 1938.
57 FO 371/31620/f5628, Bromley minute, 10 August, and Ashley Clarke, 12 August 1942.

58　FO 371/31620/f7866, Brenan minute on loan and extraterritoriality, 25 November 1942.

59　BT 11/1995, Harcourt Johnstone, 15 December 1942, and Kingsley Wood, 7 January 1943.

60　MacDougall papers, MacDougall to Noel Sabine, CO, 22 December 1942.

61　Ibid., 30 December 1942.

62　FO 371/31803/f7609, IPR conference and the future of Hong Kong, 9 November 1942. Sir John Pratt wrote to Ashley Clarke in October to confide: 'For many years I have felt that if we could not hold Hong Kong with the goodwill of the Chinese it was not worth holding at all.' He wanted to return the colony 'now', although he realised that was unlikely to be the FO–CO consensus. A point made by an illegible scribe in the FO: 'I agree . . . with most of Pratt's views. The line he takes about Hong Kong, however, would not be unanimously endorsed by the Cabinet to say the least.'

63　FO 371/35905, Pratt to Ashley Clarke, private, 26 December 1942.

64　FO 371/35905, Sir Maurice Peterson to Ashley Clarke on Pratt, 21 January 1943.

65　FO 371/34087/A1914, Pratt debrief to Committee on American Opinion and the British Empire, 22 February 1943.

66　FO 371/35680/ f412/G, Seymour to Eden, 13 January 1943.

67　FO 371/35680/ f412/G, Brenan and Ashley Clarke, January 1943.

68　FO 371/35680/f412/G, Butler, January 1943.

69　Ibid., Law, 1 February 1943.

70　FO 371/35680/ f412/G, Eden, 4 February 1943.

71　Hansard, 28 January 1943, vol. 386, p. 634.

72　FO 371/35683/f1090, reply to Halifax telex, February 1943. Ibid., Thornely, CO, to Oliver Harvey, FO, 11 February 1943.

73　Cadogan diary, p. 501, 31 December 1942.

6 London's Hong Kong planning

1　HS 1/349, 1942–45 future of Hong Kong, 27 February 1943: 'Sino-British relations', prepared by AD/O to Minister for Economic Warfare, Lord Selborne (SO). Selborne added, 'This is a very valuable paper.'

2　Lord Ismay, *The Memoirs of Lord Ismay* (London, 1960), p. 309.

3　HS 1/349, 1942–45 future of Hong Kong, 27 February 1943: 'Sino-British relations'.

4　Ibid.

5　HS 1/349, SOE paper on Sino-British relations prepared by AD/O, 23 February 1943.

6　FO 954/6/f686, Mountbatten to Eden on raising profile of Far Eastern war, 23 September 1943.

7　CO 825/35/25, CO arrangements for military administration of Hong Kong, 19 June 1943.

8　FO 825/42/15, Gent to Thornely, 16 February 1943.

9　CO 825/42/15, Monson minute, 30 June 1943.

10　CO 825/42/15, Gent minute, 1 July 1943.

11 CO 852, 375/5, commercial relations with China: Hong Kong interests in post-war policy. FO to Seymour, 22 July 1943, and Gent minute, 4 August 1943.
12 CO 825/42/15, Paskin minute, 2 July 1943.
13 Norman Miners, *Hong Kong under Imperial Rule, 1912–1941* (Oxford, 1987), p. 37.
14 CO 825/42/15, Gater to Stanley, 21 August 1943.
15 CO 825/42/15, Stanley minute, 23 August 1943.
16 CO 825/42/15, Gent minute, 1 July 1943.
17 CO 825/42/15, Paskin to Ashley Clarke, 27 August 1943.
18 CO 825/42/15, 10 August 1943. FO refusal to attend CO conference.
19 CO 825/42/15, Monson, 10 August, and Gent, 15 August 1943.
20 CO 825/42/15, Monson minute, 10 August 1943.
21 FO 371/35824/f4541, A.L. Scott minute on Paskin's letter, 1 September 1943.
22 Cadogan diary, 19 June 1945. Quoted in Thorne, p. 118.
23 FO 371/35824/f4541, Ashley Clarke minute, 2 September 1943.
24 CO 825/42/15, Paskin minute, 12 November 1943.
25 Steve Tsang, *Democracy Shelved: Great Britain, China, and Attempts at Constitutional Reform in Hong Kong, 1945–1952* (Oxford, 1988), p. 13.
26 CO 825/42/15, Gent minute, 29 December 1943.
27 CO 825/35/25, appointment of N.L. Smith, 18 August 1943.
28 CO 129/592/8.
29 F.S.V. Donnison, *British Military Administration in the Far East, 1943–46* (London, 1956), pp. 149–50.
30 Miners, pp. 41–2.
31 *The Economist*, 17 February 1945, p. 210.
32 Leo Amery diary, 16 February 1945, p. 1030.
33 FO 371/41657/f5341, for details of Stanley's, Attlee's and Churchill's statements on Hong Kong, November 1944.
34 CO 825/42/15, Gent minute, 29 December 1943.
35 CO 825/42/15, Monson minute, 8 May 1944. Also, Gent letter to Moss, 29 May 1944.
36 FO 371/41657/f2172, Moss memo to Sir Alexander Blackburn FO, May 1944.
37 *Speeches of Churchill, vol. VII*, pp. 6918–24. 'The future of the Empire', House of Commons, 21 April 1944. Churchill quoted Kipling in his own speech.
38 FO 371/41657/f2172, Moss memo to Sir Alexander Blackburn FO, May 1944.
39 HS 1/349, Selborne meets Sir George Moss, 24 June 1944.
40 FO 371/41657/f2172, Moss memo to Sir Alexander Blackburn FO, May 1944.
41 FO 371/41746/f2968, L.H. Foulds minute, June 1944.
42 FO 371/41657/f2172, *Shanghai Evening Post and Mercury* (US edition), 31 March 1944.
43 FO 371/41746/f2968, Sir Maurice Peterson minute, 28 June 1944.
44 Louis, p. 366. In 1944 Roosevelt encouraged the State Department to proceed with trusteeship plans while at the same time telling the military to plan for permanent bases throughout the Pacific. Also p. 426 for Hopkins's comments on FDR 'not being caught' by WSC's encouragement to annex islands.
45 HS 1/171, CO meeting with SOE, 13 June 1944.

46   HS 1/171, CO meeting with SOE, 10 August 1944.
47   HS 1/171, CO meeting with SOE, MI2 and MI9, 19 August 1944.
48   CO 825/42/15, CO guidance to Poynton for UN negotiations, 3 August 1944.
49   CO 968/156/Pt.1, minutes by Poynton of meeting, 27 July 1944. Also Gater to Cadogan, 28 July 1944. Quoted in Louis, pp. 382–3.
50   Louis, p. 377.
51   FO 371/41657/f3681, 12 June 1944. ICI's Chungking rep argued to Paskin of the CO that Hong Kong should not be returned to China, and this would not damage Sino-British relations. Forwarded to the FO where A.L. Scott commented, 14 August 1944.
52   NARA, JCS, RG 218, Box 342, civil affairs policy for British territory of Hong Kong and Borneo.
53   Hansard, vol. 402, pp. 407–10, 6 June 1944, parliamentary question by William Astor MP for Fulham East. With classic imperial irony, Astor denied the rights of the Chinese to claim any British territory while at the same time proclaiming that the Colonial Office administration would need people 'who can love and sympathise with the Chinese'!
54   *Speeches of Churchill, vol. VII*, pp. 6918–24. 'The future of the Empire', House of Commons, 21 April 1944.
55   CO 825/42/15, Miss Ruskin's draft Hong Kong announcement for Stanley, 6 November 1944. Also FO 371/41657/f5341, parliamentary question by William Astor MP, 8 November 1944.
56   FO 371/41657/f5341, *Daily Express*, 9 November 1944. Also CO 825/42/15, Gent minute, 18 November 1944.
57   FO 371/41746/f3665, inter-departmental meeting under chair of Sir Maurice Peterson, 3 August 1944. Also f3896 for encouragement of Washington Embassy.
58   CAB 96/5, Far East(44)1, 15 November 1944.
59   CO 825/39/7, Far Eastern committee memos and meetings 1944. Gent, 13 November 1944.
60   CAB 96/8, (45)4, British commercial interests in China – position of Hong Kong, 11 January 1945.
61   FO 371/41695/f5195, Stilwell's recall, 6 November 1944.
62   FO 371/41695/f5265, appointment of Wedemeyer, November 1944.
63   FO 371/41746/f5800, Dening to FO, 9 December 1944.
64   FO 371/41746/f5802, Dening to FO, 9 December 1944. Also Eden minute undated.
65   FO 371/41746/f5802, Dening to FO, 9 December 1944. Minute by M. Butler undated.

7   Military strategy in the Far East

1   Pownall, Louis Mountbatten's Chief of Staff at SEAC, 29 April 1944. Quoted in Thorne, p. 450.
2   Quoted in Thorne, p. 294.
3   Levine, p. 137.
4   Seagrave, p. 10.

5   Theodore H. White, *In Search of History* (NY, 1978), pp. 180–4.
6   Seagrave, pp. 419–20.
7   FO 371/35814, US authorities suppressing Chiang's book, May 1943.
8   White, p. 157.
9   FDR, Hopkins papers, Sherwood Collection, Box 331. Chiang Kai-shek to FDR, 19 April 1943.
10 FDR, FDR Official file, China 150, Box 2. T.V. Soong to Harry Hopkins, 13 May 1943. This was a curt note informing the Americans of Chinese displeasure over their ignorance of the Casablanca conference.
11 FDR, President's Secretary, Box 27, Diplomatic Correspondence, China. Gauss, 9 December 1943.
12 FDR, Hopkins papers, Box 334, book 9. John Davies to Harry Hopkins, 31 December 1943.
13 Admiral William Leahy, *I Was There* (London, 1950), p. 186.
14 NARA, RG59, Geographical files 1940–44, China Box 2237. Conversation Hornbeck and T.V. Soong, 19 August 1943.
15 FO 371/35739/f2584, Ashley Clarke minute, 19 May 1943.
16 The Chinese communists remained relatively unimportant to the British until later in the war when the Americans began to pressure Chiang to settle his differences with Mao. The Americans believed that Chiang should be fighting the Japanese, not the communists. Prior to this time, the communists were geographically isolated in Yenan and closer contacts would also have irked Chiang. Sir Horace Seymour finally met Mao on 28 August 1945 in Chungking, observing that Mao was a genuine communist but, at the same time, different from the Soviet model. The ambassador advocated that Britain continue its policy of non-intervention regarding KMT–CCP conflict, which was accepted by London. See Shian Li, 'Britain's China policy and the communists, 1942 to 1946: the role of Ambassador Sir Horace Seymour', *Modern Asian Studies*, 26, 1 (1992).
17 White, p. 108.
18 FRUS, China 1943, II, p. 845. Memo by Welles, 29 March 1943.
19 NARA, RG59, Hong Kong 1940–44, Box 5098. 7 June 1943.
20 Ibid., dated Chungking, 2 April 1943.
21 FO 371/35834/ f1591, account of dinner with Dr Currie by Col. MacHugh, 24 March 1943.
22 Seagrave, pp. 411 and 416.
23 FO 371/35824/f4382, future of Hong Kong: US attitude, August 1943.
24 Chan Kit-ching, 'The United States and the question of Hong Kong', *Journal of the Hong Kong Branch of the Royal Asiatic Society*, 19 (1979). Hornbeck memo, November 1943.
25 Seagrave, pp. 397 and 405–6.
26 FO 371/35834/f1591, Col. MacHugh on meeting with Currie, 24 March 1943.
27 FO 954/7/f31, FO memo on Pacific Strategy, 1 March 1944.
28 FDR, Presidential Secretary, Box 27, China 1943. John Davies letter, 9 March 1943.
29 FDR, Map Room, Box 165/F2. Chief of Staff summary of Stilwell messages, 18 February 1943.
30 FRUS, China 1944, p. 188. John Davies memo, 31 December 1943.

31 Wedemeyer, p. 267. British policy meeting, 8 August 1944. Wedemeyer, as Louis Mountbatten's American deputy, was present at the meeting to put forward SEAC's claim for additional resources for operations. After this incident Churchill excluded him from all further meetings.

32 Keith Sainsbury, *Churchill and Roosevelt at War* (London, 1994), pp. 160–3.

33 Gilbert, *Churchill, VII*, p. 470.

34 Thorne, p. 299. See also pp. 297–302.

35 FO 954/7/f20, Dening on political implications of Far Eastern strategy, 17 February 1944.

36 AP 20/11/91, Eden to Churchill on latter's COS (44) 168 (0), 21 February 1944.

37 PREM 3, 160/6, Churchill to COS, 12 September 1944. Quoted in Thorne, p. 412.

38 Ismay papers, IV/Pow/4/2, Ismay to Pownall, 27 May 1944. Quoted in Thorne, p. 415.

39 Char 20/188, COS(44)207, COS to Churchill, 1 March 1944.

40 Char 20/188, Churchill note to COS, 20 March 1944.

41 PREM 3, 160/7, Churchill memo, 29 February 1944.

42 FDR, PSF, Box 74, State Departmental file: Cordell Hull, January–August 1944. Roosevelt to Hull on Indo-China, 24 January 1944.

43 FO 954/6/f618, Churchill on recovery of Burma, 10 January 1943.

44 Eden diary, 25 February 1944.

45 FO 954/7/f66, Halifax to Eden, 2 May 1944.

46 Claire Chennault was the founder of the American volunteer airforce in China that became known as the Flying Tigers, see Seagrave, pp. 369–72.

47 FO 954/7/f145/f146/f154, Eden 10 and 12 July 1944.

48 FO 954/7/f132, Ashley Clarke minute, 15 June 1944. Eden underlined the Hong Kong section.

49 FO 954/7/f81, FO paper on 'Political considerations affecting Far Eastern strategy', 22 May 1944.

50 Eden diary, 6 and 14 July 1944.

51 Ismay, p. 337.

52 Levine, p. 145.

53 Levine, p. 154.

54 FO 954/22/f229, Churchill to Smuts, 25 September 1944.

55 FDR, Map Room, Box 117. FDR to Chiang Kai-shek, 6 July 1944.

56 FDR, PSF, OSS April 1944–45, Box 4. Donovan to FDR, 24 June 1944. The President requested he show the memo to Hull and Stimson.

57 FDR, PSF, OSS April 1944–45, Box 4. Donovan to FDR, 24 June 1944.

58 Hopkins Papers, 334, Book 9. John Davies to Hopkins, 30 August 1944.

59 FDR, Map Room, Box 11. Roosevelt to Chiang Kai-shek, 16 September 1944.

60 Stilwell Papers, p. 333, 19 September 1944. See also FDR, Map Room, Box 11, Hull memo to Roosevelt, 28 April 1944, for American suspicions against Madame Chiang Kai-shek's withholding US messages. Ambassador Gauss also reported on 'marital intranquillity between the Chiangs'.

61 FDR, PSF, Box 27, Diplomatic Correspondence, China: January–July 1944, 26 May 1944. Stimson, Secretary for War, also urged Roosevelt to rectify the hugely inflated rate of exchange which the Chinese kept for American

expenditure. Through this mechanism the Chinese accumulated millions of extra dollars. Roosevelt passed the issue over to Morgenthau.

62 Stilwell Papers, p. 332, 17 September 1944.
63 FO 371/41607/f3308. Views of K.C. Wu, Chinese vice-minister for foreign affairs, 10 June 1944. Also A.L. Scott minute, 19 July 1944.
64 FDR, Map Room, Box 11, Chiang Kai-shek to Roosevelt, 29 March 1944.
65 FO 954/7/f63, de Wiart to Ismay, 24 April 1944.
66 FDR, Map Room, Box 11, Roosevelt to Chiang Kai-shek, 8 April 1944.
67 FDR, Map Room, Box 11, Cordell Hull to Roosevelt, 7 April 1944.
68 Wedemeyer, p. 295.
69 For example see Stilwell papers, p. 304, 14 June 1944.
70 FDR, PSF, Box 4, Safe file: OSS, April 1944–45. Donovan to Roosevelt, 4 May 1944.
71 FO 954/7/f229, Sterndale Bennett, 7 November 1944.
72 AP 20/10/344a, Cadogan to Churchill, 16 October 1943.
73 Hong Kong PRO, HKRS 163, MacDougall to Gent, 18 April 1945.
74 CO 852/42/15, Gent minute, 29 December 1943. Sir George Sansom in Washington DC embassy also held a similar view to Seymour on Hong Kong.
75 FDR, Map Room, Box 11. John Davies, New Delhi, 15 January 1944.
76 NARA, RG 59, Box 2237 China. Notes on Wallace's conversation with Chiang, 21 June 1944.
77 Eden diary, 11 April 1944.

8 The Cairo conference

1 Stilwell papers, pp. 251–4. Meeting in Cairo after Tehran Conference, 6 December 1943.
2 Winston Churchill, *The Second World War, vol. V* (London, 1952), p. 289.
3 AP 20/3/5, notebook of war trip October–December 1943. Entry, 25 November 1943.
4 Ibid.
5 Ismay, p. 334.
6 Gilbert, *Churchill VII*, p. 561.
7 Eden, *The Reckoning*, p. 426.
8 AP 20/3/5, 25 November 1943.
9 AP 20/11/121, Eden to Churchill, attached minute by Dening, 1 March 1944.
10 Moran, p. 132, 25 November 1943.
11 Leahy, p. 185.
12 Louis, pp. 281–2.
13 Dalton diary, p. 685, 21 December 1943.
14 Leo Amery diary, p. 955, 13 December 1943.
15 Stilwell papers, pp. 236–40. See also pp. 224–5 for attempt by Soong sisters to woo Stilwell once they saw that Stilwell was their link to American aid.
16 Ch'i, Hsi-sheng, *Nationalist China at War, Military Defeats and Political Collapse, 1937–45* (Michigan, 1982), pp. 113–17. Ch'i states that during the war, the KMT 'gave up any attempt to wage revolutionary struggles [with the

result that] the national party became an empty shell and its leaders reduced to soldierless generals', inciting factional intrigues. p. 236.

17   Moran, p. 130, 23 November 1943.
18   Seagrave, p. 379. John Service minute to State Department.
19   Ibid., p. 410. John Service minute to State Department.
20   The Sian incident occurred against the backdrop of the KMT's fourth annihilation campaign against the communists. Several KMT generals wanted to stop the encroachment of the Japanese before the communists, and took Chiang hostage in an attempt to persuade him to switch priorities.
21   Ibid., p. 415.
22   Elliott Roosevelt, p. 142. He added, 'I can't think what would be happening in China, if it weren't for [Stilwell].'
23   Stilwell papers, p. 251–4. Meeting in Cairo after Tehran, 6 December 1943.
24   Seagrave, p. 378.
25   Ismay, p. 335.
26   FDR, Map Room, Box 165 (2), Hurley to Roosevelt, Cairo 20 November 1943.
27   Elliott Roosevelt, p. 193.
28   Quoted in Leahy, p. 185.
29   Quoted in Seagrave, p. 386.
30   Elliott Roosevelt, pp. 162–5.
31   Stilwell papers, pp. 251–4. Meeting in Cairo after Tehran Conference, 6 December 1943.
32   Stilwell diary, 6 December 1943. Quoted in Thorne, p. 308. Cut from published version.
33   Martin Gilbert, *Churchill VII*, pp. 595–9. Roosevelt conceded to Churchill after the fourth plenary session of the Third Cairo Conference that 'Buccaneer is off'. The Prime Minister had also spoken disparagingly about Mountbatten's plans and his apparently extravagant demands for troops and *matériel*. Mountbatten's deputy, the American General Wedemeyer, however, implies that Churchill's displeasure was born from his enthusiasm for Culverin, not his opposition. He felt that if the operational demands could be reduced the operation could still go ahead. When the Prime Minister told Wedemeyer, the American thought privately, 'Don't forget Gallipoli!' See General Albert C. Wedemeyer, *Wedemeyer Reports!* (NY, 1958), pp. 258–60.
34   FDR, PS, Box 27, Diplomatic Correspondence, China 1943, Gauss memo, 9 December 1943. With attached Morgenthau memo for President, 18 December 1943. The President was also convinced of his own powers of economic thought, and advised Morgenthau what should be done. He suggested a course of action that was still hugely beneficial to the Chinese (and not America) while doing nothing to tackle the fundamental causes of Chinese inflation. The Treasury Secretary expressed 'complete sympathy' with the President's aim of aiding China and resisting remedial action.
35   John Morton Blum, *Years of War, 1941–45, from the Morgenthau Diaries* (Boston, 1967), p. 114. Morgenthau to White, 18 January 1944.
36   Ibid., p. 107.
37   FDR, Map Room, Box 165 (2), Hurley to Roosevelt, Cairo, 20 November 1943.
38   FRUS, Cairo and Tehran 1943 (Washington, 1961), p. 554.
39   Moran, pp. 133–4.

40 FRUS, Cairo and Tehran 1943, p. 554. Tripartite dinner meeting, 29 November.
41 FO 371/35874/f6714, Sir Prideaux-Brune to Ashley Clarke, 7 December 1943.
42 Thorne, p. 312.
43 HS 1/154: 'Remorse' financial dealings. FO paper by Eric Teichman of FO Information Service, 27 October 1943. 'Remorse' was the British operational codename for playing the Chinese financial black market in an effort to subsidise their meagre finances, and avoid China's fixed exchange controls.

9 Hard choices

1 Leahy, p. 338.
2 Lord Halifax, *The Fullness of Days* (London, 1957), p. 250.
3 FO 371/46251/f1147, A.L. Scott, 8 February 1945.
4 HS 1/208, AD minute, 29 March 1945.
5 CO 825/39/7, FE(44)8, 25 November 1944. Seymour letter to Eden on post-war trade, 19 September 1944.
6 CAB 96/5, FE(44)1, 15 November 1944. Hall would later become Labour's Colonial Secretary in July 1945.
7 CAB 96/8, FE(E)(44)1, note by the CO on Hong Kong's economic importance, 12 December 1944.
8 CAB 96/8, FE(E)(45)18, British shipping interests in China, 26 February 1945.
9 CAB 96/8, FE(45)9, Dr Sun Fo's comments, 27 January 1945.
10 CO 825/39/7, FE(44)10, Sir Prideaux-Brune on Anglo-American cooperation in China, 30 November 1944.
11 FO 954/7/f338, Chiang Kai-shek thanks Britain for surplus naval craft, 22 April 1945.
12 FDR, Map Room, Box 165 (2), Wedemeyer to Roosevelt, 20 December 1944.
13 FDR, Map Room, Box 11 (8), Roosevelt to Hurley, 17 November 1944.
14 Eden diary, 4 January 1945.
15 Eden diary, 2 February 1945.
16 Herbert Feis, *The China Tangle* (Princeton, 1953), p. 249. This is the official State Department history of the period. See also Robert Conquest, pp. 264–8.
17 Wedemeyer, p. 327.
18 Eden, *The Reckoning*, pp. 513–14.
19 FO 371/54073/f9836, Churchill minute on Soviet claims in the Far East, 23 October 1944.
20 Leahy, p. 368, 9 February 1945.
21 Moran, p. 223, 4 February 1945.
22 Ibid., p. 226, 8 February 1945.
23 FDR, Map Room, Box 165(9), State Department recommendations for Far Eastern policy at Yalta, January 1945.
24 Ibid.
25 Wedemeyer, pp. 317–19.
26 Moran, pp. 227–8, 9 February 1945.
27 AP 20/12/768, Churchill to Eden, 31 December 1944.
28 Moran, p. 228, 9 February 1945.

29   FO 954/22/f276, Eden to Churchill, 8 January 1945, replying to Churchill's personal letter of 31 December 1944. The Prime Minister grudgingly approved Eden's position.
30   Gilbert, *Churchill VII*, pp. 1155–6.
31   Harvey, p. 348, 15 July 1944.
32   Taussig papers, Box 49. Memo of Roosevelt–Stanley conversation by Taussig, 16 January 1945. Quoted in Louis, pp. 437–8.
      In 1949 the State Department was compiling a handbook on Far Eastern conference discussions between heads of state and foreign ministers for the period 1943–47. In pursuit of this aim, the State Department attempted to find the letter from Chiang Kai-shek that Roosevelt referred to in his meeting with Stanley. Robert Dennison, Naval Aide to President Truman, reported on 14 May 1949 that 'a careful search has been made of all known files of President Roosevelt without result. The letter itself was not found, nor any record of the receipt of such a letter discovered.' In all probability it never existed. See NARA, RG 59, Hong Kong 1945–49, Box 5099, April 1949.
33   FO 371/44595/AN154, conversation Law and Roosevelt, 22 December 1944.
34   FO 371/41769/f5392, Sterndale Bennett minute, 18 November 1944.
35   Quoted in Louis, pp. 428–30, IPR conference, January 1945.
36   FO 954/7/f253, Carton de Wiart to Ismay, 21 November 1944. Also, Wedemeyer, p. 293.
37   Wedemeyer, p. 298.
38   CO 129/591/11, various minutes on Emergency Unit, 20 January and 20 February 1945.
39   Wedemeyer, p. 341.
40   FDR, Map Room, Box 11/8, Hurley to Roosevelt, 2 January 1945. See also PSF/Box 27, Hurley, 1 January 1945.
41   CO 129/591/11, Gent to Gater, 20 February 1945. See also HS 1/169, SOE Force 136 to London, 1 March 1945 for planned Sino-British guerrilla operation in Kwangtung whose ultimate aim was the liberation of Hong Kong. A London member of SOE called these plans 'entirely nebulous' considering the situation.
42   FO 371/46251/f4153, Colonel Ride's report, 4 July 1945.
43   CO 129/591/11, emergency planning unit, inter-departmental meeting, 5 July 1945.
44   CO 129/591/11, Seymour reply to above, 9 July 1945.
45   CO 129/591/11, Thornely minute, 23 February 1945.
46   HS 1/331, Lord Selborne's paper, 15 March 1945. Also Stanley to Churchill, 21 March 1945.
47   *Roosevelt and Churchill, their Secret Wartime Correspondence*, p. 677, Churchill to Roosevelt, 17 March 1945. Roosevelt to Churchill, pp. 682–3, 22 March 1945. See also FO 954/7/f283,f325 and f327 February–March 1945.
48   HS 1/171, inter-departmental meeting at CO summarising Hong Kong situation, 23 July 1945.
49   Carton de Wiart, *Happy Odyssey* (London, 1950), pp. 258–9.
50   HS 1/171, inter-departmental meeting at CO summarising Hong Kong situation, 23 July 1945.
51   HKRS 211/2/37, MacDougall report on visit to Chungking, March 1945.

52 HKRS 211/2/37, MacDougall to Gent on visit to Chungking, 18 April 1945.
53 FO 371/46151/f1543, Seymour to Sterndale Bennett, 21 February 1945.
54 FO 371/46251/f1147, A.L. Scott, 23 February 1945. Scott, however, was disdainful of the CO's suggestion that the lease of the New Territories could be extended. See, ibid., f1375, 8 March 1945.
55 FO 371/46251/f1543, T.H. Brewis, 14 May 1945.
56 FO 371/46325/f2663, Eden, 30 March 1945.
57 HS 1/208, Field Marshal Wilson, Washington DC, to Ismay, 27 March 1945.
58 FO 371/46325/f2144, A.L. Scott, 5 April 1945.
59 FO 371/46251/f2382, FO brief for Hurley visit, 3 April 1945. Eden added on 4 April: 'I had not known that Hong Kong was a free port. I suppose there is no qualification about this', illustrating his ignorance of Hong Kong's business role.
60 WO 203/5621, Sterndale Bennett to Seymour on Hurley's visit, 24 April 1945. The FO avoided mentioning the CO's predisposition to take into account the opinions of the inhabitants of Hong Kong, should Hurley 'exaggerate it into a possibly awkward commitment'. See FO 371/46251/f2382, CO brief, 31 March 1945.
61 FO 371/46325/f2577, Churchill minute, 11 April 1945.
62 WO 203/5621, Sterndale Bennett to Seymour on Hurley's visit, 24 April 1945.
63 Moran, p. 226, 7 February 1945.
64 Gilbert, *Churchill VII*, p. 1301, Churchill speech, House of Commons, 17 April 1945.
65 Wedemeyer, p. 272.
66 Louis, p. 441.
67 Ibid., see pp. 512–47. Truman approved the State Department's military compromise prior to the conference to enable the military to retain full control of the Pacific islands for security purposes, p. 496.
68 CAB 65/60, WM(45)61, 14 May 1945.
69 CO 968/1571/5, Seymour to Eden, 16 May 1945.
70 Charles E. Bohlen, *Witness to History* (NY, 1973), p. 223.
71 CO 129/592/8, extract from FE(E), 10 May 1945.
72 FO 371/46325/f2577, Stanley letter to Eden, 25 May 1945. Also Sterndale Bennett minute, 28 May 1945.
73 Eden, *The Reckoning*, pp. 540–1.
74 Moran, p. 251, 20 May 1945. Also, p. 255.
75 Eden diary, 17 July 1945.
76 HKRS 211/2/6, letter to MacDougall, 5 July 1945.

10 Return of the Empire

1 HS 1/210, SOE paper on scheme for British publicity in Far East, 19 April 1945.
2 FO 371/46232/f3603, Seymour to Sterndale Bennett, 16 June 1945.
3 FO 371/46251/f4008, Sterndale Bennett to Seymour, 18 July 1945.
4 FO 371/46171/f4917, A.L. Scott, 5 July 1945.
5 HS 1/331, AD4 reviews British political warfare plans for the Far East, 12 May 1945.

6   FO 371/46251/f2456, MacDougall, April 1945.
7   HS 1/171, Seymour to London, 20 July 1945.
8   Moran, p. 257, 8 July 1945.
9   Eden diary, 10 August 1945.
10 *Documents on British Policy Overseas, series 1, vol. 1* (London, 1988). The Conference at Potsdam, no. 550, I (6), Far Eastern department FO, 7 July 1945.
11 FO 371/54073/45, Clark Kerr to Eden, 18 July 1945. Also Major General Woodburn Kirby, *The War against Japan, vol. V, The Surrender of Japan* (London, 1969), pp. 202–3. Stalin demanded concessions far beyond the Yalta agreement from the Chinese in his discussions with T.V. Soong: independence for Outer Mongolia, a military zone in Manchuria, and a Russian controlling interest in Chinese Eastern and South Manchurian railways. In return Stalin offered not to support the Chinese communists.
12 HS 1/157, SOE general intelligence report China, 10 July 1945.
13 FO 371/46251/f4449, Sterndale Bennett minute, 25 July 1945.
14 CO 129/591/13, civil affairs agreement, Gater to Cadogan, 28 July 1945.
15 FO 371/46251/f4588, Stanley to Eden, 25 July 1945.
16 Eden diary, 17 July 1945.
17 Eden diary, 20 July 1945. Moran dined with the Edens and Churchill that night: 'They talked until nearly midnight as if nothing had happened. I wondered if I could have behaved with the same quiet dignity immediately after hearing that my [son] John had been killed.' Moran, p. 277, 20 July 1945.
18 Eden diary, 25 July 1945.
19 Moran, p. 287, 26 July 1945.
20 FO 371/46232/f4649, *Ta Kung Pao*, 30 July 1945.
21 Gilbert, *Churchill VIII*, p. 116, Attlee to Churchill, 1 August 1945.
22 Eden diary, 28 July 1945.
23 Moran, p. 288, 2 August 1945.
24 Cadogan diary, p. 776, 28 July 1945.
25 Gilbert, *Churchill VIII*, p. 114, King George VI to Churchill, 31 July 1945.
26 FO 371/46251/f4588, CO enquiries about Terminal, 31 July 1945.
27 CO 129/591/13, Paskin minute, 9 August 1945.
28 CO 129/591/11, inter-departmental meeting, 29 July 1945.
29 CO 129/591/11, meeting of Calvert, SAS, with CO, 3 August 1945.
30 CO 129/591/11, inter-departmental meeting, 29 July 1945.
31 Cadogan diary, p. 781, 11 August 1945. Australia and China shared the State Department's opposition but were persuaded that Japan would only surrender in an orderly manner subject to Emperor Hirohito's orders.
32 Kirby, *The War against Japan, vol. V*, pp. 205–220 *passim*.
33 NARA, RG 165, Box 505, CCS 901/1, 11 August 1945.
34 NARA, RG 165, Box 505, CCS 901/3, 12 August 1945.
35 Kirby, *War against Japan, vol. V*, pp. 283–8.
36 CO 129/591/16, Gent to Gater, 4 August 1945.
37 CO 129/591/16, FO to Chungking, 11 August 1945.
38 F.S.V. Donnison, *British Military Administration in the Far East, 1943–46* (London, 1956), pp. 77–9.
39 Kirby, *War against Japan, vol. V*, pp. 145–6.

40 NARA, RG 165, Box 505, Telephone conversation Dunn and Lincoln, 15 August 1945.
41 CO 129/591/16, Wallinger, Chungking, to FO, 14 August. The Chinese were given British plans for the Hong Kong surrender the same day.
42 CO 129/591/16, Cabinet Far Eastern committee meeting, 17 August 1945.
43 CO 129/591/16, Hall to Attlee, 10 August 1945.
44 CO 129/591/18, COS(45)200, Alan Brooke, 17 August 1945.
45 Edwin Ride, *BAAG, Hong Kong Resistance, 1942–1945* (Hong Kong, 1981), p. 287.
46 CO 129/591/16, Ride to Cartwright, HQ British troops China, 15 August 1945.
47 CO 129/591/16, FO to Chungking, 13 August 1945.
48 CO 129/591/16, de Wiart to Cartwright HQ British troops China, 17 August 1945.
49 Ride, *BAAG*, p. 288.
50 HS 1/329, B/B 131, Kunming to ADI, 17 August 1945.
51 FO 371/46251/f5166, Kitson minute, 16 August 1945.
52 CO 129/591/18, Attlee to Truman, 18 August 1945.
53 FO 800/461, Truman to Attlee, 19 August 1945. The second paragraph of Truman's message stated that Secretary of State, Byrnes, had informed T.V. Soong of the President's decision, adding that 'it did not in any way represent US views regarding the future status of Hong Kong'. The CO and FO agreed that this section should be ignored, just as they had disregarded an earlier American Chiefs of Staff's attempt to distance themselves from British Hong Kong policy.
54 CO 129/591/18, 203, Joint Service Mission, Washington DC, to London, 22 August 1945.
55 CO 129/591/18, 203, Joint Service Mission, Washington DC, to London, 22 August 1945.
56 FO 371/46212/f6055, A.L. Scott minute, 31 August 1945.
57 Harry Truman, *Year of Decisions, 1945* (London, 1955), p. 383.
58 FO 371/44538/AN2597, political summary Washington DC to London, 27 August 1945.
59 NARA, RG 218, Box 87, Hong Kong geographical 1942–45, JCAC 30, 18 June 1945.
60 FO 371/46251/f4876, Kitson minute, 14 August 1945. Kitson reiterated this point in 46171/f6104, 30 September 1945.
61 CO 129/591/18, 155, Seymour to FO, 24 August 1945.
62 Franklin Gimson diary, introduction. Japan's sudden capitulation, however, saved the lives of thousands of Allied POWs who were to be shot on the orders of Tokyo.
63 London's message to Gimson dated 13 August, reached him on 23 August. See George Wright-Nooth with Mark Adkin, *Prisoner of the Turnip Heads* (London, 1994) for details of British internment in Stanley camp.
64 Gimson diary, introduction.
65 CO 129/591/16, Ride to C in C India, 21 August 1945.
66 *The Times*, 21 August 1945.
67 FO 371/46251/f5066, Churchill parliamentary question, 23 August 1945.
68 CO 129/591/18, Seymour to FO, 26 August 1945.

69 NARA, RG 59, Hong Kong 1945–49, Winant to Washington DC, 23 August 1945.
70 CO 129/591/18, Sterndale Bennett on *Daily Telegraph* report to C.R. Price, COS Secretariat, 23 August 1945.
71 CO 129/591/18, FO to Seymour, 28 August 1945.
72 CO 129/591/18, Seymour to FO, 26 August 1945.
73 CO 129/591/18, Ismay to Gater, CO, 24 August 1945.
74 CO 129/591/18, FO to Seymour, 28 August 1945.
75 CO 129/591/18, de Wiart to Ismay, on meeting with Chiang Kai-shek on 25–26 August 1945.
76 See CO 129/591/18, Gent to Gater, 17 August, and Gent minute, 18 August 1945.
77 CO 129/591/18, de Wiart to Ismay, 27 August. Also Seymour to FO, 30 August 1945.
78 CO 129/591/18, Seymour to FO after meeting Dr K.C. Wu, 29 August 1945.
79 CO 129/591/18, Sterndale Bennett to Seymour, 30 August 1945. Sent following day, and accepted by Chiang Kai-shek. For Cabinet discussion see Gent minute 28 August 1945.
80 CO 129/591/18, Sterndale Bennett to Seymour, and reply, 30–31 August 1945.
81 Kirby, *The War against Japan, vol. V*, pp. 283–8.
82 Gimson diary, introduction.
83 The Japanese deny that the boats which left Lamma island were hostile to the British fleet and maintain that their warheads had already been dumped at sea. See Lo Tim Keung and Jason Wordie, *Ruins of War, a Guide to Hong Kong's Battlefields and Wartime Sites* (Hong Kong, 1996), p. 182. The development of the suicide boats was initiated by the Imperial Japanese Navy in April 1944. The boats sent to Hong Kong were intended for use against Allied shipping, should any attempt be made to enter the western harbour of Hong Kong. There were 127 boats called Shinyo (shaking the ocean) with 559 personnel from Japan sent in February 1945.
84 CO 129/591/18, Harcourt to Pacific Fleet, 4 September 1945.
85 Wright-Nooth, p. 187.
86 Kirby, *The War against Japan, vol. V*, pp. 286–7.
87 CO 129/591/18, Sterndale Bennett to Chiefs of Staff, 1 September 1945.
88 CO 129/591/20, various correspondence between General Hayes and COS, 30 August–9 September 1945.
89 CO 129/591/18, 27, Harcourt's war diary (for period 29 August to 16 September 1945) to Secretary of the Admiralty, 6 October 1945.

Conclusion

1 Sir Ralph Furse, *Acuparius, Recollections of a Recruiting Officer* (London, 1962), pp. 298–9.
2 Denis Judd, *British Imperial Experience from 1765 to the Present* (London, 1997), p. 321.
3 Dutton, pp. 156–7.
4 Seagrave, pp. 419–20.

5 Leahy, p. 368, 9 February 1945.
6 Porter and Stockwell, pp. 30–31.
7 Robert Conquest, *Stalin, Breaker of Nations* (London, 1991), p. 262.
8 Michael H. Hunt, *Ideology in US Foreign Policy* (London, 1987), p. 38.
9 *The Economist*, 9 October 1999, p. 41.
10 Clive Ponting, *Churchill* (London, 1994), p. 690.
11 Harvey, p. 176, 3 November 1942.
12 FO 371/46171/f4917, G.V. Kitson, 5 July 1945.
13 Moran, p. 247.
14 Sir Ralph Furse, p. 131.
15 Lord Rosebery speech, City of London Liberal Club, 5 May 1899, in *Daily News*, 6 May 1899.

Epilogue

1 NSC 5717, 9 August 1957. Access limited on a strict need-to-know basis.
2 'The break-up of the Colonial Empires and its implications for US security', 3 September 1948. Michael Warner (ed.), *The CIA under Truman* (Washington DC, 1994).
3 FO 371/75788, CBB Heathcote-Smith political summaries, April 1949.
4 Welsh, p. 440.
5 *Liverpool Post*, 2 December 1948, article: 'War threat to helpless Hong Kong', by Patrick O'Donovan.
6 FO371/75839 UK government policy towards Hong Kong 1949.
7 CO 537/3702, Paskin minute, 16 June 1948.
8 CO 537/3702, Creech Jones minute, 27 June 1948.
9 FO371/75872/f6909, Sir N. Brook, Cabinet Office to Dening, referring to Cabinet Paper FE(O)(49)25, 12 May 1949.
10 FO371/75871/f6019, F.S. Tomlinson minute to Bevin, 4 May 1949.
11 Welsh, p. 438.
12 FO371/75872/f7787, Noel Baker, Commonwealth Relations Office to PM, 12 May 1949.
13 See Mark Roberti, *The Fall of Hong Kong* (Chichester, 1994).
14 Dr Zhisui Li, *The Private Life of Chairman Mao* (London, 1995), p. 270.
15 'The cold war in Asia', *Cold War International History Project*, Winter 1995/6, No. 6–7, Washington DC.
16 NSC 6007, 11 June 1960.
17 Welsh, p. 446.
18 NSC 5717, 9 August 1957. Access limited on a strict need-to-know basis.
19 NSC 44, 26 July 1948.
20 Joint Munitions Allocation Committee to JCS, Aid to China. RG218, Geographic file 1948–50, 7 October 1949.
21 Gerald Segal, 'Does China matter?', *Foreign Affairs* (September/October 1999).
22 FO 371/75839/f13408, Cabinet conclusion CM(49)54, 29 August 1949.

Bibliography

Unpublished material

Public Records Office, London
Board of Trade, BT 11
Cabinet conclusions, CAB 23, 65, 128
Cabinet Committee of Imperial Defence, CAB 16
Cabinet memoranda, CAB 66, 129
Chiefs of Staff Committee, CAB 79
Colonial Office, CO 98, 129, 133, 547, 825, 852, 967, 968 series
Far Eastern Committee, CAB 69, 96, 134
Far Eastern Economic Sub-Committee, CAB 96
Foreign Office, general political, FO 371 series
Foreign Secretary, official papers, FO 800, 954
Prime Minister's Office files, PREM 1, 3, 4
Special Operations Executive, Far Eastern, HS 1 series
War Office, WO 203 series

Birmingham University
Anthony Eden, private papers

Oxford University, Bodleian Library
Clement Attlee papers
Conservative Party papers

Oxford University, Rhodes House Library
Arthur Creech Jones papers
Fabian Society papers
Franklin Gimson diary
David MacDougall papers

Cambridge, Churchill College, Churchill Library
Alexander Cadogan diaries
Winston Churchill papers
William Slim papers

Labour Party Archive, Manchester
Labour Party Committee on Colonial Affairs

Franklin Roosevelt Library, Hyde Park, USA
Franklin Roosevelt papers
Harry Hopkins papers

Henry Morgenthau papers
Sumner Welles papers
Taussig papers

National Archives and Records Administration, College Park, USA
Office of Strategic Services, research and analysis reports
Joint Chiefs of Staff, minutes, RG 165, 218 series
National Security Council papers
State Department papers, RG 59, 84 series

Public Record Office, Hong Kong
HKRS, 163, 211, 231 series
Cecil Harcourt papers

Published material

Articles

Christopher M. Bell, ' "Our most exposed outpost": Hong Kong and British Far Eastern strategy, 1921–1941', *Journal of Military History*, 60 (January 1996).

Chan Lau Kit-ching, 'The Hong Kong question during the Pacific war', *Journal of Imperial and Commonwealth History*, 2, 1 (1973).

——, 'The abrogation of British extraterritoriality in China 1942–43: a study of Anglo-American-Chinese relations', *Modern Asian Studies*, 2, 2 (1977).

——, 'The United States and the question of Hong Kong', *Journal of the Hong Kong Branch of the Royal Asiatic Society*, 19 (1979).

Paul Dickson, 'Crerar and the decision to garrison Hong Kong', *Journal of Canadian Military History*, 3, 1 (Spring 1994).

Kent Fedorowich, 'Doomed from the outset? Internment and civilian exchange in the Far East – the British failure over Hong Kong, 1941–45' (Unpublished).

W.J. Hinton, 'Hong Kong's place in the British Empire', *Journal of the Royal Central Asian Society*, 38 (1941).

Johannes R. Lombardo, 'A mission of espionage, intelligence and psychological operations: the American Consulate in Hong Kong, 1949–64', *Intelligence and National Security*, 14, 4 (Winter 1999).

Galen Perras, ' "Our position in the Far East would be stronger without this unsatisfactory commitment": Britain and the reinforcement of Hong Kong, 1941', *Canadian Journal of History*, 30 (August 1995).

Shian Li, 'Britain's China policy and the communists, 1942 to 1946: the role of Ambassador Sir Horace Seymour', *Modern Asian Studies*, 26, 1 (1992).

——, 'The extraterritoriality negotiations of 1943 and the New Territories', *Modern Asian Studies*, 30, 3 (1996).

James Tang, 'From Empire defence to imperial retreat: Britain's post-war China policy and the decolonization of Hong Kong', *Modern Asian Studies*, 4, 2 (1994).

Newspapers

China Morning Post, 1939–1941 and 1945
Hong Kong News, 1941–1944
The Daily Telegraph
The Economist
The Times

Secondary literature

Acheson, D., *Present at the Creation* (London, 1948).
Amery, L., *My Political Life, vol. III* (London, 1955).
Attlee, C.R., *As it Happened* (London, 1954).
Avon, Lord, *The Reckoning* (London, 1965).
Barnett, C., *The Collapse of British Power* (London, 1972).
——, *The Audit of War* (London, 1986).
——, *Lost Victory* (London, 1995).
Barnes, J. and D. Nicholson (eds), *The Empire at Bay: the Leo Amery Diaries, 1929–45* (London, 1988).
Bennett, G. (ed.), *The Concept of Empire, Burke to Attlee 1774–1947* (London, 1953).
Blum, J.M., *Roosevelt and Morgenthau* (Boston, 1970).
——, *Years of War, 1941–1945, from the Morgenthau Diaries* (Boston, 1967).
Bohlen, C.E., *Witness to History* (London, 1973).
Bosanquet, D., *Escape from China* (London, 1983).
Bullock, A., *The Life and Times of Ernest Bevin, vol. II* (London, 1967); *vol. III* (London, 1983).
Burridge, T., *Clement Attlee, a Political Biography* (London, 1985).
Butler, R.A., *The Art of the Possible* (London, 1971).
Byrnes, J.F., *Speaking Frankly* (London, 1948).
Cain, P.J. and A.G. Hopkins, *British Imperialism, Innovation and Expansion, 1688–1914* (London, 1993).
——, *British Imperialism: Crisis and Deconstruction, 1914–1990* (London, 1993).
Cantril, H. and M. Strunk, *Public Opinion, 1935–1946* (Princeton, 1951).
Ch'i, Hsi-sheng, *Nationalist China at War, Military Defeats and Political Collapse, 1937–45* (Michigan, 1982).
Chan Lau Kit-ching, *China, Britain and Hong Kong, 1895–1945* (Hong Kong, 1992).
Chennault, C.L., *Way of the Fighter* (NY, 1949).
Chiang Kai-shek, *China's Destiny and Chinese Economic Theory* (ed. P. Jaffe, NY, 1947).
Churchill, W.S., *History of the Second World War, vol. I* (London, 1948); *vol. II* (London, 1949); *vol. III* (London, 1950); *vol. IV* (London, 1951); *vol. V* (London, 1952); *vol. VI* (London, 1954).
——, *The Hinge of Fate* (London, 1964).
Colville, J., *The Fringes of Power: the Downing Street Diaries, 1939–55* (London, 1985).
Conquest, R., *Stalin: Breaker of Nations* (London, 1991).
Cruishank, C., *SOE in the Far East* (Oxford, 1983).
Cottrell, R., *The End of Hong Kong* (London, 1994).

Dalton, H., *Memoirs, 1931–1945: the Fateful Years* (London, 1957).

Davies, J.P., *Dragon by the Tail* (NY, 1972).

Dilks, D. (ed.), *The Diaries of Sir Alexander Cadogan* (London, 1982).

Documents on British Policy Overseas, Series I, Volume I, *The Conference at Potsdam* (London, 1988).

Donnison, F.S.V., *British Military Administration in the Far East, 1943–46* (London, 1956).

Dreyer, E.L., *China at War, 1900–1949* (London, 1995).

Dutton, D., *Anthony Eden, a Life and Reputation* (London, 1997).

Eiler, Keith E. (ed.), *Wedemeyer on Peace* (Stanford, 1987).

Fairbank, J.K., *The United States and China* (Cambridge, MA, 1971).

Feis, H., *The China Tangle* (Princeton, 1953).

Foreign Relations of the United States series (Washington DC, 1940–1945).

Furse, Sir R., *Acuparius, Recollections of a Recruiting Officer* (London, 1962).

Gardiner, J. and N. Wenborn (eds), *The History Today Companion to British History* (London, 1995).

Gardner, L.C., *Economic Aspects of New Deal Diplomacy* (Madison, 1964).

Gellman, I.F., *Secret Affairs: Franklin Roosevelt, Cordell Hull and Sumner Welles* (Baltimore, 1995).

Gilbert, M., *Winston S. Churchill, vol. VI* (London, 1983); *vol. VII* (London, 1986); *vol. VIII* (London, 1988).

Gittings, J., *China and the World, 1922–1972* (London, 1974).

Gladwyn, Lord, *Memoirs* (London, 1972).

Grantham, A., *Via Ports* (Hong Kong, 1965).

Gull, E.M., *British Economic Interests in the Far East* (London, 1943).

Halifax, Lord, *The Fullness of Days* (London, 1957).

Hansard, House of Commons Debates, 5th series, vols 374–411 (London, 1942–45).

Harriman, W.A. and E. Abel, *Special Envoy to Churchill and Stalin, 1941–1946* (London, 1976).

Harris, K., *Attlee* (London, 1982).

Harvey, J. (ed.), *The Diplomatic Diaries of Oliver Harvey, 1937–1940* (London, 1978).

Heussler, R., *Yesterday's Rulers* (NY, 1963).

Holland, R.F., 'The imperial factor in British strategies from Attlee to Macmillan, 1945–63', in R.F. Holland and G. Rizvi (eds), *Perspectives on Imperialism and Decolonization: Essays in Honour of A.F. Madden* (London, 1984).

Hull, C., *Memoirs, vol. II* (London, 1948).

Hunt, Michael H., *Ideology and US Foreign Policy* (London, 1987).

Ismay, Lord, *Memoirs* (London, 1960).

James, L., *The Rise and Fall of the British Empire* (London, 1994).

Jeffries, Sir C., *The Colonial Empire and its Civil Service* (Cambridge, 1938).

Judd, D., *British Imperial Experience from 1765 to the Present* (London, 1997).

Kennan, G., *Memoirs, 1925–1950* (London, 1968).

Kimball, W.F., *The Juggler: Franklin Roosevelt as Wartime Statesman* (Princeton, NJ, 1991).

Kirby, S.W., *The War against Japan, vol. I* (London, 1957); *vol. II* (London, 1958); *vol. III* (London, 1961); *vol. IV* (London, 1965); *vol. V* (London, 1969).

Lanxin Xiang, *Recasting the Imperial Far East: Britain and America in China, 1945–1950* (London, 1995).

Leahy, W.D., *I Was There* (London, 1950).

Levine, A.J., *The Pacific War* (London, 1995).

Lippmann, W., *United States War Aims* (NY, 1944).

Loewenheim F.L., H.D. Langley and M. Jonas (eds), *Roosevelt and Churchill, their Secret Wartime Correspondence* (NY, 1990).

Louis, W.R., *Imperialism at Bay* (Oxford, 1977).

Macmillan, H., *The Blast of War, 1939–1945* (London, 1967).

Millis, W. (ed.), *The Forrestal Diaries*, (London, 1952).

Miners, N., *Hong Kong under Imperial Rule, 1912–1941* (Oxford, 1987).

Moran, Lord, *Winston Churchill: the Struggle for Survival, 1940–1965* (London, 1966).

Lord Louis Mountbatten, *Report to the Combined Chiefs of Staff by the Supreme Allied Commander South East Asia* (London, 1951).

Parker, R.A.C., *Chamberlain and Appeasement* (London, 1993).

Peterson, M., *Both Sides of the Curtain* (London, 1950).

Pimlott, B. (ed.), *The Second World War Diary of Hugh Dalton, 1940–45* (London, 1986).

Ponting, C., *Churchill* (London, 1994).

Porter, A.N. and A.J. Stockwell, *British Imperial Policy and Decolonization, 1938–64* (London, 1987).

Reynolds, D., *The Creation of the Anglo-American Alliance, 1937–41* (London, 1981).

——, *Rich Relations, the American Occupation of Britain 1942–1945* (London, 1995).

Rhodes James, R. (ed.), *Winston S. Churchill, his Complete Speeches, vol. VI 1935–42* (London, 1974); *vol. VII, 1942–49* (London, 1974).

——, *Anthony Eden* (London, 1986).

Ride, E., *BAAG, Hong Kong Resistance, 1942–1945* (Hong Kong, 1981).

Roberti, M., *The Fall of Hong Kong* (Chichester, 1994).

Roberts, A., *The Holy Fox, a Biography of Lord Halifax* (London, 1991).

Romanus, C. and R. Sutherland, *Stilwell's Mission to China* (Washington DC, 1953).

Roosevelt, E., *As He Saw It* (NY, 1946).

Sainsbury, K., *Churchill and Roosevelt at War* (London, 1994).

Sbrega, J.J., *Anglo-American Relations and Colonialism in East Asia* (NY, 1983).

Seagrave, S., *The Soong Dynasty* (NY, 1985).

Seaman, L.C.B., *Victorian England* (London, 1973).

Shai, A., *Britain and China, 1941–47* (London, 1984).

Slim, W., *Defeat into Victory* (London, 1960).

Snow, E., *Red Star over China* (London, 1968).

Spector, R., 'American seizure of Japan's strategic points, summer 1942–1944', in S. Dockrill (ed.), *From Pearl Harbour to Hiroshima* (London, 1994).

Stettinius, Edward R., *The Diaries of Edward R. Stettinius Jnr, 1943–46* (NY, 1975).

Stockwell, A.J. (ed.), *Documents on the End of Empire: Malaya, II* (London, 1994).

Tedder, Lord, *With Prejudice* (London, 1966).

Truman, H.S., *Year of Decisions, 1945* (London, 1955).

Tsang, S., *Democracy Shelved: Great Britain, China, and Attempts at Constitutional Reform in Hong Kong, 1945–1952* (Oxford, 1988).

Tuchman, B., *Sand against the Wind: Stilwell and the American Experience in China, 1911–1945* (London, 1971).

Tung, W.L., *Wellington Koo and China's Wartime Diplomacy* (NY, 1978).

Wedemeyer, A.C., *Wedemeyer Reports!* (NY, 1958).

Wellington Koo, *Wellington Koo Memoirs*, translated by the Institute of Modern History, Chinese Academy of Social Science (Peking, 1987).

Welsh, F., *A History of Hong Kong* (London, 1994).

White, T.H. (ed.), *The Stilwell Papers* (NY, 1948).

——, *In Search of History: a Personal Adventure* (NY, 1978).

Wiart, C. de, *Happy Odyssey* (London, 1950).

Winant, J.G., *A Letter from Grosvenor Square* (London, 1947).

Wordie, J. and Lo Tim Keung, *Ruins of War, a Guide to Hong Kong Battlefields and Wartime Sites* (Hong Kong, 1996).

Wright-Nooth, G. with M. Adkin, *Prisoner of the Turnip Heads* (London, 1994).

Index